366 Days of

Claudette Joy Spence

ISBN: 978-0-9760911-1-0

Contributors

Bekeo Adijun
Denise Brantley
Reginald Brantley
Phyllis Coachman
Ian Edwards
Deirdre FieldsWilson
Jeffrey Gardere
Devon Harris
Leighton Hollar
Ken Irish
Alpheus Lewis
Anthony Lewis
Everett Lewis
Lascelles Lewis
Delroy McCormack
Jasmin Pitter
Rosetta Pringle
Wesley Pringle Jr.
Claudette Joy Spence
Gbenga Subair
Sophia Walsh-Newman
Gerald White-Davis
Errol Williamson
Ruby Wilson

Foreword

Dr. Carter G. Woodson once wrote, "If a race has no history, if it has no worthwhile traditions, it becomes a negligible factor in the thought of the world and stands in danger of being exterminated." Woodson explained this in his 1933 book, *The Mis-education of the Negro*, and the impact this lack of one's own historical and cultural knowledge has had on Black people. As an instructor of Black Studies at York College (CUNY), I see this negative impact on students that have little to no knowledge of Black History. Some are local students, others are recent immigrants to America, but most are products of our own school system, where Black History was passed over or is limited in the curriculum.

A historian and Principal at Washington, D.C. Washington, D.C.'s all-Black Armstrong Manual Training School, Dr. Woodson designated the week of February 12th and 14th as Negro History Week in 1926, to share and highlight accomplishments, contributions and participation of people of African Ancestry to his high school students. The designation of Negro History Week was a major contribution to American education. This Week spread to other schools and was hosted in churches, becoming nationally recognized, if only for the shortest month of the year. This Week was later expanded to the month of February in the 1970's and renamed, Black History Month.

Another significant contribution was the creation of the African American 7-day cultural celebration of Kwanzaa by historian/educator Dr. Maulana Karenga in 1966. Celebrated December 26th through January 1st, this event highlights Seven Principles called the Nguzo Saba, one principle for each day: Unity, Self-Determination, Collective Work and Responsibility, Cooperative Economics, Creativity, Purpose and Faith. Principles to live our lives by and put into practice 365 days of the year. Although an African American celebration based on African values, Kwanzaa is now practiced in countries around the world as it represents the shared values of People of African Descent throughout the Diaspora. The value of having our own cultural celebration during the recognized Holiday season offers Black People time to celebrate themselves in the midst of their religious celebrations.

The creation of the first Black Studies Department and inclusion of an Africana curriculum began at San Francisco State College in 1968 as an outgrowth of the 1960's Black Power Movement. Black Studies was a revolutionary concept and one of the most critically relevant additions to college/university education. These courses are a direct response to Dr. Woodson's claim of widespread 'mis-education' in the United States of America.

This latest work by Sister Claudette Spence serves as the latest remedy for 'mis-education' as it apprises us of those whose contributions are not in history books but may be recognized as local heroes and sheroes, known to their families and in their local communities. *366 Days of Liberation* provides a new voice for the Diaspora, 366 days to read and learn who and what was done in various ways, means and forms. This book tells our stories about the lives of our people. As an educator and activist, I recommend *366 Days of Liberation* as these profiles fill a void in our knowledge base of prominent as well as common men and women who made a difference, made sacrifices and for the betterment of their families and communities future, and for our People. Ashe!

Food for thought:

"Until the lion has his own storyteller, tales of the hunt will always glorify the hunter." (African Proverb)

Andrew P. Jackson (Sekou Molefi Baako)

Introduction

Five years ago while struggling with making sense of medical and physical conditions that immobilized me and brought to me fear of living with the limitations of my circumstance, I questioned how I would continue to live a vibrant and vivacious life that stoked my youth and adulthood. One day while brooding, I heard, "I am going to make you get up and walk because I have work for you to do. Your work here is not done yet." I have learned to swim, in my elder years, as one major step in my healing and wellness. And as I tried to figure out what work God wanted me to do, I came to the realization that it was connected to utilizing my talents, experiences, academic training and other God-given gifts to (continue to) work for my people. My African people. Many opportunities have presented themselves since I have been back on my feet – although still a little wobbly. *366 Days of Liberation* is one such opportunity.

366 Days of Liberation is created to promote African-consciousness, liberation, and the African principles of community.

It is my hope that *366 Days of Liberation* will inform and educate. That it will inspire and encourage. That it will reaffirm the value of those among us who work from a Pan-African perspective. And that it will shine a light into action for those among us who dismiss or are ignorant of our approach to loving all Africans, so as a larger community we will be conquerors of the obstacles that present themselves and together we will implement solutions that move masses of us into better material and spiritual wealth. – those at home and those abroad.

This body of work is assembled as a research project based on my academic studies in political science and communications and my experience in community-building and justice work done primarily in New York communities. Access to the internet and writers who submitted their literary contributions made this assignment possible.

To celebrate the life of our ancestors, as I have grown to know, is important. Without them we would not be here. And their energies are valuable. I am thankful God has allowed me the time to come to this realization. *366 Days of Liberation* celebrates our ancestors.

Many of the ancestors celebrated in *366 Days of Liberation* are well-known Africans who have worked diligently towards the liberation of Africans from the spiritual, mental and physical cages of our society. They have played their roles on the international stage. You may recognize many of them and maybe even learn something new about them. Others have played no less of a significant role at the local community stage and at the family stage. All these stages of engagement are important and are valuable to the lives of our people.

And just as the ancestors highlighted in this work have made a positive contribution towards removing barriers to our success and victory and replacing them with systems for our spiritual and physical elevation, one can find another side to their persona that could easily negate their positive contributions. I have chosen to include them in this work because of the good they have done and because their presence brings us face to face with the duality of humankind. And herein it calls us to be reflective on how our materialistic approach to living tarnishes the innate love, peace, and compassion from us and relegates us to a realm where we inflict pain and suffering on others, and even on our selves. May we be reminded here to be introspective to untarnish and nurture our love.

I have also included people who are not of Black African ancestry because they have demonstrated their love of and for Africans and have consistently worked to improve the living conditions of large numbers of Africans in their nation state and worldwide. I respect them for their convictions of doing the right things for Africans – at home and abroad.

To everyone who contributed a piece about the liberating presence of their ancestors while they were with us on the physical stage, we are thankful. You are a gift. You work is a gift. And this gift will keep on living and giving.

To everyone who was supportive of this idea and offered encouragement in so many ways, I thank you. These include and are not limited to: my pastor, Reverend Reginald Brantley at Corona Congregational Church United Church of Christ (UCC); my sister friend Reverend Dr. Ruby Wilson who has supported me through the publication of my first book in 2005; my colleague E. Wayne McDonald of the Caribbean Cultural Center who helps to keep me centered in the diversity of the Caribbean experience; my colleague and church family Sekou Molefi Baako (Andrew Jackson) who has been supportive of me and my work from back in the 1980's when I was a communications major completing undergraduate work at Queens College, City University of New York. He engaged me to videotape projects at the Langston Hughes Community Library and Cultural Center – one of my first assignments included documenting Cheryl Byron's performance. Thank you Brother Andrew for the ways in which you teach and guide our community. You exude pure love. To my colleague and friend Jasmin Pitter President of Division 432 of the Universal Negro Improvement Association and African Communities League, thank you for your patience while I pulled this book together. Thank you to colleague and friend Causewell Vaughan for taking on the gigantic project of editing this body of work. I apprecilove the effort you have put into editing parts of this work. To sister friend Denise Brantley, thank you for your keen eyes and clarity on this work. To all my colleagues, family and friends, I thank you for supporting me and by extension supporting our African community. May your generosity return to you exponentially and when you least expect.

To my Brahma Kumaris (BK) family whose love and teachings have been a Light to my path on the journey while I acknowledge my ancestral presence and grow in understanding my spiritual being, I thank you. With a special mention of Sister Carmen Palmer, Brothers Carl B. Moxie and Eric Larson the first instruments of learning at the BK, thank you for your guidance.

As we grow, coming into the fullness of ourselves, I present to you a gift: *366 Days of Liberation*

With Love, Peace and Power, ***ClaudetteJoy***

Welcome

to

366 Days of Liberation

Created to be read one-a-day for the year.

Our ancestors must have experienced freedom in the mind so that they could and did bring benefit to others. They knew love at an elevated level that allowed them to share kind actions for everyone… for most people, consistently. They knew they were created for a purpose; they knew it, they lived it; in service to humanity. And in remembrance of our ancestors we would like to believe they lived a life of which their ancestors can be proud. May we find among these pages gems that remind us and embolden us to make our contributions to making our space a kinder world for Africans. The arena is broad; your gifts are many and unique, may we use them for the collective good.

Herein too are some principles that guide family, community-living and the lives of some of our ancestors.

366 Days of Liberation is designed for you to read one-a-day, like vitamins for the mind and spirit, for the year. May you discover that which nurtures. In Love & Peace, Welcome.

ClaudetteJoy Spence

January 1 *(The Seventh Day of Kwanzaa)*

Imani - *Faith*

Kwanzaa is a seven day festival that celebrates African and African American culture and history from 26th December to 1st January. It is founded on traditional African principles and brought forward into the 20th century in 1966 by Dr. Maulana Karenga, professor and chairman of Black Studies at California State University, Long Beach, created Kwanzaa in 1966.

African theologists and philosophers say Ma'at is an ancient Kemetic concept. The Nguzo Saba is a term popularized by Dr. Maulana Karenga. As used by the Ancient Africans, Ma'at was a concept that stood for "universal order." Ma'at represents realty in all its manifestations both spiritual and material. It is the divine force that encompasses and embraces everything that is alive and exists. As an ethical system, Ma'at is often discussed as seven cardinal virtues (truth, justice, righteousness, harmony, balance, reciprocity, and order). As part of Karenga's Kawaida philosophy, the Nguzo Saba are seven principles (Umoja, Unity; Kujichagulia, Self-determination; Ujima, Cooperative Work and Responsibility; Ujamaa, Collective Economics; Nia, Purpose; Kuumba, Creativity; and Imani, Faith). The Nguzo Saba is most widely recognized in relation to the seven days of Kwanzaa.

Faith, some say, is the belief in something unseen, confident that it will manifest in the physical form. Sometimes our faith fluctuates, and I image that's all right. However, doubt interrupts the flow of energy for the manifestation of that which we desire with a pure and unselfish heart. May our faith in the One God of us fluctuate less and less.

January 2
Queen Nanny – One of Jamaica's National Heroes

Nanny, a woman from the Ashanti tribe in Ghana, was a leader of the Maroons - enslaved Africans in Jamaica who had escaped the plantation life at the beginning of the 18th century. She was an outstanding military leader who was a thorn in the side of first the Spanish and then the British in their battles as she outsmarted, out-planned and outmaneuvered the British at every turn. The Spanish and British were baffled and infuriated by her brilliant guerrilla warfare tactics.

Besides inspiring her people to ward off the troops, Nanny was also a chieftainess or wise woman of the village, who passed down legends and encouraged the continuation of customs, music and songs, that had come with the people from Africa, and which instilled in them confidence and pride. She also had responsibility for the welfare of the women and children in the community; even the king had to call upon her for advice, especially those relating to women.

For more than 30 years Nanny freed more than 800 enslaved people and helped them settle into Maroon communities. In her lifetime and after, she was seen as a symbol of unity and strength for her people during their time of crisis, and her settlement, called Nanny Town, remained under Maroon rule.

January 3

Evelyn Lewis

Contributor: Claudette Joy Spence, M.Sc. (Daughter)

Born in Golden Grove, St. Ann, Jamaica as the second child for her mother Carmen and father Samuel, Evelyn was the sister to seventeen brothers and sisters and numerous nieces and nephews who loved her affectionately. The mother of one son and three daughters, Evelyn was creative and enterprising in her efforts to generate income to support her family who she loved dearly. While in Jamaica, she was one of the best dressmakers and hairdressers of her time. She worked exceptionally well at keeping the women beautiful in the way in which beauty was defined.

Lewis became a pioneer by emigrating to the USA and paving a way for some of her siblings and her children to seek opportunities in the US. With the community awaiting her delayed genius, she earned her high school diploma and earned credentials to be in the nursing field as a nurse aide. Her passion was caring for the elderly and she worked in a nursing home. Her patients and their families loved her as did her co-workers. Her sense of justice and ability to speak up and speak out brought her to be elected as their union representative at the Service Employees International Union (SEIU). She represented them well.

As I write this I realize I learned, among so many other things, compassion from my mother. I love you Mama.

January 4
Alexander Spence

Alexander Spence (Center), L. Donald Tankoy, R. Claudette Joy Spence
Contributor: Claudette Joy Spence, M.Sc. (Daughter)

A highly skilled furniture-maker, Alexander loved the sea. And he loved his family. For more than sixteen years he worked on board a cargo ship that travelled the world delivering the ore of Jamaica, the land of his birth to European countries for their refinement of it. He was well read and well-travelled.

In my childhood, Al was the first person I heard say that civilization began in Africa and the movement of people has taken them across the world land mass.

Daddy introduced me to reel-to-reel audio recording; while on shore leave, he would record voices of his family members and take them to sea with him. He introduced me to the Kodak "Brownie" camera. He introduced me to a Smith-Corona typewriter and even to an accordion which I never really mastered but had fun trying to do so. I now see that those early introductions to media tools are now ones I have used and still use in my craft.

Daddy painted oil on canvas. Though not a trained artist he loved to draw. He told the story of painting a portrait of Bustamante and taking it to him as a gift. He loved his two daughters and their mother. Later in life while in retirement in Jamaica, missing the sea and his daughters who had emigrated to the US, Al questioned his decision to work so far away from home and from his children and not having a greater influence on them. Despite his pondering, he taught us to be creative, adventurous, and practical. He introduced us to critical thinking skills, inspired us to follow our dreams, and to love.

January 5

Dutty Boukman

Boukman was born in Jamaica but was allegedly deported to Saint-Domingue (Haiti) after he had been caught teaching other enslaved Africans to read. The moniker "Dutty" was not complimentary. It summed up how people who owned and enslaved Africans viewed enslaved Black men and women who were literate.

Boukman, who held positions as a commander (slave driver) and later a coach driver, held secret meetings with the enslaved Africans in Haiti.

Boukman declared at a meeting that "God who has created the shining sun above … is watching us and sees the misdeeds of the whites! The God of the whites demands crime. Our God is benevolent. Our God who is so good orders us to take vengeance!" A week later, on Aug. 24, 1791, the Haitian Revolution began. Boukman has been noted for his leadership skills, courage and fearlessness during the successful revolution.

January 6

Samuel Lewis

R. Samuel Lewis, L. Mr. and Mrs. Ezekiel and Margaret Lewis, Lucille Spied, Mrs. Leante Lewis
Contributor: Alpheus Lewis (Son)

Samuel Lewis of Golden Grove, St. Ann, Jamaica was a community man and political operative. He attended the Beechamville Methodist Church on Sunday mornings and because of limited transportation at the time he walked to get there and back. Uncle Sam as he was affectionately called was a disciplined man. However, unlike most fathers at the time, he did not flog his children. He would give a stern look of caution that everyone understood.

Uncle Sam was an active and helpful member of his community. He assisted people in his village to sell their agricultural produce (fruits, vegetables and coffee berries) at the best prices. Uncle Sam also engaged in his own agricultural activities where he planted short and long term crops such as yam, banana, potato and rearing animals to feed his family and to generate income. He was an active political operative of the People's National Party and he was lead spokesman for political representative Dr. Iron Lloyd. He was celebrated for his engaging and lively political speeches at community meetings.

Uncle Sam often assisted people in his village who could not read by writing their letters and interpreting documents for them. He was referred to as the community lawyer.

He fought in World War I with the British army as a sergeant. He later travelled to Panama to help build the Canal and then to Cuba to work on a farm. He returned to Jamaica and married Leante Johnson. The marriage produced three girls and three boys. He also had a son and a daughter before his marriage. We all learned to value farming, family, community, and justice from him.

January 7

Carmen Williamson Garrick

Contributor: Delroy McCormack (Grandson)

Daughter to a mother of Maroon descent and a European father, Carmen was the mother to many in the district of her birth. With eleven children in the home, she was the consummate mother and wife focused on creating home for her children and the children of many others in the district. She passed her wisdom on to her many grandchildren. And the love and care she had for other people's biological children are passed on to her children and grandchildren. Today one of her grandchildren follows her footsteps in the district of her birth in Golden Grove, St. Ann, Jamaica, W.I.

She was a disciplinarian who wouldn't miss hitting you with a flying object as we were running away from her to avoid a flogging. She was also someone with whom we could talk.

She taught us punctuality and the importance of keeping your word, "your word is your bond," she would say. She was an ardent church-goer: twice on Sundays and once on a week day. Auntie stressed the importance of education because she knew the value of being able to read and write. She would often scold us about the crab-toe writing and encouraged our better penmanship.

I grew up with Auntie from I was nine months old. I learned from her about her enterprising and entrepreneurial spirits and the hard work she never shunned in her pursuit of caring for herself and her family.

January 8

Zumbi
Zumbi dos Palmares: Hero of Brazil

"The legend of the Palmares quilombo…and its greatest leader, Zumbi, are central to the history and modern day struggle of Brazilians who recognize their African ancestry. All over Brazil, there are or have been hundreds of organizations and cultural groups named after this legendary leader, as well as a national holiday in recognition of Black consciousness and also Brazil's first and only predominantly Black college." - https://www.blackhistorybuff.com/blogs/the-black-history-buff-blog/zumbi-dos-palmares-hero-of-brazil

It is believed that Zumbi dos Palmares was born free in the Palmares region of Brazil in the year 1655. Although free, He was not content with the enslavement of Africans so he decided to liberate his people. He was the last of the military leaders of the Quilombo (Kimbundu word: "kilombo," of the North Mbundu Bantu language in Angola, meaning "warrior village or settlement") of Palmares. The Quilombo dos Palmares was a free society, which included the present day Brazilian coastal state of Alagoas.

Today, Zumbi is known as one of the great historic leaders of Brazil Quilombo dos Palmares was a self-sustaining republic of maroons located in "a region perhaps the size of Portugal in the hinterland of Bahia" (Braudel 1984). The Bahia Alagoas region of Brazil is where this free African settlement was located. At its height in the early 1600s, Palmares had a population of over 30,000. By 1630, it was described by the commentators as "the Promised Land" for escaped African slaves. King Ganga Zumba of Palmares offered emancipation for enslaved Africans entering its territories.

January 9

Harriet Tubman

c. 1820 - 1913

Harriet Tubman is perhaps the most well-known of all the Underground Railroad's "conductors." During a ten-year span she made 19 trips into the South and escorted over 300 Africans to freedom. She is reported to have said to Frederick Douglass, in all of her journeys she "never lost a single passenger."

Tubman was born into slavery in Maryland around 1820. At age five or six, she began to work as a house servant. Seven years later she was sent to work in the fields. While still in her teens, she suffered an injury that followed her for the rest of her life. Always ready to stand up for someone else, Tubman blocked a doorway to protect another field-hand from an angry overseer. The overseer picked up and threw an object at the field hand. The object fell short, striking Tubman on the head. She never fully recovered from the blow, which subjected her to spells in which she would fall into a deep sleep.

Around 1844 she married a free Black named John Tubman and took his last name. (She was born Araminta Ross; she later changed her first name to Harriet – her mother's name.) In 1849, in fear that she, along with the other enslaved Africans on the plantation, was to be sold, Tubman decided to run away. She set out one night on foot with some assistance from a friendly white woman. She followed the North Star by night, making her way to Pennsylvania and soon after to Philadelphia, where she found work and saved her money.

Tubman even carried a gun for protection and which she used to threaten Africans if they became too tired and wanted to stop or decided to turn back, telling them, "You'll be free or die."

January 10
Marcus Mosiah Garvey – Jamaica's First National Hero
April 17, 1887 - 1940

Marcus Mosiah Garvey Jr., Jamaica's first national hero, was born in St. Ann, Jamaica. After immigrating to the United States, Garvey preached his doctrine of self-pride and freedom to Black people. He, along with Amy Ashwood, founded the Universal Negro Improvement Association (UNIA), which touched the lives of over 8 to 11 million Black people living in North and Latin America, the West Indies and Africa. Garvey launched successful businesses, encouraged entrepreneurship and urged millions of people to buy from Black-owned businesses.

Garvey was inspired by Booker T. Washington's philosophy and practice.

Garvey inspired other Black leaders and activists such as Louis Farrakhan, President Nnamdi Azikiwe, Elijah Muhammad, President Kwame Nkrumah, Kwame Ture, President Jomo Kenyatta, President Nelson Mandela, President Patrice Lumumba, President Julius Nyerere, Malcolm X and Martin Luther King Jr. Mr. Garvey's influence, teachings and legacy still live on today as he is recognized as the first Black man to awaken the dignity of the Black race in Jamaica, North America and Africa.

Divisions of the UNIA in North America, Latin America, the Caribbean and Africa continue the work of living into the aims and objectives of the UNIA.

Marcus Garvey was married to Amy Ashwood. His second wife was Amy Jacques.

Garvey founded the People's Political Party in 1929 – after his return from the US - which had a manifesto that included land reform to benefit tenant farmers, minimum wage, protection for native industries, technical schools in each parish, and city status for Montego Bay and Port Antonio. It was the first political party in Jamaica and in a general election, Garvey was elected councilor for Allman Town, Kingston in 1929 and 1930.

January 11

Tacky

Tacky, in the 1700s, was a Coromantee chief of the Akan people from Ghana. He led one of the most significant rebellions in Jamaica and the Caribbean. Tacky's position as an overseer on the Frontier plantation in the St. Mary's parish of Jamaica gave him the opportunity to draw plans for a rebellion. According to the *Jamaica Gleaner*, "on Easter Monday, 1760, Tacky and his warriors went to Port Maria, St. Mary, where they killed the shopkeeper of Fort Haldane and took gunpowder, muskets and cannon balls. They then went to the plantations killing white people, and by morning light hundreds more enslaved Africans had joined them.

In the end, a reported 60 whites, and 300-400 enslaved Africans were killed." Tacky's rebellion helped spur on uprisings on estates in the other parishes including Westmoreland in the west, St. John in the south center of the island (now merged into St. Catherine), St. Thomas in the east, Clarendon, and St. Dorothy (now merged into St. Catherine). The Maroons helped in the capture of Tacky whose head was placed on display in St. Catherine.

January 12

Nomzamo Winifred Zanyiwe Madikizela

September 26, 1936 - April 2, 2018

Madikizela-Mandela's Xhosa name was Nomzamo ("She who tries"). She was born in a village that is now the Eastern Cape Province. Her parents, Columbus and Gertrude, who had a white father and Xhosa mother, were both teachers. Columbus was a history teacher and a headmaster, and Gertrude was a domestic science teacher. Winnie's mother died when Winnie was nine years old.

Madikizela-Mandela became the head girl at her high school in Bizana went on to study social work at the Jan Hofmeyr School of Social Work in Johannesburg. She earned a degree in social work in 1956, and several years later earned a bachelor's degree in international relations from the University of the Witwatersrand. One of her first jobs was as a social worker at Baragwanath Hospital in Soweto.

Winnie Madikizela-Mandela **OLS MP** served as an anti-apartheid activist and politician, and the second wife of Nelson Mandela. Together they had two children. She served as a Member of Parliament from 1994 to 2003, and from 2009 until her death, and was a deputy minister of arts and culture from 1994 to 1996. A member of the African National Congress (ANC) political party, she served on the ANC's National Executive Committee and headed its Women's League. Madikizela-Mandela was known to her supporters as the "Mother of the Nation."

In 1963, after Nelson Mandela was imprisoned following the Rivonia Trial, Winnie Mandela became his public face during the 27 years he spent in jail. During that period, she rose to prominence within the domestic anti-apartheid movement. She was detained by apartheid state security services on various occasions, tortured, subjected to banning orders and spent several months in solitary confinement.

January 13

Cudjoe

Cudjoe and his brother, Accompong, led the Maroon "Freedom Fighters" in what was dubbed the First Maroon War against the English Occupation Army that had claimed Jamaica.

Cudjoe possessed all the qualities of a born commander. He defeated the British in every encounter. Before planning a plantation raid, he would have his spies mingle freely with the enslaved Africans in the markets and on the plantations, gathering information on when and where to strike.

Cudjoe's war against the white European inhabitants of Jamaica had brought him great fame among the white planters and the Africans who had run away from enslavement as he left burning properties and a trail of white bodies behind him. According to *gutenburg.org*, Cudjoe's men were "always supplied with arms and ammunition; and as his men were perfect marksmen, never wasted a shot, and never risked a battle, his forces naturally increased, while those of his opponents were decimated."

January 14
Samuel Sharpe – One of Jamaica's National Heroes
1801 - 1832

"I would rather die upon yonder gallows, than live in slavery," are the famous words of Samuel Sharpe before he was put to death. Sharpe was a Baptist deacon, a freedom fighter and the main instigator of the 1831 Christmas Rebellion, which was instrumental in bringing about the abolition of slavery in Jamaica. In 1831, the British Parliament began discussions concerning the abolition of slavery — a move European plantation owners and owners of enslaved Africans were against. Sharpe became aware of this and brought it to the attention of his congregation. He devised a plan of resistance in 1831, by which the enslaved people would refuse to work on Christmas Day of 1831 and afterwards, unless their grievances were addressed. The rebellion was a key moment in the fight for the abolition of slavery as just a few years later, in 1834, slavery would be abolished and a system of "apprenticeship" would be instituted.

Samuel Sharpe was the main instigator and organizer of the 1831 Slave Rebellion, which began on the Kensington Estate in St. James and which was largely instrumental in bringing about the abolition of slavery.

Because of his intelligence and leadership qualities, Sam Sharpe became a "daddy", or leader of the Africans who were Baptists in Montego Bay, St. James. Religious meetings were the only permissible forms of organised activities for the slaves. Sam Sharpe was able to communicate his concern and encourage political thought, concerning events in England which affected the enslaved Africans in Jamaica.

In 1982 the Right Excellent Sam Sharpe was conferred the Order of the National Hero as per Government Notice 23 Jamaica Gazette along with Nanny of the Maroons.

January 15

Martin Luther King, Jr. – Nobel Prize Recipient

January 15, 1929 - April 4, 1968

During the less than thirteen years of Dr. Martin Luther King, Jr.'s public leadership of the modern American Civil Rights Movement, from around 1955 until April 4, 1968, a few more African Americans achieved more progress towards justice in America than the previous 350 years had produced. Dr. King is widely regarded as America's pre-eminent advocate of nonviolence and one of the greatest nonviolent leaders in world history.

Drawing inspiration from his Christian faith and the peaceful teachings of Mahatma Gandhi, Rev. Dr. King led a nonviolent movement in the late 1950's and '60s to achieve legal equality for African-Americans in the United States.

While others were advocating for freedom by any means necessary, including violence, Martin Luther King, Jr. used the power of words and acts of nonviolent resistance, such as protests, grassroots organizing, and civil disobedience to achieve seemingly impossible goals. He went on to lead similar campaigns against poverty and international conflict, always maintaining fidelity to his principles that men and women everywhere, regardless of color or creed, are equal members of the human family.

January 16

Toussaint L'Overture
1743-1803

Toussaint L'Ouverture was a former enslaved African who rose to become the leader of the only successful slave revolt in modern history known as the Haitian Revolution.

Born into slavery on May 20, 1743 in the French colony of Saint Dominque, L'Ouverture was the eldest son of Gaou Guinon, an African prince who was captured by slavers. At a time when revisions to the French Code Noir (Black Code) legalized the harsh treatment of enslaved Africans as property, young L'Overture instead inspired kindness from those in authority over him. His godfather, the priest Simon Baptiste, for example, taught him to read and write. Impressed by L'Ouverture, Bayon de Libertad, the manager of the Breda plantation on which L'Ouverture was born, allowed him unlimited access to his personal library.

By the time he was twenty, the well-read and tri-lingual L'Ouverture—he knew French, Creole, and Latin—had also gained a reputation as a skilled horseman and for his knowledge of medicinal plants and herbs. More importantly, L'Ouverture had secured his freedom from de Libertad even as he continued to manage his former owner's household personnel and to act as his coachman. Over the course of the next eighteen years, L'Ouverture settled into life on the Breda plantation marrying fellow Catholic Suzanne Simon and parenting two sons, Isaac and Saint-Jean.

The events of August 22, 1791, the "Night of Fire", in which enslaved Africans revolted by setting fire to plantation houses and fields and killing whites, convinced the 48-year-old L'Ouverture that he should join the growing insurgency, although not before securing the safety of his wife and children in the Spanish-controlled eastern half of the island (Santo Domingo) and assuring that Bayon de Libertad and his wife were safe aboard a ship bound for the United States.

January 17

Ruth Smith
1900s

Ruth Smith was a member of the Women's Motor Corp. the second most prominent women's auxiliary of the Universal Negro Improvement Association (UNIA). (The most prominent was the Black Cross Nurses.) The Women's Motor Corp. also known as the Universal African Motor Corps was the female counterpart to the men's Universal African Legion, a para-military auxiliary. In the Women's Motor Corp. women received military training, dressed in military uniform and trained to become auto mechanics and skilled drivers.

Smith's reputation for being able to handle herself and an automobile attracted the attention of Madame DeMena – an international organizer for the UNIA. She became DeMena's personal driver and secretary.

Smith was born in Gadsden, Alabama in 1909 and relocated with her family to Detroit when she was a child. It was in Detroit where Smith's mother joined the UNIA and Smith also joined at the age of ten.

January 18

Amy Ashwood Garvey
January 18, 1897 - May 3, 1969

Amy Ashwood Garvey – Founder of the Universal Negro Improvement Association (UNIA) in Jamaica in 1914. Born in Jamaica, Amy Ashwood was one of three children of Michael Delbert Ashwood and Maudriana Thompson. She was raised in Panama, where her father ran a restaurant and worked as a printer. Supported by her family in her desire for education, she returned to Jamaica to attend a high school for girls.

Ashwood became the first secretary and a member of the board of management of the newly formed UNIA in 1914 - 1915. She worked with Marcus Garvey in organizing the inaugural meeting in Collegiate Hall in Kingston, the weekly Tuesday night elocution meetings, and the office that was soon established in a house on Charles Street rented by the Ashwood family. She also helped to establish the Ladies' auxiliary wing of the movement and was involved in early plans to build an industrial school.

Ashwood became the general secretary of the organization in 1919 and was one of the first directors of the Black Star Line – the shipping lines formed through the UNIA. She put her life on the line for Marcus Garvey, helping to shield him when he was shot by George Tyler at the UNIA offices in October 1919. Amy Ashwood and Marcus Garvey were married on December 25, 1919. After the marriage ended in 1922, Ashwood became a world traveler remaining active in the arts and Pan-African movement internationally.

January 19
Paul Bogle – One of Jamaica's National Heroes
c. 1820 - October 24, 1865

Paul Bogle, it is believed, was born free about 1822 in Jamaica, W.I. The trading of Africans into slavery was abolished there in 1807 by the British. He was a Baptist deacon in Stony Gut, in the parish of St. Thomas, and was generally regarded as a peaceful man who shunned violence.

"In 1865, the American civil war and a severe drought had dramatically increased food costs in Jamaica, while collapsing sugar prices had cut estate wages and made work scarce," reported the *Jamaica Gleaner*. Poverty and injustice in the society and lack of public confidence in the central authority, urged Bogle and his brother Moses Bogle to lead a protest march. The people of Stony Gut walked to Spanish Town in the parish of St. Catherine – about 45 miles - to air their grievances to the governor. They were denied an audience with him.

After returning to St. Thomas, Bogle put in place a plan for a peaceful protest. A few days later he led another protest to the courthouse in Morant Bay. This erupted into violence initiated by a volunteer militia that was set up to halt the protestors and protect property. This encounter escalated into what is known as the Morant Bay rebellion. Bogle was held accountable, tried and executed.

In the long-term, the rebellion achieved its objectives. It paved the way for the establishment of just practices in the courts and it brought about a change in official attitude, which made possible the social and economic betterment of the some African living in Jamaica.

January 20

Kwame Nkrumah
September 21, 1909 - April 27, 1972

The first African-born Prime Minister of Ghana, Kwame Nkrumah was a prominent Pan-African organizer whose radical vision and bold leadership helped lead Ghana to independence in 1957. Nkrumah served as an inspiration to Martin Luther King, who often looked to Nkrumah's leadership as an example of nonviolent activism.

Nkrumah was born in the British colony of Nkroful, on the Gold Coast (now Ghana). Although raised in a small fishing village, Nkrumah was educated in the United States. He received both his Bachelor of Arts and Bachelor of Theology from Lincoln University and continued his education at the University of Pennsylvania, where he received a Masters of Philosophy and a Masters of Education (1942, 1943). While in college, Nkrumah became increasingly active in the Pan-African movement, the African Students Association of America, and the West African Students' Union. In 1945 Nkrumah played a central role in organizing the Fifth Pan-Africanist Congress.

In 1947 Nkrumah's activism attracted the attention of Ghanaian politician J. B. Danquah, who hired Nkrumah to serve as general secretary of the United Gold Coast Convention, an organization pursuing independence for the British colony. However, ideological differences between the two men led Nkrumah to found his own party, the Convention People's Party (CPP), in 1949.

Nkrumah and the CPP sought self-government through the nonviolent strategy of positive action which employed the tactics of protest and strike against the colonial administration. In 1951 Nkrumah and the CPP received a decisive majority of votes in Ghana's first general elections, and on March 22, 1952, Nkrumah became the first prime minister of the Gold Coast. It would be five more years before full independence was realized, and the Gold Coast became the self-governed nation of Ghana.

January 21

Booker Taliaferro Washington
April 18, 1856 – November 14, 1915
Founder and First President of Tuskegee Normal and Industrial Institute
(now Tuskegee University)

Booker Taliaferro Washington was a foremost Black educator of the late 19th and early 20th centuries. He had a major influence on race relations and was an influential presence in Black public affairs from 1895 until his death. He was an author, orator, a pre-eminent leader in the African American community and of the Black elite who was an adviser to many presidents of the United States.

Born in Franklin County, Virginia, Washington's mother was an enslaved African who worked as a cook. During his childhood and young adulthood Washington worked in a salt mine and a coal mine in West Virginia. He attended school while working in the mines.

Washington was from the last generation of Black American leaders born into slavery and became the leading voice of the former enslaved Africans and their descendants. They were newly oppressed in the South by disenfranchisement and the Jim Crow discriminatory laws enacted in the post-Reconstruction Southern states in the late 19th and early 20th centuries.

Washington was a key proponent of education and the creation and success of African-American businesses and one of the founders of the National Negro Business League. He was the founder of the Tuskegee Normal and Industrial Institute (now Tuskegee University) in 1881.

January 22

Richard Allen
February 14, 1760 - March 26, 1831

Richard Allen and his associate Absalom Jones were the leaders of the Black Methodist community in Philadelphia in 1793 when a yellow fever epidemic broke out. Many people, Black and white, were dying and hundreds more fled the city. City officials approached Allen and asked if the Black community could help serve as nurses to the suffering and help bury the dead.

Allen and Jones recognized the racism inherent in the request: asking Black folks to do the risky, dirty work for whites. But they consented—partly from compassion and partly to show the white community, in one more way, the moral and spiritual powers of Blacks.

Allen, born into slavery in Philadelphia, converted to Christianity at age seventeen and began preaching on the plantation on which he worked and at local Methodist churches. He preached whenever he had the chance. His owner, one of Allen's early converts, was so impressed with him that he allowed Allen to purchase his freedom.

The Reverend Richard Allen was the founder and first bishop of the African Methodist Episcopal Church, a major denomination in the U.S.

January 23

Wyatt Tee Walker
August 16, 1929 - January 23, 2018

Walker, as the Reverend Wyatt T. Walker, was a major figure in the Civil Rights Movement of the 1950s and 1960s, as well as a prominent minister, theologian of the Black religious tradition, and scholar and composer of Black gospel music. Walker was also a developer of affordable housing in New York City and co-founder of the first charter school approved by the State University of New York.

Walker's civil rights activities began while he was pastor of Gillfield Baptist Church in Petersburg, Virginia. There he worked to integrate the Petersburg Public Library and the lunch counters at bus stop cafes in the city. He left Gillfield to become the first full-time executive director of the Southern Christian Leadership Conference (SCLC), where he worked closely with Dr. Martin Luther King, Jr., whom he had met while in seminary at Virginia Union University in Richmond, Virginia. Working with SCLC Walker was a key strategist for several major civil rights protests, including the Birmingham Movement. Walker, along with his wife Theresa Ann, was arrested as part of the Freedom Rides in Jackson, Mississippi in 1961.

Walker, born in Brockton, Massachusetts, earned a B.S. in Chemistry and Physics, *magna cum laude* from Virginia Union University, a M.A. from its Graduate School of Divinity, and in 1975 he earned his D. Min. degree from the Colgate-Rochester Divinity School.

The Rev. Dr. Wyatt T. Walker moved to Harlem to become the senior pastor for Canaan Baptist Church of Christ. While there, Dr. Walker also worked with Governor Rockefeller as Special Assistant for Urban Affairs and became the largest single developer of affordable housing in New York City. Dr. Walker is responsible for the construction of the Adam Clayton Powell, Jr. State Office Building.

January 24

Fannie Lou Hamer
October 6, 1917 - March 14, 1977

Fannie Lou Hamer was an American voting and women's rights activist, community organizer, and a leader in the civil rights movement.

The forced (without her consent) hysterectomy experienced by Fannie Lou Hamer in 1961 was one of the moments that set her on the path to the forefront of the Mississippi Civil Rights movement. However, the incident that brought her into a public leadership role came a year later. On August 31, 1962, not long after attending a voting rights meeting organized by the Student Nonviolent Coordinating Committee (SNCC), Hamer joined 17 of her neighbors on a bus to Indianola, the county seat. Officials blocked most of the group from even attempting to register. Hamer and one man were the only ones allowed to fill out the application and take the literacy test, which both failed.

Hamer was a founder of the Mississippi Freedom Democratic Party (MFDP). It was formed to expand Black voter registration and challenge the legitimacy of the state's all-white Democratic Party. In 1964, with the support of the MFDP, Hamer ran for Congress.

Voting rights remained a priority, even after the passage of the Voting Rights Act in 1965, and Hamer took the lead in lawsuits that led to the first elections in which large numbers of Black residents of Sunflower County were registered and eligible to vote in 1967. She also organized plaintiffs for a school desegregation lawsuit, instituted livestock and agricultural co-ops to improve economic prospects in the Mississippi Delta, and was involved in the introduction of Head Start programs for low-income children of all races. Hamer had mixed success, particularly as her worsening health limited her capacity for public speaking and made raising funds to sustain these initiatives difficult.

January 25

Amy Jacques Garvey
December 31, 1895 - July 25, 1973

Amy Jacques Garvey was born in Jamaica and in adulthood expressed herself through a Pan-African lens. She was a Garveyite who worked diligently for the aims of the Universal Negro Improvement Association (UNIA). Her organizing and journalistic skills preserved many of the UNIA's activities and Marcus Garvey's speeches.

Amy Jacques Garvey compiled Marcus Garvey's work into the published book *Philosophy and Opinions of Marcus Garvey*. In the preface she says, "The history of contact between white and Black races for the last three hundred years or more, records only a series of pillages, wholesale murders, atrocious brutalities, industrial exploitation, disfranchisement of the one on the other; the strong against the weak; but the sun of evolution is gradually rising, shedding its light between the clouds of misery and oppression, and quickening and animating to racial consciousness and eventual national independence Black men and women the world over."

Amy Jacques was the second wife of the Honorable Marcus Mosiah Garvey.

January 26

Fidel Castro
August 13, 1926 - November 25, 2016

Fidel Alejandro Castro Ruz was a Cuban revolutionary and politician who served as Prime Minister of Cuba from 1959 to 1976 and President from 1976 to 2008. Ideologically he was a Marxist–Leninist and Cuban nationalist. Under his administration the Republic of Cuba became a one-party communist state; industry and business were nationalized, and state socialist reforms were implemented throughout society.

Fidel, as many call him, has come to be known as a fighter for freedom and justice for Africans. His leadership in the revolution in Cuba transformed the aspirations and the quality of life for Cubans many of whom are of African ancestry.

Fidel and his administration created the foundation and a system for all Cubans to be literate and have good quality health care. Cuba built a healthcare system whose medical teams have brought care to the developing world.

During the war for Angola's independence from Portugal, in the 1970s, Cuban troops were sent to support the indigenous Africans in Angola in their fight for liberation.

In 2020 worldwide pandemic, the administration that leads Cuba continues to practice Fidel's philosophy of serving humanity through a justice lens. Cuba has sent medical teams to nations such as Italy, Venezuela, Jamaica, Brazil, Togo, and Barbados.

Born in Birán, Oriente province (now Holguin Province) in eastern Cuba, Fidel Castro was the son of a wealthy Spanish farmer. While studying law at the University of Havana, Castro adopted leftist, anti-imperialist ideas from understanding society is divided between rich and poor, and that an imperialist system subjugates and exploits people. He saw the injustice and inhumanity in that and worked to change that.

January 27

Frederick Douglass
c. 1818 - February 20, 1895

Frederick Douglass was a leader in the abolitionist movement, an early champion of women's rights, and author of several autobiographies that describe his experiences in slavery and life after the Civil War, including *Narrative of the Life of Frederick Douglass, an American Slave* (1845) and *What to the Slave Is the Fourth of July?*(1852).

Douglass was born into slavery, from which he escaped, sometime around 1818 in Maryland. While he had minimal formal education, he became one of the most famous intellectuals of his time, advising US presidents and lecturing to thousands on a range of topics, including women's rights and Irish home rule. Douglass' full name at birth was Frederick Augustus Washington Bailey. His mother, Bailey, was of Native American ancestry and his father of African and European ancestry. He took the name Douglass after he escaped.

While invited to and well-received in many places, crowds were not always hospitable to Douglass. While participating in an 1843 lecture tour through the Midwest, Douglass was chased and beaten by an angry mob before being rescued by a local Quaker family.

Before becoming well-known as an orator and champion for justice, Douglas was a ship caulker who pooled his money with other African entrepreneurs to purchase a ship-building yard in Baltimore Harbor. They did this so the Africans, who were fired from their jobs, because the Irish men complained about working with them, would have employment. Douglass, George Alexander Hackett and others founded the Chesapeake Marine Railway and Drydock Company, an African American owned ship-building company that operated from 1855 to 1873. They were assisted in their purchase by a white sympathizer when business owners refused to sell them a business.

January 28

George Wells Parker
September 18, 1882 - July 28, 1931

George Wells Parker was an African-American political activist and writer who co-founded the Hamitic League of the World. His parents were born in Virginia and South Carolina, and his family moved to Omaha when Parker was young. He attended Creighton University and later graduated from Harvard University, one of the first African-Americans to do so.

As a Black nationalist and contemporary of Marcus Garvey, Parker's views on Africa as the cradle of civilization foreshadowed increased fascination with Egyptian imagery by African-Americans.

In 1916 Parker started helping African Americans resettle in Omaha and, by 1917, he helped found the Hamitic League of the World to promote African pride and Black economic progress.

As a historian committed towards accelerating racial self-awareness, Parker's work called for the revision of all textbooks that falsified and deleted the truth concerning Black folk. His lecture on *The African Origin of the Grecian Civilization* was delivered to supporters in Omaha and then published in the *Journal of Negro History* in 1917. Parker argued that new anthropological research had demonstrated that Mesopotamian and Greek civilization originated in Africa. In 1918 the League published his pamphlet *Children of the Sun*, which further developed his arguments for the African origins presented in classical Egyptian, Asian and European civilizations.

Parker had an ideological counterpart in Cyril Briggs, a Caribbean-born journalist based in New York City who founded the African Blood Brotherhood. The organizations created by these two men often clashed and collaborated.

January 29

Elinor Young White
September 26, 1900 - September 23, 1975

Elinor White was born in Mississippi to Lawson Robinson and Clara Young. She moved to Chicago where she met and married William White. They had one daughter, Clara (Clarine).

Mother White, as she was respectfully called, believed in providing service to her people, so she was involved in her community: she worked within her church, served as Village Clerk and ran for Mayor of Robbins, Illinois.

Mother White was deeply engaged in the Universal Negro Improvement Association (UNIA). She was secretary of the Chicago Division; one of the select few chosen to attend the Honorable Marcus M. Garvey's School of African Philosophy; a UNIA Commissioner of the State of Illinois; a juvenile organizer; and appointed personal representative to the Honorable Marcus M. Garvey. She attended every Convention from 1922, the year she joined the UNIA, until she made her transition in 1975.

Mother White was a researcher, a lecturer, a writer, and an inspiration to us all. She was a true Garveyite.

Source: *Women of the UNIA*, Gwendolyn Martin, Brenda Amoakon, T. M. Myers

January 30

Carlos Cooks
June 23, 1913 - May 5, 1966

Carlos A. Cooks was born in the Dominican Republic to James Henry Cooks and Alice Cooks, who were originally from the neighboring island of St. Martin. He received formal education in Santo Domingo until he moved to New York in 1929 where he went on to higher learning. Cooks was known for his love of sports and his expertise in boxing. His intellect was recognized from an early age and he attended the leadership school in the Voodoo *Sacré* Society.

Cooks' grew up among a Garveyite family. His father and his uncle were among the many St. Martiners who were members of the Marcus Garvey-led Universal Negro Improvement Association (UNIA). He was a key link in the history of Black American nationalism between Marcus Garvey before him and Malcolm X, whom he influenced. Carlos Cooks administered the Advance Division of the UNIA after Marcus Garvey was deported. He founded the African Nationalist Pioneer Movement and spoke the concept "Buy Black."

It was Cooks who maintained an African Nationalist Legion who were mentally prepared and physically ready to join the African Liberation struggle, who designated August 17th – the birthday of Marcus Garvey – as the first Black holiday, official or unofficial, and who formed an independent school, complete with a course in Kiswahili (1954). Kiswahili is a Bantu language and the indigenous language of the Swahili people of Eastern and Central Africa.

Cooks did not receive much publicity because he honored an oath to not promote himself. He was focused on doing the work.

January 31
John Henrik Clarke (born John Henry Clark)
January 1, 1915 - July 12, 1998

John Henrik Clarke was an African American historian, writer, professor, and founder of the African Heritage Studies Association and the Black Caucus of the African Studies Association that influenced academia through the African Studies departments in many US colleges and universities.

Born in Union Springs Alabama, Clarke moved to Harlem in 1933. There he developed as a writer and lecturer. Study circles such as the Harlem History Club and the Harlem Writers' Workshop influenced him. He studied at New York University, Columbia University, Hunter College, the New School of Social Research and the League for Professional Writers, and he earned a bachelors (1992) and doctorate degree (1994), from Pacific Western University (now California Miramar University). He was an autodidact whose mentors included the scholar Arturo Alfonso Schomburg.

He served as a non-commissioned officer in the United States Army Air Forces attaining the rank of master sergeant.

Clarke was co-founder of the *Harlem Quarterly* (1949–51), book review editor of the *Negro History Bulletin* (1948–52), associate editor of the magazine, *Freedomways,* and a feature writer for the Black-owned *Pittsburgh Courier.*

He taught at the New School for Social Research, was the founding chairman of the department of Black and Puerto Rican Studies at Hunter College, and was the Carter G. Woodson Distinguished Visiting Professor of African History at Cornell University's Africana Studies and Research Center. He lectured at several places in Africa including the University of Ghana and the University of Ibadan, Nigeria. While in Ghana he met President Kwame Nkrumah whom he

Dr. John Henrik Clarke's devotion to the Pan-African ideal was exemplified through his ability to bring people together throughout the African world.

February 1

Marianne Samad
1920 - 2019

Marianne Samad was born in New York to parents who were Garveyites. She lived by the principles of Garveyism and was moved to create clothing for the African boys and young men in schools in Harlem where she worked. Her creation was inspired by her desire to foster pride in their African heritage.

Samad was impressed with the royalty of the attire of she saw African men who were visiting the United Nations wearing. That gave her the idea to create something similar for the boys and men of Harlem. They wore her design with pride.

That creation became known as the dashiki.

Samad who met her husband Clarence Thomas in New York, relocated with him to the land of his birth, Jamaica and carried on the mantle of teaching Garveyism to eager and inquisitive minds.

February 2

Coretta Scott King

April 27, 1927 - January 30, 2006

Although better known for being the wife of famed civil rights leader Dr. Martin Luther King Jr., Coretta Scott King created her own legacy in the movement to end injustice. She was an author, an advocate for African American equality, and a singer who often incorporated music in her civil rights work. She also worked to continue her husband's legacy after his death.

Coretta Scott was born in Marion, Alabama to parents were both entrepreneurs and a mother who was musically talented. As a child, Scott expressed interest in music and quickly excelled in grade school as lead in the choir. She was the valedictorian at her high school and went on to receive her BA in music from Antioch College in Yellow Springs, Ohio. Scott was awarded a scholarship to further her music studies at the New England Conservatory of Music in Boston, Massachusetts. While studying at the school Scott was introduced to then, doctoral student Martin Luther King Jr.

Working side by side with her husband throughout the 1950s and '60s, Scott-King took part in the Montgomery Bus Boycott of 1955, journeyed to Ghana to mark that nation's independence in 1957, traveled to India on a pilgrimage in 1959 and worked to pass the 1964 Civil Rights Act. She also worked as a public mediator and liaison to peace and justice organizations.

February 3

Eduardo Chivambo Mondelane
June 20, 1920 - February 3, 1969

Eduardo Chivambo Mondlane was the architect of Mozambique's national unity. He had a vision of a free, united and independent Mozambique, unshackled from Portugal's colonial authorities. Although he was assassinated while in exile, his legacy lives on.

Mondlane served as the founding president of the Mozambican Liberation Front (FRELIMO) from 1962, the year that FRELIMO was founded in Tanzania, until his assassination. He was an anthropologist by profession who also worked at the United Nations and as a history and sociology professor at Syracuse University in New York State.

Mondlane, the son of a tribal chief was born in Mandlakazi in the province of Gaza in Portuguese East Africa (Mozambique). He worked as a shepherd until the age of 12 attending several different primary schools in Mozambique and South Africa. He was expelled from South Africa in 1949, following the rise of the Apartheid government. He studied at the University of Lisbon, Portugal and earned his academic degrees from universities in the USA.

Through Mondlane's leadership, FRELIMO was supported by several Western countries and the Union of Soviet Socialist Republics, as well as by many African states. FRELIMO began a guerrilla war in 1964 to obtain Mozambique's independence from Portugal. Mondlane wanted not merely to fight for independence but also for a change to a socialist society.

In 1969, a bomb planted in a book sent to Mondlane at the FRELIMO Headquarters in Dar es Salaam, Tanzania exploded when he opened the package - killing him.

February 4

Thomas Isidore Noel Sankara

December 21, 1949 - October 15, 1987

Thomas Isidore Noël Sankara was a Burkinabé military captain, Marxist revolutionary, Pan-Africanist theorist, and President of Burkina Faso from 1983 to 1987. Viewed by supporters as a charismatic and iconic figure of the revolution, he is commonly referred to as "Africa's Che Guevara" after the Argentine revolutionary.

Sankara's leadership turned his West African country with the colonial designation of Upper Volta to a dynamic progressive nation renamed Burkina Faso ("Land of the Honorable People"). He led one of the most ambitious programs of sweeping reforms ever seen in Africa. It sought to fundamentally reverse the structural social inequities inherited from the French colonialists.

Among Sankara's accomplishments were the vaccination of 2.5 million children against meningitis, yellow fever and measles in a matter of weeks; the start of a nation-wide literacy campaign, increasing the literacy rate from 13% in 1983 to 73% in 1987, and the planting more than 10 million trees to prevent desertification.

Sankara built roads and a railway, without foreign aid, to tie the nation together. He held women in high esteem, appointing them to high governmental positions, recruited them into the military, and granted them pregnancy leave while they pursued an education. And he outlawed female genital mutilation, forced marriages and polygamy.

Sankara helped the nation's economy by selling off the government's fleet of Mercedes cars and made the Renault 5 (the cheapest car sold in Burkina Faso at that time) the official service car of the ministers. He reduced the salaries of all public servants, including his own, and forbade the use of government chauffeurs and first class airline tickets. He redistributed land from the feudal landlords and gave it directly to the peasants. Wheat production rose, making the country more self-sufficient.

February 5

Muhammad Ali

January 17, 1942 - June 3, 2016

Muhammad Ali (born Cassius Marcellus Clay Jr.) was an American professional boxer, activist and philanthropist. Nicknamed "the Greatest", he is widely regarded as one of the most significant and celebrated figures of the 20th century and as one of the greatest boxers of all time.

Years after he burst upon the scene as a gold-medal winner at the 1960 Olympics, in Rome, Ali remained a magical figure, known and loved throughout the world. Ali brought unprecedented speed, grace, and showmanship to boxing. His charm and wit radically changed the public's expectation of a boxing champion. His accomplishments in the ring are legendary.

In 1966 Ali refused to be drafted into the military citing his religious beliefs and ethical opposition to the Vietnam War. He was found guilty of draft evasion and was stripped of his Heavyweight Boxing Champion title. He stayed out of prison as he appealed the decision to the Supreme Court, which overturned his conviction in 1971, but he had not fought for nearly four years and lost a period of peak performance as an athlete.

Ali's actions as a conscientious objector to the Vietnam War made him an icon for the larger counterculture generation, and he was a high-profile figure of racial pride for African Americans during the civil rights movement. As a Muslim, Ali was initially affiliated with Elijah Muhammad's Nation of Islam. Ali's embrace of the Nation of Islam in the 1960s and his insistence on being called Muhammad Ali instead of his "slave name," Cassius Clay, heralded a new era in Black pride.

As a humanitarian Ali helped people in nations worldwide and lives on through the Muhammad Ali Center in Louisville, Kentucky.

February 6

John Robert Lewis
February 21, 1940 - July 17, 2020

John Robert Lewis, American statesman, civil rights activist and longtime Georgia Congressman, was a strategist and practitioner for justice for African Americans in the USA. The son of Alabama sharecroppers, Lewis was a central figure in the key civil rights battles of the 1960s, including the Freedom Rides and the Selma to Montgomery voting rights march.

Lewis brought his fight for human rights and racial reconciliation to Congress where he served Georgia's 5th Congressional District from 1987 until his death. He sponsored bills primarily in the areas of taxation, health, crime and law enforcement, education, international affairs, families, transportation and public works, and social welfare.

Lewis was attracted to the liberation movement as a young adult when he heard about the Montgomery Bus Boycott in 1955. His activism started in Nashville, Tennessee when he was a student at Fisk University where he earned a bachelor's degree in Religion and Philosophy. He was part of a group of young activists studying the philosophy of nonviolence. He served as chairman of the Student Nonviolent Coordinating Committee.

Lewis was arrested more than 40 times. He was involved in lunch counter sit-ins; freedom rides on interstate buses; and he was the youngest speaker at the 1963 March on Washington. He was consistent in the practice of the non-violence philosophy. The most visibly brutal attack on the peaceful protesters by the sheriffs, of March 1965, as they tried to cross the Edmund Pettus Bridge over the Alabama River did not change Lewis' perspective. He and hundreds of protestors marching for their voting rights were violently beaten by police.

Representative John Lewis was presented with the 2010 Medal of Freedom by President Barack Obama in 2011. The medal is the highest honor awarded to civilians.

February 7

Nancy M. Strong

July 25, 1909 - February 17, 2000

Nancy M. Strong was of a quiet demeanor but seemed to have carved out a niche for herself that was helpful for speeding services to the officials of the organization – Universal Negro Improvement Association and African Communities League (UNIA-ACL) and members at large. She could always be found in her chosen spot in the dining hall where she could see all coming and going as they received their food and she could make sure they paid for what they received and did it with a smile.

When her services were complete at the close of meals, she could be seen upstairs in the Convention Hall quietly observing the business of the hour as an observer and participant in the organizational affairs.

Elder Strong was born to Charlie and Nannie Mills in Yancey's Mill, Virginia. When she became of adult age, she relocated to Philadelphia, Pennsylvania. There she became employed as a Housekeeping Assistant and went on to graduate from Apex Beauty School. She later joined the African Methodist Episcopal (AME) Church. Even though she was wheelchair-bound for over twenty years, she was referred to as being the best in everything. One of her favorite expressions when things didn't go as she thought they should, she would say, "Mercy, Mercy, Mercy."

Some of her favorite things were cooking, knitting, and singing.

Elder Strong loved people and received many awards for supporting people yet it seemed her most cherished community decision was her membership into the UNIA-ACL. She led by her peaceful and consistent participation as a follower as a Garveyite.

February 8

Nganga Nzumbi – Ganga Zumba
Ca. 1630 - 1678

Nganga Nzumbi was the first leader of the massive runaway slave settlement of Quilombo dos Palmares, or Angola Janga, in the present-day state of Alagoas, Brazil. Zumba was an enslaved African who escaped bondage on a sugar plantation and eventually rose to the position of highest authority within the kingdom of Palmares and earned the corresponding title of *Ganga Zumba*.

Although some Portuguese documents regard Ganga Zumba as his proper name, and this name is widely used today, the most important of the documents translate the name as "Great Lord." In Kikongo, *nganga a nzumbi* was "the priest responsible for the spiritual defense of the community" which was a *kilombo* or military settlement made up multiple groups. A letter written to him by the governor of Pernambuco in 1678 and now found in the Archives of the University of Coimbra, calls him "Ganazumba," which is a better translation of "Great Lord" (in Kimbundu).

Ganga is believed to have been the son of princess Aqualtune, daughter of a king of Kongo in Africa. He, other family members, and court officials were captured by the Portuguese. It is believed that some were sent to Spanish America and others to northeast Brazil which at the time was controlled by the Dutch.

February 9

Charles Edward Anderson Berry

October 18, 1926 - March 18, 2017

Charles Edward Anderson Berry, popularly known as Chuck Berry, was an American singer, songwriter and guitarist, and one of the pioneers of rock and roll music. Nicknamed the "Father of Rock and Roll", Berry refined and developed rhythm and blues into the major elements that made rock and roll distinctive with songs such as *Maybellene* (1955), *Roll Over Beethoven* (1956), *Rock and Roll Music* (1957), and *Johnny B. Goode* (1958).

Writing lyrics that focused on teen life and consumerism and developing a music style that included guitar solos and showmanship, Berry was a major influence on subsequent rock music.

Born into a middle-class African-American family in St. Louis, Berry had an interest in music from an early age and gave his first public performance at Sumner High School. While still a high school student he was convicted of armed robbery and was sent to a reformatory, where he was held from 1944 to 1947. After his release, Berry settled into married life and worked at an automobile assembly plant.

By early 1953, influenced by the guitar riffs and showmanship techniques of the blues musician T-Bone Walker, Berry began performing with the Johnnie Johnson Trio. His break came when he traveled to Chicago in May 1955 and met Muddy Waters, who suggested he contact Leonard Chess, of Chess Records. With Chess, he recorded *Maybellene*—Berry's adaptation of the country song *Ida Red* - which sold over a million copies, reaching number one on *Billboard* magazine's rhythm and blues chart.

February 10

Medgar Wiley Ever

July 2, 1925 - June 12, 1963

Medgar Wiley Evers was born in Decatur, Mississippi, attending school there until he was inducted into the U.S. Army in 1943. Despite fighting for his country as part of the Battle of Normandy, Evers soon found that his skin color gave him no freedom when he and five friends were forced away at gunpoint from voting in a local election. Despite his resentment over such treatment, Evers enrolled at Alcorn State University, majoring in business administration. He competed on the university's football and track teams, debate team and performed in the choir. He was also president of the junior class.

Evers applied to the then-segregated University of Mississippi Law School in 1954. When his application was rejected, Evers became the focus of a National Association for the Advancement of Colored People (NAACP) campaign to desegregate the school, a case aided by the U.S. Supreme Court ruling in the case of Brown v. Board of Education 347 US 483 that segregation was unconstitutional. In December of that year, Evers became the NAACP's first field officer in Mississippi. He played an instrumental role in desegregating the University of Mississippi.

His public investigations into the murder of Emmett Till and his vocal support of Clyde Kennard left him vulnerable to attacks. On May 28, 1963, a Molotov cocktail was thrown into the carport of his home, and five days before his death, he was nearly run down by a car after he emerged from the Jackson NAACP office. A local television station had granted Evers time for a short speech, his first in Mississippi, where he outlined the goals of the Jackson Movement. Following the speech, threats on Evers' life increased.

February 11

Jimmie Lee Jackson
December 16, 1938 - February 26, 1965

Jimmie Lee Jackson was an African American veteran and civil rights activist in Marion, Alabama, and a deacon in the Baptist church. On February 18, 1965, while unarmed and participating in a peaceful voting rights march in his city, he was beaten by troopers and fatally shot by an Alabama state trooper. He was trying to protect his grandfather and mother during a state troopers attack on the marchers. Jackson died eight days later in the hospital.

His death helped inspire the first of three Selma to Montgomery marches on March 7, 1965, a major event in the civil rights movement that helped gain congressional passage of the Voting Rights Act of 1965. This opened the door to millions of African Americans being able to vote again in Alabama and across the Southern United States, regaining participation as citizens in the political system for the first time since the turn of the 20th century. Most had been disenfranchised since then by state constitutions and discriminatory practices that made voter registration and voting more difficult.

Jackson was honored at his memorial service, eulogized as a martyr to a moral cause. He was buried in Heard Cemetery, an old slave burial ground, next to his father. His headstone was paid for by the Perry County Civic League. In the decades since, his headstone has been vandalized, bearing the marks of at least one shotgun blast.

February 12

Maya Angelou

April 4, 1928 - May 28, 2014

An acclaimed American poet, storyteller, activist, and autobiographer, Maya Angelou was born Marguerite Johnson in St. Louis, Missouri. Angelou had a career as a singer, dancer, actress, composer, and Hollywood's first female Black director, but became most famous as a writer, editor, essayist, playwright, and poet.

As a civil rights activist, Angelou worked for Dr. Martin Luther King Jr. and Malcolm X. She was also an educator and served as the Reynolds Professor of American Studies at Wake Forest University.

In some settings Angelou was recognized "as a spokesperson for… all people who are committed to raising the moral standards of living in the United States."

She served on two US presidential committees, for Gerald Ford in 1975 and for Jimmy Carter in 1977. In 2000, Angelou was awarded the National Medal of Arts by President Bill Clinton. In 2010, she was awarded the Presidential Medal of Freedom, the highest civilian honor in the U.S., by President Barack Obama. Angelou was awarded over 50 honorary degrees before her death.

Two of Angelou's most famous works are *I Know Why the Caged Bird Sings* (1969) and *Mrs. Flowers: A Moment of Friendship* (1986).

February 13

J. A. George Irish
May 17, 1942 - February 12, 2019

Contributor: Ken G. Irish-Bramble, PhD. (Son)

J.A. George Irish O.E. was born in Baker Hill, Montserrat W.I. Starting from humble beginnings he grew to become an icon whose legacy extends throughout the Americas - known for his cultural and academic work and for his social activism in his earlier years. Irish was an accomplished academic, musician, community activist, social-engineer, and leader. He exemplified the ideals of Black pride, nationalism, self-reliance and cultural pride. He published more than 32 books and received more than 120 awards.

Irish left a legacy. As a folklorist, he wrote, composed and published numerous folksongs, poems and short-stories. He believed that the preservation and promotion of native "creole" culture was a priority. He founded cultural groups such as the Emerald Community Singers and, the Montserrat Theatre Group. Through the Caribbean Diaspora Press, *Wadabagei: A Journal of the Caribbean and its Diasporas* he offered scholars the opportunity to publish their works on the Caribbean Diasporic experience. He founded Caribbean regional debating competitions to encourage regional networking among young scholars. He founded Montserrat Allied Workers Union (MAWU), a political party United National Front (UNF), several schools and developed programs in Latin America to empower sustainable community development.

Irish earned a degree in Modern Languages and a Ph.D. in Spanish from the University of the West Indies (UWI), Jamaica. He taught at UWI, at Medgar Evers College City University of New York, and he was the director of Caribbean Research Center at Medgar. He believed that through support of each other's aspirations we could accomplish great things. And that it begins with a sense of pride in who we are and a recognition that we have internally all the human resources we need to succeed.

February 14

Jean-Jacques Dessalines
1758-1806

Reviled for his brutality yet honored as one of the founding fathers of Haiti, Jean-Jacques Dessalines was second in command under Toussaint L'Overture during the Haitian Revolution and was the general who emerged after L'Overture's capture to lead the insurgents in declaring Haitian independence on January 1, 1804.

Dessalines was born into slavery in the French colony of Saint Dominque. Born to Congolese parents, he was originally given the name Duclos, after the plantation's owner. He later adopted the surname Dessalines after the free Black landowner who purchased him and from whom he escaped. Dessalines was treated harshly as an enslaved African and violence became a way of life that marked him throughout his military and brief political career contributing both to his success on the battlefield and to his eventual downfall.

Unable to read or write in the language of the enslavers, Dessalines was nonetheless a quick study under L'Overture earning the nickname "The Tiger" for his fury in battle. In 1794 Dessalines's military skill and leadership was vital to L'Overture's success in capturing the Spanish-controlled eastern half of the island, and in return, L'Overture made him governor of the south.

For a brief period of time after L'Overture's capture in 1802 Dessalines appeared to be siding with the French, but the move was nothing more than a ruse designed to trick the French into trusting Dessalines so that he could regroup the insurgents and continue the fight for independence. It was successful. When Dessalines proclaimed Saint Dominque's independence, he chose the name Haiti for his country, the name used by the island's aboriginal inhabitants.

February 15

Roger Gardere
1908 – 1981

Contributor: Jeffrey R. Gardere, M.Phil., M.S., D.Min., Ph.D., ABPP (Son)
Board Certified Clinical Psychologist

Roger Gardere was born in 1908 in Gonaives, Haiti to a very wealthy and aristocratic family. However, his political views, personal convictions and passions were always with the "people." In other words, he dedicated himself to working with those who were poor and struggling. At one point he became a lawyer and the first Superintendent of Schools in Gonaives, Haiti. His purpose and mission was to bring a quality education to the financially struggling families of Haiti.

Unfortunately, his liberal political views brought he and his brother into the cross hairs of Dr. Francois "Papa Doc" Duvalier, the self-appointed president for life of Haiti. When my uncle was murdered by the Tonton Macoutes (vicious thug secret police), because he shared my father's same political views, my mother Renee Gardere whisked my father to New York, where he lived in exile for the rest of his life.

Though my father became a U.S. citizen, he always held on to his Haitian heritage, and never stopped believing in the people of Haiti and their relentless fight for freedom. My father instilled these same values of egalite (equality) into me as I eventually became a healer and an advocate for mental health and social justice.

February 16

Family Roots: Abner Vandiver

1831-circa 1910

Contributor: Denise S. Brantley, AuD, MPH

The year was 1900 and Mt. Moriah Baptist Church in Anderson, South Carolina, was celebrating its 22nd anniversary. "Among the congregation at that time were all five original trustees of the church", including my maternal great, great grandfather --Abner Vandiver. (*The Vandiver-Williams Newsletter*, 2000). He and the other trustees apparently worked to pay for the land and then signed the deed for the land on which the church was built. Oral history and content from the church's dedication program in 1991 indicated that the evolution of the church included the labor of Blacks as well as the support of some of the white community. At a time when lynching was still prevalent and segregation was the order of the day, the creation of this church (which still thrives today) surely reflects the epic power of God.

Abner's father Isaac Vandiver was an African. I can only imagine that Isaac, born in 1782, was likely caught up in the Trans-Atlantic Slave Trade that took place between 1701 and 1800. During that time six million Africans were captured from the West Coast of Africa and transported across the Atlantic to the Americas. Isaac's son, Abner along with his wife and four children appear on the 1870 Census of Anderson County

I am proud to be a fifth-generation descendant of an African and the great, great granddaughter of a man whose character reflected his perseverance and faithfulness as a church founder. I know the strength and spirit of my ancestors has been passed down through my family over the generations. For that I am grateful.

February 17

Nnamdi Azikiwe PC

November 16, 1904 - May 11, 1996

President Nnamdi Benjamin Azikiwe, **PC** usually referred to as "Zik", was a Nigerian statesman and political leader who served as the first President of Nigeria from 1963 to 1966. Considered a driving force behind the nation's independence, he came to be known as the "father of Nigerian Nationalism."

The most central figure in Nigeria's efforts to obtain independence was Nnamdi Azikiwe who began his efforts as a journalist in the 1930s. He is said to have introduced populist, revolutionary journalism to Africa. Azikiwe learned his journalism in the United States, where he also experienced at first hand American racism and the efforts of radical journalists to combat it. When he returned to Africa, he helped to launch political movements and parties through his newspapers.

From Nnamdi Azikiwe, *Zik* (Cambridge, England, 1961) - from an address delivered at the Plenary Session of the British Peace Congress held at the Lime Grove Baths, Goldhawk Road, Hammersmith, London, on October 23, 1949:

Take a look at the map of Africa. You will notice that its contour presents a shape which reminds one of a ham bone. To some people this ham bone has been designed by destiny for the carving knife of European imperialism; to others, it is a question mark which asks whether Europe will act up to its ethical professions of peace and harmony. Yet the paradox of Africa is that its wealth and resources are among the root causes of wars. Since the Berlin Conference, the continent of Africa has been partitioned and dominated by armies of occupation in the guise of political trustees and guardians, represented by the following European countries: Britain, France, Belgium, Portugal, Spain, Italy, and also the Union of South Africa.

February 18

Herbert Lee

January 1, 1912 - September 25, 1961

Herbert Lee was an American civil rights activist in Mississippi remembered as a proponent of voting rights for African Americans in that state, who had been disenfranchised since 1890. He was a charter member of the National Association for the Advancement of Colored People (NAACP) in Amite County and sought to enfranchise Black Americans by encouraging voter registration.

Herbert Lee who worked with civil rights leader Bob Moses to help register Black voters was killed by a state legislator who claimed self-defense and was never arrested. Louis Allen, a Black man who witnessed the murder, was later also killed.

February 19

George Washington Lee

December 25, 1903 - May 7, 1955

Rev. George Washington Lee, one of the first Black people registered to vote in Humphreys County, Mississippi, used his pulpit and his printing press to urge others to vote. White officials offered Lee protection on the condition he end his voter registration efforts, but Lee refused and was murdered.

In 1954, Blacks in Belzoni, Mississippi outnumbered whites 2-to-1. But like all Southern Blacks, they were not allowed to attend white schools. They were forbidden to eat in white restaurants. They would be arrested if they sat in bus seats reserved for whites. And they did not vote.

Rev. Lee also ran a local grocery store and printing press and it is believed he had no illusions that integration would come in his lifetime or that it would come without a struggle. He believed the change would have to begin at the ballot box.

With the help of his friend Gus Courts, Lee started a chapter of the National Association for the Advancement of Colored People. They printed leaflets and held meetings, urging Blacks to pay the poll tax (a fee for voting that was later outlawed by the Voting Rights Act) and to register to vote.

Whites in town immediately organized a White Citizens Council to fight back. The names of Blacks registered to vote were put on a list and circulated to white businessmen who retaliated by firing them from their jobs, denying them credit and raising their rent.

White officials offered Lee protection on the condition he end his voter registration efforts. Lee refused.

February 20

Aretha Louise Franklin
March 25, 1942 - August 16, 2018

Aretha Louise Franklin was an American singer, songwriter, actress, pianist, and civil rights activist who began her musical career as a child singing gospel at New Bethel Baptist Church in Detroit, Michigan.

Franklin was born on, to Barbara (née Siggers) and Clarence LaVaughn "C. L." in Franklin, Tennessee. Her father was a Baptist minister and circuit preacher originally from Shelby, Mississippi, and her mother was an accomplished piano player and vocalist.

From her time growing up in the home of her prominent African-American preacher father to the end of her life, Franklin was immersed and involved in the struggle for civil rights and women's rights. She provided money for civil rights groups, at times covering payroll, and performed at benefits and protests. When Angela Davis was jailed in 1970, Franklin told *Jet* magazine: "Angela Davis must go free ... Black people will be free. I've been locked up (for disturbing the peace in Detroit) and I know you got to disturb the peace when you can't get no peace. Jail is hell to be in. I'm going to see her free if there is any justice in our courts, not because I believe in communism, but because she's a Black woman and she wants freedom for Black people".

Franklin and several other American icons declined to take part in performing at President Donald Trump's 2017 inauguration as a large-scale act of musical protest.

Franklin was a strong supporter for Native American rights. Also, she supported Indigenous Peoples' struggles worldwide and numerous movements that supported Native American and First Nation cultural rights.

February 21

Malcolm X

May 19, 1925 - February 21, 1965

Malcolm X, originally Malcolm Little, was born in Omaha, Nebraska. After moving to the Midwest with his family at a young age, he suffered great tragedy with the alleged suicide of his father and the subsequent institutionalization of his mother. After spending his remaining childhood years in foster homes with his siblings, Malcolm dropped out of middle school, and a few years later moved to Boston and found work on the streets as a shoe-shiner, drug dealer, gambler and burglar.

It was while serving a ten year sentence in prison for burglary that Malcolm became passionately committed to furthering his education. It was also at this time that Malcolm's brother introduced him to the teachings of the Nation of Islam (NOI) and encouraged Malcolm to convert to the Muslim faith. Intrigued by the NOI, Malcolm began studying the work of Elijah Muhammad who preached about systemic oppression and fought for a world separate from one inhabited by white people.

By the time Malcolm was released from prison, he was a transformed man strong in the knowledge of himself and African-centered history. He was a devout follower of NOI and soon after meeting Muhammad he agreed to work for NOI and changed his surname to "X". The change was intended to symbolize the shedding of what he called his slave name and the "X" signified the branding many enslaved Africans received their upper arm.

Malcolm X was appointed as a minister and national spokesperson for Nation of Islam. He was also charged with establishing new mosques around the country. He established several mosques and delivered messages to guide Black Americans into self-pride and self-determination – a familiar philosophy he heard from his parents who were Garveyites.

February 22

Walter Rodney

March 23, 1942 - June 13, 1980

Walter Anthony Rodney was born to Edward and Pauline Rodney in Georgetown, Guyana. He developed into an intellectual and a scholar and is recognized as one of the Caribbean's most brilliant minds.

Rodney pursued his undergraduate studies at the University of the West Indies in Jamaica. He earned a Ph.D. in African History from the School of Oriental and African Studies in London.

Rodney combined his scholarship with activism and became a voice for the under-represented and disenfranchised – this distinguished him from his academic colleagues. His interest in the struggles of the working class began at a young age with an introduction to politics by his father, and continued with his involvement in debating and study groups throughout his student years. His Ph.D. thesis illustrated his strength as an intellectual and activist as he challenged the prevailing assumptions about African history and put forth his own ideas and models for analyzing the history of oppressed peoples. Influenced by the Black Power Movement in the U.S., Developing World revolutionaries and Marxist theory, Rodney began to actively challenge the status quo.

In 1968, while a UWI professor in Jamaica, he joined others to object to the socio-economic and political direction of the government. Rodney's activities attracted the Jamaican government's attention and after attending the 1968 Black Writers' Conference in Montreal, Canada he was banned from re-entering the country.

Rodney returned to Guyana in 1974 to begin an appointment as Professor of History at the University of Guyana, but the government rescinded the appointment. He remained in Guyana and served to engender a new political consciousness in the country. He developed and shared his ideas in speeches and writings on the self-emancipation of the working people, People's Power, and multiracial democracy.

February 23

Jomo Kenyatta

c. 1897 - August 22, 1978

Jomo Kenyatta was the first president of Kenya and is still today often referred to as *mzee* (the Father of the Nation). He was elected in 1963 and named president in 1964.

Kenyatta's parents died while he was young, and he was moved to Muthiga to live with his grandfather where he attended the Church of Scotland's Thogoto mission school, converted to Christianity, and was baptized as Johnstone.

Kenyatta studied anthropology at the London School of Economics, gave public lectures, wrote to newspapers, traveled across Europe and participated in the Pan-African Congress. In 1938 he wrote a book on the Kikuyu people titled *Facing Mount Kenya* under the name Jomo Kenyatta.

On his return to Kenya in 1946, Kenyatta became president of the Kenya African Union (KAU). Though there was little evidence that he was involved, Kenyatta and 97 other KAU leaders were arrested in 1952 and put on trial for the murder of Chief Waruhiu Kungu and for managing the Mau Mau Rebellion. Kenyatta was sentenced to seven years imprisonment and indefinite restriction thereafter.

Kenyatta was released in 1961 after national and international protests. He then joined KANU (Kenya African National Union) and became its president. In the 1963 general elections which brought Kenya into independence, KANU won the majority of seats in the new national assembly and the following year (1964) Kenyatta was named president. Kenyatta urged reconciliation among the various Kenyan political factions and devised the national slogan, *Harambbee* ("pull-together").

Kenyatta established systems that offered assistance to indigenous Kenyans, granted former settler farms to squatters and ex-Mau Mau members, abolished British colonial laws which allowed racial discrimination, and promoted educational reforms.

February 24

Stokely Carmichael/Kwame Toure

June 29, 1941 - November 15, 1998

A civil rights leader, antiwar activist, and Pan-African revolutionary, Stokely Carmichael is best known for popularizing the slogan "Black Power," which in the mid-1960s galvanized a movement toward more militant and separatist assertions of Black identity, nationalism, and empowerment and away from the liberal, interracial pacifism of Martin Luther King and the Southern Christian Leadership Conference (SCLC).

Carmichael was born in 1941 in Port of Spain, Trinidad. His family moved to New York City when he was eleven. He showed promise as a young student and was accepted into the mostly white Bronx High School of Science in 1956. He attended Howard University and joined the newly formed Student Non-Violent Coordinating Committee (SNCC) in 1960. He participated in SNCC sit-ins and Freedom Rides throughout the Deep South, and when SNCC turned its attention to voter registration, Carmichael led the campaign that established the Lowndes County Freedom Organization, a symbolic forerunner to the Black Panther Party.

In 1964, Carmichael graduated from Howard and, along with other young SNCC activists, became increasingly frustrated with the movement's reliance on white liberals and its advocacy of non-violent reform, especially in the wake of the Democratic Party's betrayal of the Mississippi Freedom Democratic Party. In May 1965, Carmichael was elected to replace John Lewis as SNCC chairman, formalizing the shift in SNCC's ideology.

Carmichael spent the last decades of his life abroad, denouncing U.S. racism and imperialism while working to build the All African People's Revolutionary Party. He changed his name to Kwame Ture in 1968, in honor of his friends and political allies, Pan-African leaders Sekou Touré and Kwame Nkrumah. In 1969, Ture settled permanently in Conakry, Guinea where he died of prostate cancer in 1998.

February 25

Lorraine Hansberry
May 19, 1930 - January 12, 1965

Lorraine Vivian Hansberry was a playwright and writer. She was the first African-American female author to have a play performed on Broadway. Her best known work, the play *A Raisin in the Sun*, highlights the lives of Black Americans living under racial segregation in Chicago. The title of the play was taken from the poem *Harlem* by Langston Hughes. At the age of 29, she won the New York Drama Critics' Circle Award — making her the first African-American dramatist, the fifth woman, and the youngest playwright to do so.

Hansberry was born on the South Side of Chicago as the youngest of Nannie Perry Hansberry and Carl Augustus Hansberry's four children. Her father founded Lake Street Bank, one of the first banks for Blacks in Chicago, and ran a successful real estate business. Her uncle was William Leo Hansberry, a scholar of African studies at Howard University in Washington, D.C.

Despite their middle-class status, the Hansberrys were subject to segregation. When she was eight years old, Hansberry's family deliberately attempted to move into a restricted neighborhood where white property owners agreed not to sell to Blacks. Carl Hansberry, with the help of Harry H. Pace, president of the Supreme Liberty Life Insurance Company and several white realtors, secretly bought and moved into property at Rhodes Avenue. The family was threatened by a white mob.

The Supreme Court of Illinois upheld the legality of the restrictive covenant and forced the family to leave the house. The U.S. Supreme Court reversed the decision on a legal technicality. The result was the opening of 30 blocks of South Side Chicago to African Americans. The case did not argue that racially restrictive covenants were unlawful.

February 26

Beverly Jones

1955 - 1973

The Black Power Movement (BPM) was an experience in Trinidad and Tobago's history where issues that affected Black people were brought to the forefront. Many Black men and women fought and died for some of the things that are taken for granted on a daily basis. The BPM started in February 1970, and some of the issues they highlighted included institutional racism, unemployment and alienation of the working class.

Women were pivotal contributors to this BPM movement and struggle. They played an active role in both the mass demonstrations and the subsequent guerrilla struggle. Ayesha Mutope and Josanne Leonard played leading roles in the secondary school movement through the National Organisation of Revolutionary Students. Women also supported the movement by distributing pamphlets, provision of administrative skills as well as food and refreshments for meetings. They also held discussions with people in poorer communities, debating the meaning of Black Power and the revolutionary literature in circulation.

Beverly Jones, along with her sister Jennifer Jones represented women in the armed struggle during the Black Power Movement. They were both part of the National Union of Freedom Fighters (NUFF), a more radicalized organisation that was due to the excessive and exploitative treatment by some branches of the police force. Beverly was killed in the Caura- Lopinot hills on, two weeks before her 18th birthday.

NUFF was anti-imperialist and anti-capitalist in its ideology, and opposed both the foreign investors who controlled much of the economy and the local economic elites. They were notable for the extent to which women played an active role in the organisation, and included women among its guerrilla fighters.

February 27

Miriam Subair

Contributor: Gbenga Subair

Keep Moving Forward Always

This past February of 2020 makes it ten years since my mom Mrs. Mariam Subair left to join the ancestors. Every day I think about her and wish she was around to see what I have become with much more to accomplish. But I know she is watching from above with a smile knowing I am on the right path and will continue to stay on that path to achieve unlimited success each and every day.

My mom, born in Nigeria, instilled in me the essence of hard work, good work ethic, good discipline and the necessary tools needed to succeed in life and to continue to aim high and accomplish goals I set no matter what the obstacles and challenges were. These were skills she learned growing up during her younger days and which she extended to me and my other siblings.

She taught me at a young age to be kind to people, the value of self-reliance and independence, the value of education and the impact I must have to help and uplift others no matter who they are, their culture, history, background or where they come from. We all have roles to play to help as much as we can at all times.

In the years since she has joined the ancestors, my approach to life is to continue to uplift people around me, keep moving forward always with no regrets and continuing to achieve nonstop success each and every day. I cherish these life lessons I have learned from my mother.

February 28

Elijah Muhammad

October 7, 1897 – February 25, 1975

Elijah Muhammad (born Elijah Robert Poole) was a religious leader who led the Nation of Islam (NOI) from 1934 until his death. He was known as The Messenger of Allah (God), to the Nation of Islam believers who were not historically traditional Muslims.

The Nation of Islam provided teachings to African Americans that boosted their pride in the knowledge of their African history and discipline to be organized in self-reliance and economic support of their community while living in a racist USA. A follower of the teachings of Marcus Mosiah Garvey, Muhammad was also the teacher and mentor of Malcolm X, Louis Farrakhan, and Muhammad Ali.

February 29

James Brown
May 3, 1933 - December 25, 2006

James Brown was talented artiste who was an inspiration to young college students who were active in the liberation struggles of the 1960s and 70s. *Say it Loud, (I'm Black and I'm Proud)* was one of Brown's popular songs written by him during the violent 1960s civil rights movement.

Nearly stillborn, then revived by an aunt in a country shack in the piney woods outside Barnwell, South Carolina, Brown was determined to be live and thrive.

By the time he was in his 30s, James Brown was more than a dominant musical voice. He was an outstanding African-American personality who was drawn into the waters of national politics as an inspiration and role model.

"JAMES BROWN is a concept, a vibration, a dance," he reported. "It's not me, the man. JAMES BROWN is a freedom I created for humanity."

Brown proclaimed himself "The Hardest Working Man in Show Business." His admirers and fans agreed with him.

March 1

Ahmed Sekou Toure
January 9, 1922 - March 26, 1984

Ahmed Sekou Toure was a Guinean politician who played a key role in the African independence movement. As the first president of the Republic of Guinea, he led his country to gain its independence from France in 1958. He was known as a charismatic and radical figure in Africa's post-colonial history.

Toure's activism for independence and decolonisation bore fruit in 1958, when an overwhelming population of Guinea voted in favor of independence, rejecting French President Charles de Gaulle's offer of joining a new federal community.

Toure's words regarding de Gaulle's offer strongly resonated across the Guinean public. He famously said: "Guinea prefers poverty in freedom than riches in slavery." It was a comment that angered de Gaulle. "Then all you have to do is to vote 'no'. I pledge myself that nobody will stand in the way of your independence," Gaulle said in response to Toure's assertion.

Guinea became the first independent French-speaking state in Africa and it was the only country which did not accept the proposal of the French president.

In 1958, Toure became the first president of what became known as The Republic of Guinea.

The French reacted by recalling all their professional people and civil servants and by removing all transportable equipment. As France threatened Toure and Guinea through economic pressure, Toure accepted support from the communist bloc and at the same time sought help from Western nations.

Born in 1922 in Faranah, Guinea, Toure came from humble origins. His parents were uneducated and poor. Some sources say he was the grandson of Samory Toure, the legendary leader who resisted France in the late 19th Century.

March 2

Zora Neale Hurston
January 7, 1891 - January 28, 1960

Zora Neale Hurston was an American author, anthropologist, and filmmaker. She portrayed racial struggles in the early-1900s American South

Zora Neale Hurston knew how to make an entrance. On May 1, 1925, at a literary awards dinner sponsored by *Opportunity* magazine, the earthy Harlem newcomer turned heads and raised eyebrows as she claimed four awards: a second-place fiction prize for her short story *Spunk,* a second-place award in drama for her play *Color Struck*, and two honorable mentions.

Over a career that spanned more than 30 years, she published four novels, two books of folklore, an autobiography, numerous short stories, and several essays, articles and plays.

In October 1927 Hurston published an account of the Black settlement at St. Augustine, Florida, in the *Journal of Negro History*; also in this issue: *Cudjo's Own Story of the Last African Slaver*. This was published as a book *Barracoon* in 2018. Hurston had refused to publish the manuscript in the 1920s because the publisher had wanted her to change Cudjo's language to that of standardized English.

Born in Notasulga, Alabama, Hurston moved with her family to Eatonville, Florida, when she was still a toddler. Her writings reveal no recollection of her Alabama beginnings. For Hurston, Eatonville was always home.

March 3

James Baldwin
August 2, 1924 - December 1, 1987

James Baldwin was an essayist, playwright, novelist and voice of the American civil rights movement known for works including *Notes of a Native Son*, *'The Fire Next Time,* and *Go Tell It on the Mountain.*

Baldwin published the 1953 novel *Go Tell It on the Mountain*, receiving acclaim for his insights on race, spirituality and humanity. Other novels included *Giovanni's Room*, *Another Country*, and *Just Above My Head,* as well as essays like *Notes of a Native Son* and *The Fire Next Time.*

Baldwin was born in Harlem, New York. One of the 20th century's greatest writers, Baldwin broke new literary ground with the exploration of racial and social issues in his many works. He was especially known for his essays on the Black experience in America.

He served as a youth minister in a Harlem Pentecostal church from the ages of 14 to 16.

Baldwin's novels, short stories, and plays fictionalize fundamental personal questions and dilemmas amid complex social and psychological pressures. Themes of masculinity, sexuality, race, and class intertwine to create intricate narratives that run parallel with some of the major political movements toward social change in mid-twentieth-century America, such as the civil rights movement and the gay liberation movement.

Baldwin's protagonists are often, but not exclusively African American, while gay and bisexual men also frequently feature as protagonists in his literature. These characters often face internal and external obstacles in their search for social- and self-acceptance. Such dynamics are prominent in Baldwin's second novel, *Giovanni's Room*, which was written in 1956, well before the gay liberation movement.

March 4

Zenzi Miriam Makeba
March 4, 1932 - November 9, 2008

Zenzi Miriam Makeba was a South African singer and human rights campaigner who put African music onto the international map in the 1960s. Makeba is well known throughout the world known as 'Mama Africa' and the 'Empress of African Song'.

Zenzi Miriam Makeba was born in 1932 in the segregated neighbourhood of Prospect, Johannesburg during a time of economic depression. Her mother Nomkomndelo Christina, a domestic worker, was imprisoned for six months for illegally brewing beer to help make ends meet, and Miriam went to prison with her as she was just 18 days old..

In 1959, Makeba traveled to Europe, following the success of the film *Come Back, Africa* made by the American filmmaker Lionel Rogosin. This film demonstrated her talent to an international audience. After Makeba's marriage to the African American activist Kwame Ture in 1969, she was exiled to Guinea. She achieved great success on the African continent and played a major symbolic role as a militant Pan-African.

In 1963 and 1971, Makeba spoke at the United Nations with the support of Guinea. She was named "Woman of the Century" by the Bedford Stuyvesant Community of New York City. She also received Commander of the Order of Arts and Letters and the French Legion of Honour. Her autobiography was published in 1988, and is translated into five languages. Her records, more than 30, achieved global success. In 1990, Nelson Mandela persuaded Mama Africa to return to South Africa, where she worked with her charitable foundations.

March 5

Toni Morrison
February 18, 1931 - August 5, 2019

Toni Morrison was a Nobel Prize- and Pulitzer Prize-winning novelist, editor and professor. Her novels are known for their epic themes, exquisite language and richly detailed African American characters who are central to their narratives. Among her best-known novels are *The Bluest Eye*, *Sula*, *Song of Solomon*, *Beloved*, *Jazz*, *Love* and *A Mercy*. Morrison has earned a plethora of book-world accolades and honorary degrees, also receiving the Presidential Medal of Freedom in 2012.

Born Chloe Anthony Wofford in Lorain, Ohio, Morrison was the second oldest of four children. Her father, George Wofford, worked primarily as a welder but held several jobs at once to support the family. Her mother, Ramah, was a domestic worker. Morrison later credited her parents with instilling in her a love of reading, music and folklore along with clarity and perspective.

Morrison earned a bachelor's degree in English from Howard University and a Master of Arts in English from Cornell University. She taught English first at Texas Southern University and then at Howard.

March 6

Baynard Rustin
March 17, 1912 - August 24, 1987

Bayard Rustin was an American leader in social movements for civil rights, socialism, nonviolence, and gay rights. Rustin worked with A. Philip Randolph on the March on Washington Movement, in 1941, to press for an end to racial discrimination in employment. He was a brilliant theorist, tactician, and organizer.

Rustin spent 28 months in federal prison after being arrested in 1943 when, as a conscientious objector, he refused to report to his draft board for a physical examination.

Rustin organized Freedom Rides, and helped to organize the Southern Christian Leadership Conference to strengthen Martin Luther King Jr.'s leadership. He was the chief organizer for the 1963 March on Washington for Jobs and Freedom. Rustin worked alongside Ella Baker, a co-director of the Crusade for Citizenship, in 1954; and before the Montgomery bus boycott, he helped organize a group, called "In Friendship." They provided material and legal assistance to those being evicted from their tenant farms and households.

In the 1960s A. Philip Randolph, former head of the Brotherhood of Sleeping Car Porters, an early Black trade union, and Bayard Rustin, founded the A. Philip Randolph Institute (APRI) to forge an alliance between the civil rights movement and the labor movement

Rustin was born in West Chester, Pennsylvania, to Florence Rustin and Archie Hopkins and raised by his maternal grandparents, Julia (Davis) and Janifer Rustin. They were active church and civic association members. Leaders of the National Association for the Advancement of Colored People were frequent guests in their home. And in his youth, Rustin campaigned against Jim Crow laws.

During the 1970s and 1980s, Rustin served on many humanitarian missions, such as aiding refugees from Communist Vietnam and Cambodia and to Haiti.

March 7

Hattie McDaniel
June 10, 1895 - October 26, 1952

Hattie McDaniel, born in Wichita, Kansas, U.S., was an American actress and singer who was the first African American to win an Academy Award. She received the honour for her performance as Mammy in *Gone with the Wind* (1939).

McDaniel was raised in Denver, Colorado, where she early exhibited her musical and dramatic talent. She left school in 1910 to become a performer in several traveling minstrel groups and later became one of the first Black women to be broadcast over American radio.

With the onset of the Great Depression, however, little work was to be found for minstrel or vaudeville players, and to support herself McDaniel went to work as a bathroom attendant at Sam Pick's club in Milwaukee, Wisconsin. Although the club as a rule hired only white performers, some of its patrons became aware of McDaniel's vocal talents and encouraged the owner to make an exception. McDaniel performed at the club for more than a year until she left for Los Angeles, where her brother found her a small role on a local radio show, *The Optimistic Do-Nuts*; known as Hi-Hat Hattie, she became the show's main attraction before long.

March 8

Carter G. Woodson
December 19, 1875 - April 3, 1950

Carter Godwin Woodson was an American historian, author, journalist, and the founder of the Association for the Study of African American Life and History (ASALA). He was one of the first scholars to study the history of the African diaspora, including African-American history. A founder of *The Journal of Negro History* in 1916, Woodson has been called the "father of Black history". In February 1926 he launched the celebration of Negro History Week, the precursor of Black History Month.

Born in Virginia, the son of formerly enslaved Africans, Woodson had to put off schooling while he worked in the coal mines of West Virginia. He graduated from Berea College, and became a teacher and school administrator. He earned graduate degrees at the University of Chicago and in 1912 was the second African American, after W. E. B. Du Bois, to obtain a Ph.D. degree from Harvard University.

Most of Woodson's academic career was spent at Howard University, a Historically Black University in Washington, D.C., where he eventually served as the Dean of the College of Arts and Sciences.

Like DuBois, Woodson believed that young African Americans in the early 20th century were not being taught enough of their own heritage, and the achievements of their ancestors. To get his message out, Woodson first turned to his fraternity, Omega Psi Phi, which created Negro History and Literature Week in 1924. Woodson wanted a wider celebration, and he decided the ASALA should take on that assignment.

March 9

Alex Haley
August 11, 1921 - February 10, 1992

Author Alex Haley was best known for works depicting the struggles of African Americans. Raised in Henning, Tennessee, he began writing to help pass the time during his two decades with the U.S. Coast Guard. After conducting interviews with Malcolm X for *Playboy* magazine, he turned the material into his first book, *The Autobiography of Malcolm* (1965). Haley's subsequent novel, *Roots* (1976), was a fictionalized account of his family's history, traced through seven generations. It was adapted into a 1977 miniseries that became the most-watched broadcast in TV history, a record it would hold for years.

Alex Haley was born Alexander Murray Palmer Haley on August 11, 1921, in Ithaca, New York. At the time of his birth, Haley's father, Simon Haley, a World War I veteran, was a graduate student in agriculture at Cornell University, and his mother, Bertha Palmer Haley, was a teacher.

For the first five years of his life, Haley lived with his mother and grandparents in Henning, Tennessee, while his father finished his studies. When Simon Haley completed his degree, he joined the family in Tennessee and taught as a professor of agriculture at various southern universities. Alex Haley was always remarkably proud of his father, whom he said had overcome the immense obstacles of racism to achieve high levels of success and provide better opportunities for his children.

March 10

Michael Norman Manley

December 10, 1924 - March 6, 1997

Michael Norman Manley served as the Prime Minister of Jamaica in 1972 to 1980 and in 1989 to 1992.

Manley was born in the suburbs of Kingston, Jamaica to Norman and Edna Manley. His mother was an influential artist and art educator and his father a brilliant was a brilliant lawyer and Jamaican statesman.

During his more than forty years in public life, Manley's contribution to local, regional and international politics was one of the most enlightened, profound and impactful. He was affectionately called Joshua and was one of the most accomplished and outstanding political figures in the post-colonial history of Jamaica and the Caribbean. He constantly explored new ideas and implemented strategies to give every Jamaican a role in the process of national development.

In Jamaica, as a politician with the People's National Party, Manley attacked the human-rights record of the sitting government. He advocated a deepening of democracy, donned bushjacket suits and mobilized reggae artists to perform his message "Power for the People". In 1972 his Party won the election and he was sworn in as Jamaica's fourth Prime Minister.

Manley has been credited as the prime minister who had done the most to improve the socio-cultural, political and economic conditions for the majority of Jamaicans, and to help muster national consciousness among the people.

Michael Manley and the PNP government embarked on the most profound and wide-ranging program of social and economic reform in Jamaica's history. His efforts to bring equanimity to the majority of people in Jamaica were sabotaged by externally-triggered interference. Manley achieved considerable success in international honours and awards, mainly for his contributions towards the struggle against South African apartheid.

Manley was buried in Jamaica's National Heroes Park in Kingston.

March 11

Roy Wilkins
August 30, 1901 - September 8, 1981

Roy Wilkins was a prominent civil rights activist in the United States from the 1930s to the 1970s. Wilkins was active in the National Association for the Advancement of Colored People (NAACP) and between 1931 and 1934 was assistant NAACP secretary under Walter Francis White. When W. E. B. Du Bois left the organization in 1934, Wilkins replaced him as editor of *Crisis*, the official magazine of the NAACP.

Roy Wilkins was born in St. Louis, Missouri. He grew up in the home of his aunt and uncle in a low-income, integrated community in St. Paul, Minnesota. Working his way through college at the University of Minnesota, Wilkins graduated with a degree in sociology in 1923. He worked as a journalist at *The Minnesota Daily* and became editor of *St. Paul Appeal*, an African-American newspaper.

In 1950, Wilkins, along with A. Philip Randolph, founder of the Brotherhood of Sleeping Car Porters, and Arnold Aronson, a leader of the National Jewish Community Relations Advisory Council founded the Leadership Conference on Civil Rights (LCCR). LCCR had become the premier civil rights coalition and coordinated the national legislative campaign on behalf of every major civil rights law since 1957.

In 1955, Wilkins was named executive secretary of the NAACP. One of his first actions was to provide support to civil rights activists in Mississippi who were being subjected to a "credit squeeze" by members of the White Citizens Councils.

Wilkins backed a proposal where Black businesses and voluntary associations shifted their accounts to the Black-owned Tri-State Bank of Memphis, Tennessee. By the end of 1955, about $280,000 had been deposited in Tri-State for this purpose. The money enabled Tri-State to extend loans to credit-worthy Blacks who were denied loans by white banks.

March 12

James Chaney, Andrew Goodman, and Michael Schwerner
James Earl Chaney - May 30, 1943 - June 21, 1964
Andrew Goodman - November 23, 1943 - June 21, 1964
Michael Schwerner - November 6, 1939 - June 21, 1964

James Earl Chaney, Andrew Goodman and Michael Schwerner were social workers and activists.

The murders of Chaney, Goodman, and Schwerner, also known as the Freedom Summer murders, the Mississippi civil rights workers' murders or the Mississippi Burning murders, refers to three activists who were abducted and murdered in Neshoba County, Mississippi in June 1964 during the Civil Rights Movement. Chaney from Meridian, Mississippi, and Goodman and Schwerner were from New York City.

All three were associated with the Council of Federated Organizations (COFO) and its member organization, the Congress of Racial Equality (CORE). They had been working with the Freedom Summer campaign attempting to register African Americans in Mississippi to vote. Since 1890 and through the turn of the century, southern states had systematically disenfranchised most Black voters by discrimination in voter registration and voting.

Chaney, Goodman, and Schwerner had traveled from Meridian to the community of Longdale to talk with congregation members at a Black church that had been burned. The churches were centers of community organizing. The trio was arrested following a traffic stop for speeding outside Philadelphia, Mississippi, escorted to the local jail, and held for a number of hours. As the three left town in their car, they were followed by law enforcement and others. Before leaving Neshoba County, their car was pulled over. The three were abducted, driven to another location, and shot to death at close range. The three men's bodies were taken to an earthen dam where they were buried.

March 13

Sidilla Editha "Cedella" Booker

July 23, 1926 - April 8, 2008

Sidilla Editha "Cedella" Booker (née Malcolm and previously Marley) was a Jamaican singer and writer. She was the mother of reggae musician Bob Marley.

In 1993, Cedella Booker conceived and created what is today called the 9 Mile Music Festival, an annual music event held every year in Miami to help keep alive Bob Marley's message of peace, love and unity. As part of the admission fee to the one-day music festival, attendees bring canned goods that are collected and donated to help feed the needy in the Miami area through various local charities.

Called "the keeper of the flame," Cedella grew voluminous dreadlocks, adopted her grandson Rohan Marley, Bob Marley's son by Janet Hunt, and occasionally performed live with Marley's children, Ky-Mani, Ziggy, Stephen, Damian and Julian Marley. Later, she released the music albums *Awake Zion and Smilin' Island of Song*. Cedella Booker participated in the festivities in Addis Ababa, Ethiopia commemorating Marley's 60th birthday in 2005. She also wrote two Marley biographies.

March 14

New Beginning Movement
Coordinating Council of Revolutionary Alternatives for Trinidad and the Caribbean

The New Beginning Movement (NBM) (1971–1978) in Trinidad functioned as a voice of direct democracy and workers self-management through popular assemblies, and as a global coordinating council of a Pan-Caribbean International with linkages across the region, in Britain, the United States, and Canada.

A crucial philosophical and strategic leaven in the 1970 Black Power Revolt led by Geddes Granger's and Dave Darbeau's National Joint Action Committee (NJAC) and the 1975 United Labour Front (ULF) in Trinidad, NBM aspired to interpret Afro-Trinidadians and Indo-Trinidadians equally, and on their own autonomous terms, toward self-directed emancipation.

Led by Bukka Rennie, Wally Look Lai, and Franklyn Harvey, NBM was inspired by C.L.R. James's intellectual legacies. Through publications such as *New Beginning*, *Caribbean Dialogue*, and *The Vanguard*, these partisans advocated labor's self-emancipation and critical perspectives on capitalism and state power, and exposed the limits of elite party politics and representative government.

https://www.pdcnet.org/clrjames/content/clrjames_2017_0023_43102_0267_0305?file_type=pdf

March 15

Louise Bennett-Coverley or Miss Lou, OM, OJ, MBE
September 7, 1919 - July 26, 2006

Louise Simone Bennett-Coverley was a Jamaican poet, folklorist, writer, and educator. She brought a revival of Jamaican creole and folk songs into the mainstream culture. Miss Lou, as she was affectionately known, was a strong and leading advocate for the use of Jamaican patois (blend of English and African languages of Twi and Ga of West Africa) as mainstream language in Jamaica.

Dr. Basil Bryan, when he served as Consul General of Jamaica to New York (1998-2007), praised Bennett as an inspiration to Jamaicans as she "proudly presented the Jamaican language and culture to a wider world and today we are the beneficiaries of that audacity." She along with Harry Belafonte led the way in introducing Jamaica folk songs to international audiences.

She was acclaimed by many for her success in establishing the validity of local languages – widely known as patois - for literary expression. An important aspect of her writing was its setting in public spaces such as trams, schools and churches allowing readers to see themselves, pre- and post-independence, reflected in her work. Her writing has also been credited with providing a unique perspective on the everyday social experiences of working-class women in a postcolonial landscape.

March 16

Langston Hughes
February 1, 1901 - May 22, 1967

Langston Hughes was a central figure in the Harlem Renaissance, the flowering of Black intellectual, literary, and artistic life that took place in Harlem. A major poet, Hughes also wrote novels, short stories, essays, and plays. He sought to honestly portray the joys and hardships of working-class Black lives, avoiding both sentimental idealization and negative stereotypes. As he wrote in his essay *The Negro Artist and the Racial Mountain*, "We younger Negro artists who create now intend to express our individual dark-skinned selves without fear or shame. If white people are pleased we are glad. If they are not, it doesn't matter. We know we are beautiful. And ugly too."

This approach was not without its critics. Much of Hughes's early work was roundly criticized by many Black intellectuals for portraying what they thought to be an unattractive view of Black life. In his autobiographical *The Big Sea*, Hughes commented:

"*Fine Clothes to the Jew* [Hughes's second book] was well received by the literary magazines and the white press, but the Negro critics did not like it at all. Some called the book a disgrace to the race, a return to the dialect tradition, and a parading of all our racial defects before the public. … The Negro critics and many of the intellectuals were very sensitive about their race in books. (And still are.)…."

March 17
Montserrat Slave (Enslaved Africans) Revolt, 1768
For all who worked to make this revolt possible

Africans enslaved in Montserrat executed an island-wide attack on St Patrick's Day in 1768 hoping to take the Irish planters by surprise. Yet, despite months of plotting, their plans had been leaked and their revolt was unsuccessful resulting in nine hangings. In memory of the failed rebellion, Montserratians remember the day with Masquerade. Islanders dance the Irish jigs one night, then mock their one-time masters the next by cracking whips while dressed in tall hats like bishops' miters.

March 18

Elijah Cummings
January 18, 1951 - October 17, 2019

Born in Baltimore, Elijah Cummings a statesman and civil rights activist got an early start in justice work when at the age of eleven he and friends worked to integrate a segregated swimming pool in South Baltimore. Cummings would go on to be elected as the U.S. House of Representative for his home city for the 7th Congressional District in Maryland. His district included the city of Baltimore and the suburbs.

Cummings graduated from Baltimore City College high school and earned a Bachelor's degree in political science from Howard University. He earned a Juris Doctor degree from Maryland University Law School was admitted to the Maryland bar and practiced law until he was elected to Congress.

While in Congress, Cummings sponsored bills primarily in the issue areas of government operations and politics, health, education, crime and law enforcement, and finance and financial sector. Simultaneously he was a formidable orator who advocated for the poor in his Black-majority district.

"As Chairman of the House Oversight Committee, he showed us all not only the importance of checks and balances within our democracy, but also the necessity of good people stewarding it," former President Obama said in a statement, describing Cummings (on his transition) as "steely yet compassionate, principled yet open to new perspectives."

March 19

Eric Williams

September 25, 1911 - March 29, 1981

The Hon. Eric Eustace Williams TC CH served as the first Prime Minister of Trinidad and Tobago from 1962 until his transition. He was also a noted Caribbean historian.

Dr. Eric Williams was a teacher, historian and a philosopher. Before and during his tenure as prime minister of Trinidad and Tobago, he wrote many articles and books on the Caribbean, education, and politics. Some of his works include: *Capitalism and Slavery*, *Historical Background of Race Relations in the Caribbean*, and *The Blackest Thing in Slavery Was Not the Black Man*.

Williams was the son of Elisa and Henry Williams, a minor Post Office official in Trinidad and Tobago. He was educated at Queen's Royal College and won the Island Scholarship to Oxford University. He received the Doctor of Philosophy degree in 1938. His doctoral thesis, *The Economic Aspect of the West Indian Slave Trade and Slavery*, was considered an important contribution to research on the subject and was published in 1944 in Williams' *Capitalism and Slavery*. Much of Williams' educational pursuits at Queen's Royal College and Oxford University are documented in his book, *Inward Hunger: The Education of a Prime Minister*.

In 1939, Williams emigrated to the United States to teach at Howard University. He became an assistant professor of social and political sciences. He developed a three-volume work called *Documents Illustrating the Development of Civilization* (1947). While at Howard, Williams began to work as a consultant to the Anglo-American Caribbean Commission, a body set up after WWII to study the future of the region. In 1948, he left Howard to head the Research Branch of the Caribbean Commission. He later (1955) resigned from the Commission in protest against its crypto-colonialist policies.

March 20

Sister Rosetta Tharpe
March 20, 1915 - October 9, 1973

Sister Rosetta Tharpe, born in Cotton Plant, Arkansas was an American singer, songwriter, guitarist, and recording artist, born in Cotton Plant, Arkansas. She attained popularity in the 1930s and 1940s with her gospel recordings, characterized by a unique mixture of spiritual lyrics and rhythmic accompaniment that was a precursor of rock and roll. She was the first great recording star of gospel music and among the first gospel musicians to appeal to rhythm-and-blues and rock-and-roll audiences, later being referred to as "the original soul sister" and "the Godmother of rock and roll". She influenced early rock-and-roll musicians, including Little Richard, Johnny Cash, Carl Perkins, Chuck Berry, Elvis Presley and Jerry Lee Lewis.

Tharpe's parents Katie Bell Nubin and Willis Atkins picked cotton for a living and were both musicians. Her father was a singer and her mother was also a singer and a mandolin player, deaconess-missionary, and women's speaker for the Church of God in Christ (COGIC), which was founded in 1894 by Charles Harrison Mason, a Black Pentecostal bishop, who encouraged rhythmic musical expression, dancing in praise and allowing women to sing and teach in church. Encouraged by her mother, Tharpe began singing and playing the guitar as Little Rosetta Nubin at the age of four and was cited as a musical prodigy.

Willing to cross the line between sacred and secular by performing her music of "light" in the "darkness" of nightclubs and concert halls with big bands behind her, Sister Tharpe pushed spiritual music into the mainstream and helped pioneer the rise of pop-gospel, beginning in 1938 with the recording *Rock Me* and with the 1939 hit *This Train.*

She was posthumously inducted into Rock & Roll Hall of Fame in 2018.

March 21

Haile Selassie

July 22, 1892 - 27 August 27, 1975

Haile Selassie, I born Lij Tafari Makonnen, was Regent Plenipotentiary of Ethiopia from 1916 and the Emperor of Ethiopia from 1930 to 1974. He is a defining figure in modern Ethiopian and world history. He was a member of the Solomonic dynasty who traced his lineage to Emperor Menelik I.

Selassie attempted to modernize the country through a series of political and social reforms, including the introduction of Ethiopia's first written Constitution and the abolition of slavery. He led the failed efforts to defend Ethiopia during the Second Italo-Ethiopian War and spent the period of Italian occupation in exile in England. He returned to lead Ethiopia in 1941 after the British Empire defeated the Italian occupiers in the East African campaign. He dissolved the Federation of Ethiopia and Eritrea, which was established by the UN General Assembly in 1950, and integrated Eritrea as a province of Ethiopia while fighting to prevent their independence.

Selassie's internationalist views led to Ethiopia becoming a charter member of the United Nations. In 1963, he presided over the formation of the Organisation of African Unity, the precursor of the African Union, and served as its first chairman. He was overthrown in a 1974 military coup by a Soviet Union-backed junta and was murdered by the junta.

Among some members of the Rastafari movement (which was founded in Jamaica in the 1930s) Haile Selassie is referred to as the returned messiah of the Bible, God incarnate. Haile Selassie was a Christian and adhered to the tenets and liturgy of the Ethiopian Orthodox church.

March 22

Ralph Johnson Bunch
August 7, 1904 - December 9, 1971

Ralph Johnson Bunche was an American political scientist, academic, and diplomat who received the 1950 Nobel Peace Prize for his late 1940s mediation in Palestine. He was the first African American to be so honored. He was involved in the formation and administration of the United Nations and played a major role in numerous peacekeeping operations sponsored by the UN. In 1963, he was awarded the Presidential Medal of Freedom by President John F. Kennedy.

Bunche believed in the work of mediation in Palestine. The Nobel Committee referred to one of his lectures, in which Bunche "speaks of the qualities mediators should possess: 'They should be biased against war and for peace. They should have a bias which would lead them to believe in the essential goodness of their fellowman and that no problem of human relations is insoluble. They should be biased against suspicion, intolerance, hate, religious and racial bigotry'."

Bunche explained his philosophy in his Nobel Lecture: “There are some in the world who are prematurely resigned to the inevitability of war. Among them are the advocates of ‘preventive war’, who in their resignation to war, wish merely to select their own time initiating it. To suggest that war can prevent war is a base play on words and a despicable form of warmongering. The objective of any who sincerely believe in peace clearly must be to exhaust every honorable recourse in the effort to save the peace.”

March 23

Horace Julian Bond
January 14, 1940 - August 15, 2015

Horace Julian Bond was a leader of the American Civil Rights Movement. While a student at Morehouse College in Atlanta, he helped found the Student Nonviolent Coordinating Committee (SNCC). He was elected Board Chairman of the National Association for the Advancement of Colored People (NAACP) in 1998.

Born in Nashville, Tennessee, Bond's family moved to Pennsylvania when he was five years old when his father, Horace Mann Bond, became the first African American President of Lincoln University (Pennsylvania), his alma mater. Bond attended Morehouse College in Atlanta and won a varsity letter for swimming. He also founded a literary magazine called *The Pegasus* and served as an intern at *Time* magazine.

In the 1960s Bond led student protests against segregation in public facilities in Georgia and served as communications director for SNCC. He graduated from Morehouse and helped found the Southern Poverty Law Center (SPLC) where he served as organization's president from 1971 to 1979.

Bond was elected to the Georgia House of Representatives in 1965. White members of the House refused to seat him because of his opposition to the Vietnam War. In 1966, the United States Supreme Court ruled that the House had denied Bond his freedom of speech and had to seat him.

Bond was active as Chairman Emeritus of the NAACP, after serving 11 years as Chair, and working to educate the public about the history of the Civil Rights Movement and the struggles that African Americans experience. He hosted *America's Black Forum* from 1980 until 1997.

He published *A Time To Speak, A Time To Act*, a collection of his essays, as well as *Black Candidates Southern Campaign Experiences*.

March 24

Clara Hale
April 1, 1905 - December 18, 1992

In 1940, Clara Hale learned that she could become a foster mother. During the next 25 years, she became "Mommy" Hale to over 40 children of all ethnic and religious backgrounds.

As problems associated with drug abuse exploded in the Harlem community, Clara Hale's family begged her to take action. Within six months, she had 22 babies of heroin-addicted women in her five-room apartment. Soon, she had helped establish a home for infants addicted before birth. It was the first--and only known program--in the U.S. designed to deal with infants born addicted to non-prescription drugs.

In 1975, Hale House became the "Center for the Promotion of Human Potential," a licensed voluntary childcare agency. At that time, it was the only Black voluntary agency in the country.

Hale married shortly after high school and moved to New York City where she studied business administration, cleaned, and worked as a domestic. She was 27 when her husband died from cancer. She had three children, Nathan, Lorraine and adopted son Kenneth, and Hale struggled to support her children through the Great Depression.

Clara McBride was born in Elizabeth City, North Carolina and raised in Philadelphia, Pennsylvania.

March 25

Gilbert Scott-Heron
April 1, 1949 - May 27, 2011

Gilbert Scott-Heron was an American soul and jazz poet, musician, and author, known primarily for his work as a spoken-word performer in the 1970s and 1980s.

Scott-Heron's collaborative efforts with musician Brian Jackson featured a musical fusion of jazz, blues, and soul, as well as lyrical content concerning social and political issues of the time, delivered in both rapping and melismatic vocal styles by Scott-Heron. His own term for himself was "bluesologist," which he defined as "a scientist who is concerned with the origin of the blues."

March 26

Elizabeth Catlett
April 15, 1915 - April 2, 2012

Elizabeth Catlett was an African-American artist who explored themes relating to race and feminism in her range of sculpture, paintings, and prints. Like her peer Norman Lewis, Catlett highlighted the struggle of Black people with her art. Responding to segregation and the fight for civil rights, Catlett's depictions of sharecroppers and activists showed the influence of Primitivism and Cubism. "I have always wanted my art to service my people—to reflect us, to relate to us, to stimulate us, to make us aware of our potential," she once stated.

Born Alice Elizabeth Catlett in Washington, D.C., she was awarded a scholarship to attend the Carnegie Institute of Technology in Pittsburgh—only to have the offer rescinded on the basis of her race. She then enrolled at Howard University and went on to study under Grant Wood at the University of Iowa, becoming the first African-American woman to graduate with an MFA from the school. In the 1940s, she traveled to Mexico on a fellowship and began to paint murals influenced by the work of Diego Rivera and Frida Kahlo. The Mexican muralist's spirit of activism inspired Catlett to produce images of hardship by African-American women in the South, as depicted in *Sharecropper* (1952)—one of her most famous works.

While in Mexico, Catlett created a series of linocut prints featuring prominent Black figures to promote literacy in the country. From 1975 until her death, she lived and worked between Cuernavaca, Mexico and New York.

The artist's works are held in the collections of The Museum of Modern Art in New York, the National Gallery of Art in Washington, D.C., the Hammer Museum in Los Angeles, and the Art Institute of Chicago.

March 27

Robert Nestor Marley OM
February 6, 1945 - May 11, 1981

Robert Nesta Marley was a Jamaican singer, songwriter, and musician. Considered one of the pioneers of reggae, his musical career was marked by fusing elements of reggae, ska, and rocksteady, as well as his distinctive vocal and songwriting style. Marley's contributions to music increased the visibility of Jamaican music worldwide, and made him a global figure in popular culture for over a decade.

Over the course of his career Marley became known as a Rastafari icon, and he infused his music with a sense of spirituality. He is also considered a global symbol of Jamaican music and culture and identity, and was controversial in his outspoken support for the legalization of marijuana, sang socially and politically conscious songs, and advocated for Pan-Africanism. The lyrics to some of his more popular politically conscious songs are based on speeches made by Emperor Haile Selassie.

March 28

Thurgood Marshall
July 2, 1908 - January 24, 1993

Thurgood Marshall was an American lawyer and civil rights activist who served as Associate Justice of the Supreme Court of the United States from October 1967 until October 1991. Marshall was the Court's first African-American justice. Prior to his judicial service, he successfully argued several cases before the Supreme Court.

Born in Baltimore, Maryland, Marshall graduated from the Howard University School of Law in 1933. He established a private legal practice in Baltimore before founding the National Association for the Advancement of Colored People (NAACP) Legal Defense and Educational Fund, where he served as executive director. In that position, he argued several cases before the Supreme Court, including *Smith v. Allwright*, *Shelley v. Kraemer*, and *Brown v. Board of Education*, the latter of which held that racial segregation in public education is a violation of the Equal Protection Clause.

Thurgood Marshall was the younger of two sons of a railroad porter who later worked on the staff of a whites-only country club. His mother was a school teacher. Marshall graduated from Lincoln University in 1930 and applied to University of Maryland Law School but was turned down because of his race. He then attended Howard University Law School, though his mother had to pawn her wedding and engagement rings to pay the tuition. He graduated first in his class in 1933, just as America was feeling the full impact of the Great Depression.

March 29

Amílcar Cabral
September 12, 1924 - January 20, 1973

"Tell no lies. (…) Claim no easy victories" - (Amilcar Cabral, 1965)

Amílcar Lopes da Costa Cabral was a Bissau-Guinean and Cape Verdean agricultural engineer, Pan-Africanist, intellectual, poet, theoretician, revolutionary, political organizer, nationalist and diplomat. He was one of Africa's foremost anti-colonial leaders.

Also known by the *nom de guerre* Abel Djassi, Cabral led the nationalist movement of Guinea-Bissau and Cape Verde Islands and the ensuing war of independence in Guinea-Bissau. He was assassinated on 20 January 1973, about eight months before Guinea-Bissau's unilateral declaration of independence.

Born in Cape Verde and assassinated in 1973, Cabral is remembered as the leader of the liberation wars in Cape Verde and Guiné Bissau. A brilliant strategist, diplomat and guerrilla tactician, Cabral was also known notable for his humane and uniquely independent political vision.

Cabral's childhood was marked by both a love of learning and the witnessing of colonial injustices, in particular during the 1940s drought and famine. In 1945, earning one of very few scholarships of its kind, Cabral secured a place to learn agronomy in Lisbon.

The next seven years in the 'Metropolis' would be highly significant for Cabral in that it would provide access to the writings of Pan-Africanist cultural/political movements; as well as with connections with fellow lusophone African students (e.g. Mario de Andrade, Marcelino dos Santos, Agostinho Neto). Through the Centre for African Studies in Lisbon, important bonds were formed among key figures of the liberation struggles in Angola and Mozambique. Deeply impressed by Leopold Senghor's and Aimé Cesaire's *Négritude* as well as by Nkrumah's political visions, Cabral's placed an emphasis on the need for re-Africanisation of Africa.

March 30

Raiford Chatman "Ossie" Davis
December 18, 1917 - February 4, 2005

Raiford Chatman "Ossie" Davis was an American film, television and Broadway actor, director, poet, playwright, author, and civil rights activist.

Raiford Chatman Davis was born in Cogdell, Clinch County, Georgia, a son of Kince Charles Davis, a railway construction engineer, and his wife Laura (née Cooper; July 9, 1898 – June 6, 2004). He inadvertently became known as "Ossie" when his birth certificate was being filed and his mother's pronunciation of his name as "R. C. Davis" was misheard by the courthouse clerk in Clinch County, Georgia.

Davis experienced racism from an early age when the Klu Klux Klan threatened to shoot his father, whose job they felt was too advanced for a Black man to have. His siblings included scientist William Conan Davis, social worker Essie Morgan Davis, pharmacist Kenneth Curtis Davis, and biology teacher James Davis.

Following the wishes of his parents, Davis attended Howard University but dropped out in 1939 to fulfill his desire for an acting career in New York after a recommendation by Alain Locke; he later attended Columbia University School of General Studies. His acting career, which spanned eight decades, began in 1939 with the Rose McClendon Players in Harlem. During World War II, Davis served in the United States Army in the Medical Corps. He made his film debut in 1950 in the Sidney Poitier film *No Way Out.*

Davis and his wife Ruby Dee were involved in organizing the 1963 civil rights March on Washington for Jobs and Freedom and served as its emcees.

March 31

Amiri Baraka

October 7, 1934 - January 9, 2014

Poet, writer, teacher, and political activist Amiri Baraka was born Everett LeRoi Jones in Newark, New Jersey. He attended Rutgers University and Howard University, spent three years in the U.S. Air Force, and returned to New York City to attend Columbia University and the New School for Social Research. Baraka was well known for his strident social criticism, often writing in an incendiary style that made it difficult for some audiences and critics to respond with objectivity to his works. Throughout most of his career his method in poetry, drama, fiction, and essays was confrontational, calculated to shock and awaken audiences to the political concerns of Black Americans. For decades, Baraka was one of the most prominent voices in the world of American literature.

Baraka's own political stance changed several times, thus dividing his oeuvre into periods: as a member of the avant-garde during the 1950s, Baraka—writing as Leroi Jones—was associated with Beat poets like Allen Ginsberg and Jack Kerouac; in the '60s, he moved to Harlem and became a Black Nationalist; in the '70s, he was involved in third-world liberation movements and identified as a Marxist. More recently, Baraka was accused of anti-Semitism for his poem *Somebody Blew up America*, written in response to the September 11 attacks.

Baraka, it is said, incited controversy throughout his career. He was praised for speaking out against oppression as well as accused of fostering hate. Critical opinion has been sharply divided between those who agree, with *Dissent* contributor Stanley Kaufman, that Baraka's race and political moment have created his celebrity and those who feel that Baraka stands among the most important writers of the twentieth century.

April 1

Marvin Gaye
April 2, 1939 - April 1, 1984

Marvin Pentz Gaye, Jr. was a soul singer-songwriter in the 1960s and 1970s. He went on to produce his own records and often addressed controversial themes. Gaye, Jr., also known as the "Prince of Soul," was born in Washington.

Marvin Gaye sang in his father's church and in the Moonglows before signing with Motown. He recorded songs by Smokey Robinson before becoming his own producer on the protest album *What's Going On* (1971). This album was inspired by escalating violence and political unrest in the U.S. over the nation's involvement in the Vietnam War.

Throughout his childhood, Gaye often found peace in music, mastering the piano and drums at a young age. Until high school, his singing experience was limited to church revivals, but soon he developed a love for R&B and doo-wop that would set the foundation for his career. In the late 1950s, Gaye joined a vocal group called The New Moonglows.

The talented singer had a phenomenal range that spanned three vocal styles and he soon impressed the group's founder, Harvey Fuqua. It wasn't long before Gaye and Fuqua both came to the attention of Detroit music impresario Berry Gordy Jr. and were signed to Gordy's legendary Motown Records.

Towards the end of his career, Gaye admitted he no longer made music for pleasure; instead, he said, "I record so that I can feed people what they need, what they feel. Hopefully, I record so that I can help someone overcome a bad time." Three years after his death, Gaye was inducted into the Rock & Roll Hall of Fame.

April 2

Ellsworth Rodman Groce
August 23, 1898 – March 18, 1990
Contributor: Deirdre FieldsWilson, (Daughter)

Ellsworth Rodman Groce was born in Providence Rhode Island. He was the husband of Mildred Josephine Wyatt, the only daughter of Willis B. Wyatt. Willis moved his family from Providence to Harlem, New York. Ellsworth met and married his first wife, raising nine children in Bedford Stuyvesant, Brooklyn. He became the first organist of the Mount Sinai Baptist Church.

Ellsworth graduated from Kennedy King College located in Chicago Illinois where he received his Arts Degree in Music. As a Doctor of Music he opened a music school in Chicago, Illinois where he received an award for 50 years of community service in music.

Ellsworth also received an award for 20 years of community service from the American Red Cross where he taught over 2000 students First Aid and swimming lessons. He also received a citation from the Mayor Daley in Chicago, Illinois and was entered into the Senior Citizen Hall of Fame. He served his country during World War I with the US Navy.

April 3

Lamar Smith

1892 – August 13, 1955

Lamar "Ditney" Smith was an American civil rights figure, African-American farmer, World_War I veteran, and an organizer of Black voter registration. In 1955, he was shot dead in broad daylight around 10 a.m. at close range on the lawn of the Lincoln County courthouse in Brookhaven, Mississippi.

Smith was a voting rights activist and a member of the Regional Council of Negro Leadership (RCNL). On August 2, he voted in the primary and helped get others out to vote. There was a run-off primary scheduled for August 23. On August 13, Smith was at the courthouse helping other Black voters to fill out absentee ballots so they could vote in the runoff without exposing themselves to violence at the polls. He was shot to death in front of the courthouse in Brookhaven, Lincoln County.

Reports say there were at least 30 white witnesses, including the local sheriff, who saw a white man covered with blood leaving the scene. In spite of a public effort by prosecutor E.C. Barlow to obtain testimony, no witnesses came forward. The three men who had been arrested went free.

April 4

Menen Asfaw

April 3, 1889 - February 15, 1962

Empress Menen Asfaw (Baptismal name Walatta Giyorgis) was the Empress consort of the Ethiopian Empire. She was the wife of Emperor Haile Selassie.
Menen was born Itege Menen Asfaw in Ambassel (Amhara Region in Ethiopia) and was the daughter of Asfaw, Jantirar of Ambassel. Her maternal grandfather was Negus Mikael of Wollo and her uncle was Emperor Iyasu V (Lij Iyasu).

Menen married in 1911 at the age of 20. The future Emperor was impressed by her character and friendly disposition. Over time, Empress Menen Asfaw gave husband, Emperor Haile Selassie six children; Princess Tenagnework, Prince Asfaw Wossen, Princess Tsehai, Princess Zenebework, Prince Makonnen and Prince Sahle Selassie. When Haile Selassie became Emperor of Ethiopia his wife was crowned Empress alongside him. As consort, Empress Menen was very active and undertook a number of charitable duties focused on women, children and religious issues. The Empress also supported numerous charitable causes for the poor, the infirm and the handicapped.

Empress Menen Asfaw served as Patroness of the Ethiopian Red Cross, and the Ethiopian Women's Charitable Organization. She was also a patroness of the Jerusalem Society that arranged for pilgrimages to the Holy Land. She founded the Empress Menen School for Girls in Addis Ababa, the first all-girls school which had both boarding and day students. She gave generously from her personal funds towards the building of the new Cathedral of St. Mary of Zion at Axum but did not live to see it completed and dedicated.

Empress Menen Asfaw was buried in the imperial crypt at the Holy Trinity Cathedral.

April 5

Richard Wayne Penniman
December 5, 1932 - May 9, 2020

Richard Wayne Penniman (known as Little Richard), was an American musician, singer, and songwriter. He was an influential figure in popular music and culture for seven decades. Nicknamed "The Innovator," "The Originator," and "The Architect of Rock and Roll", Little Richard's most celebrated work dates from the mid-1950s when his charismatic showmanship and dynamic music, characterized by frenetic piano playing, pounding back beat and raspy shouted vocals, laid the foundation for rock and roll.

Little Richard's innovative emotive vocalizations and up-tempo rhythmic music also played a key role in the formation of other popular music genres, including soul and funk. He influenced numerous singers and musicians across musical genres from rock to hip hop; his music helped shape rhythm and blues for generations.

In addition to his musical style, Richard was cited as one of the first crossover Black artists, reaching audiences of all races. His music and concerts broke the color line drawing Blacks and whites together despite attempts to sustain segregation. In 2015, the National Museum of African American Music honored Richard for helping to shatter the color line on the music charts changing American culture forever.

April 6

Keith Anderson CD
October 28, 1944 - March 27, 2020

Young, Gifted and Black was just one of Keith Anderson's (Bob Andy) socially conscious songs. Others, such as *Fire Burning* and *Check It Out*, castigated capitalism and the ruling classes. But he suffered from health issues, including migraines, and put music to one side for a number of years from the late 1970s onwards, broadening into acting.

Born in Kingston, Jamaica and better known by his stage name of Bob Andy, Anderson was a Jamaican reggae vocalist and songwriter. He was widely regarded as one of reggae's most influential songwriters.

As a child, to escape beatings from his mother, Anderson tried to get in to Maxfield Park Children's Home. Through intervention of the courts, Anderson became a ward of the state and was allowed to live at the Home. While there he taught himself to play piano and began singing in Kingston Parish Church Choir. There, he met Garth "Tyrone" Evans and along with Junior Menz, and Leroy Stamp were the original founding members *The Paragons* – a popular 1960s ska and rocksteady vocal group.

In the 1970s Bob Andy performed a hit version of *Young, Gifted and Black* as part of a duo with Marcia Griffiths. It reached No. 5 in the United Kingdom. They performed it as an up-tempo recording of the Nina Simone original. They also reached No. 11 in 1971 with *Pied Piper*, which spent 13 weeks in the charts.

Bob Andy also wrote songs that would be recorded by reggae stars including Gregory Isaacs, Ken Boothe and Delroy Wilson, along with solo numbers for Marcia Griffiths.

In 2006, he was awarded Order of Distinction in the rank of Commander (CD) by the Jamaican government for his services to music.

April 7

Paul Robeson
April 9, 1898 - January 23, 1976

Paul Leroy Robeson was an American bass baritone concert artist and stage and film actor who became famous both for his cultural accomplishments and for his political activism.

Educated at Rutgers College and Columbia University, Robeson was a star athlete in his youth. He also studied Swahili and phonetics at the School of Oriental and African Studies in London in 1934.

Robeson's political activities began with his involvement with unemployed workers and anti-imperialist students whom he met in Britain and continued with support for the Republican cause in the Spanish Civil War and his opposition to fascism. In the United States he became active in the Civil Rights Movement and other social justice campaigns. His sympathies for the Soviet Union and for communism, and his criticism of the United States government and its foreign policies, caused him to be blacklisted during the McCarthy era.

April 8

Robert Mugabe
February 21, 1924 - September 6, 2019

Robert Gabriel Mugabe was a Zimbabwean revolutionary and politician who served as Prime Minister of Zimbabwe from 1980 to 1987 and then as President from 1987 to 2017. He served as Leader of the Zimbabwe African National Union (ZANU) and led its successor political party, the ZANU – Patriotic Front (ZANU–PF), from 1980 to 2017. Ideologically an African nationalist, during the 1970s and 1980s he identified as a Marxist–Leninist and as a socialist after the 1990s.

Having dominated Zimbabwe's politics for nearly four decades, Mugabe was a controversial figure. He was praised as a revolutionary hero of the African liberation struggle who helped free Zimbabwe from British colonialism, imperialism, and white minority rule. Critics accused Mugabe of being a dictator responsible for economic mismanagement, widespread corruption in Zimbabwe, anti-white racism, human rights abuses, and crimes against humanity.

April 9

José Antonio Aponte
1760 - 1812

José Antonio Aponte, often known as "Black" José Aponte, was a Cuban political activist and military officer of Yoruba origin who organized one of the most prominent slave rebellions in Cuba, the Aponte Conspiracy of 1812. He held the rank of first corporal (*cabo primero*) in Havana's Black militia, and was the leader of his local Yoruba association. Aponte was a free Black carpenter in Havana was proclaimed to be the leader of a plot to rebel against the Cuban government, free the slaves and uplift free people of color, and overthrow slavery in Cuba. The movement struck several sugar plantations on the outskirts of Havana, but it was soon crushed by the government.

In Cuba, in the late eighteenth century, there were numerous rebellions led by enslaved and free Africans; in 1812, Aponte continued this legacy as he organized one of the most prominent revolts in Cuba, known as Aponte's Rebellion of 1812.

Aponte was the creator of an unusual work of art—a "book of paintings" full of historical and mythical figures, including Black kings, emperors, priests, and soldiers that he showed to and discussed with fellow conspirators. Aponte's vision of a Black history connected a diasporic and transatlantic past to the possibility of imagining a sovereign future for free and enslaved Africans in colonial Cuba.

April 10

Prisolter Bartholomew

Contributor: Bekeo Adigun, (Grandson)

I must remember Prisolter Bartholomew, my paternal grandfather who was born in Grenada. I was twelve years old, when one morning, he said, "Son, take this donkey; we are going to the land." Each of us rode on a separate donkey for about two hours we came to that land where I was expected to work. "Pick up a few mangoes and wait for me over there," he said. He went and cut some pieces of sugar cane and came and joined me.

"Son," he said, "working to advance our people is not easy. You will have to be prepared to sacrifice yourself for the advancement of your community and at times expect them to betray you."

"Why?" I asked.

"When our people who are supposed to fight for themselves spend time drinking and smoking they will compromise themselves. They will tell your plans to their enemies. The thing they put in their body will control their behavior. If you are going to work to better conditions for us, you must not drink or smoke. And do not trust those who do with any serious plans. Take the actions you must by yourself he said, you will gain more success." I had several lessons from Grandpa.

April 11

Yosef A. A. Ben-Jochannon
December 31, 1918 - March 19, 2015

Yosef Alfredo Antonio Ben-Jochannon, referred to by his admirers as "Dr. Ben", was an American writer and historian. He was considered by some Black nationalists to be one of the more prominent Afrocentric scholars.

"It must be emphatically stated and reiterated that he unapologetically wrote solely for the African world. And as expected, his intentions not to ease the conscience of white America rubbed its academicians and sympathizers the wrong way, especially given his poignant critique of the falsehood of white racial norms. As an Ethiopian Jew and an ethnic member of arguably the world's oldest remnant of legitimate ancient Israelite stock, his identity alone shattered ideas of an exclusive white Jewish racial myth." – *Amsterdam News*.
http://amsterdamnews.com/news/2015/may/14/dr-yosef-ben-jochannan-transitioning-immortality/

April 12

Percy Sutton

November 24, 1920 - December 26, 2009

Percy Ellis Sutton was a prominent Black American political and business leader. An activist in the Civil Rights Movement and lawyer, he was also a Freedom Rider and the legal representative for Malcolm X. He was the highest-ranking African-American elected official in New York City when he was Manhattan borough president from 1966 to 1977. He was an entrepreneur whose investments included the *New York Amsterdam News*, the Apollo Theater in Harlem, and Inner City Broadcasting which operated the first African American-owned radio station in the New York market with programming for its community.

Although he was a San Antonio, Texas native, it was in New York City where Sutton sowed seeds of success cultivated with integrity and indomitable will. The youngest son of a former enslaved Africans, Sutton made his way to New York before joining the Tuskegee Airmen as an intelligence officer in World War II after being rejected by white Southern recruiters in his hometown. Following a stint in the Air Force, Sutton and his brother Oliver opened a Harlem law office in 1953. His firm represented slain activist Malcolm X, his wife, Betty Shabazz, and the Black Panthers, among others.

In the 1970s, Sutton, who served in the New York State Assembly, was a member of a group of Black politicians from Harlem dubbed the "Gang of Four," which included Charles Rangel, Basil Paterson, and David Dinkins.

April 13

Huey P. Newton
February 17, 1942 - August 22, 1989

Huey Percy Newton was an African-American political activist, author and revolutionary who, along with fellow Merritt College student Bobby Seale, co-founded the Black Panther Party (1966–1982). Together with Seale, Newton created a ten-point program which laid out guidelines for how the African-American community could achieve liberation.

In the 1960s, under Newton's leadership, the Black Panther Party founded over 60 community support programs (renamed survival programs in 1971) including food banks, medical clinics, sickle cell anemia tests, prison busing for families of inmates, legal advice seminars, clothing banks, housing cooperates, and their own ambulance service. The most famous of these programs was the Free Breakfast for Children program which fed thousands of impoverished children daily during the early 1970s. Newton also co-founded the Black Panther newspaper service which became one of America's most widely distributed African-American newspapers.

"A poster of Huey Newton sitting in a rattan throne chair wearing a beret and a black leather jacket while holding a rifle in his right hand and a spear in his left hand. Leaning against the wall on either side of the chair is a leaf-shaped, Zulu style shield with designs of horizontal line markings across the front. Beneath the chair is a zebra print rug. Along the bottom of the print is the text: The racist dog policemen must withdraw immediately from our communities, cease their wanton murder and brutality and torture of Black people, or face the wrath of the armed people." - https://nmaahc.si.edu/object/nmaahc_2011.58

April 14

Leopold Sédar Senghor
October 9, 1906 - December 20, 2001

Léopold Sédar Senghor was a Senegalese poet, politician and cultural theorist who, for two decades, served as the first president of the Republic of Senegal (1960–80). Ideologically an African socialist, he was the major theoretician of Négritude - a literary and ideological movement led by French-speaking Black writers and intellectuals from France's colonies in Africa and the Caribbean in the 1930s.

Senghor was imprisonment during the Second World War.

Léopold Sédar Senghor embodied peace, humility, and he was a perfectionist in his work. He was a great scholar who was passionate about languages. He became the first Black writer to be elected as a member of the Académie française - the famous French language council - in 1984. He was also arguably the first head of state in Africa to resign of his own will.

Phrases attributed to Léopold Sédar Senghor: "Emotion is Negro, just as reason is Hellenic." Despite the critics, he never denied the role of emotion. He reproached his opponents for not trying to understand it. According to him, emotion is the intuitive reason in opposition to the European definition of reason, the discursive one.

"Assimilate not to be assimilated." Through this other famous quotation, Senghor urges the African youth to assimilate everything that stems from ancient culture and to raise this knowledge to a new height which used to be unattainable for people from the ancient society.

"The Civilization of the Universal." The saying emanates from the famous Senghorian theory of assimilation and openness, of giving and receiving. It explains the mixing of the Negro side and the Hellenic part which should lead to the "New Negro", a full and fecund man.

April 15

African Liberation Day

African Liberation Day, also known as ALD, was founded in 1958 by Dr. Kwame Nkrumah on the occasion of the First Conference of Independent States held in Accra, Ghana and attended by eight independent African states. The 15th of April was declared "African Freedom Day," to mark each year the onward progress of the liberation movement, and to symbolize the determination of the people of Africa to free themselves from foreign domination and exploitation.

On May 25, 1963, thirty one African leaders convened a summit to found the Organization of African Unity (OAU) and they adopted May 25 as African Liberation Day.

April 16

Dudley Laws
May 7, 1934 - March 24, 2011

Dudley Laws was a controversial race activist, beloved by many in the community that he served.

A constant flow of well-wishers visited him in his hospital room where he had been confined for the last month and a thousand supporters turned out for a ceremony to honour his activism just days before his death.

In 1988, after a number of Black men were shot and killed in confrontations with Toronto-area police, Laws co-founded the Black Action Defence Committee along with Charles Roach, Sherona Hall and Lennox Farrell.

The group pushed for independent police oversight, and Laws became a tough and vocal critic of the force's relationship with his community. And he accused police of targeting Black youth.

Laws was born in Saint Thomas, Jamaica.

A welder and mechanic by trade, Laws worked at Standard Engineering Works until he emigrated to the United Kingdom in 1955 and became involved in defending the West Indian community. He influenced the development and launch of the Somerleyton and Geneva Road Association in Brixton and also joined the Standing Conference of the West Indies and the St Johns Inter-Racial Club. In 1965, he relocated to Toronto, Ontario, Canada, where he worked as a welder and taxi driver. He joined the Universal African Improvement Association, a Garveyite organization.

Laws became prominent in the 1970s and 1980s as a critic of the then Metropolitan Toronto Police Force, due to a number of young Black men being shot by police constables, as well as levelling other allegations of racist practices against the police. He was also prominent as an advocate for immigrants and refugees and worked as an immigration consultant in the 1990s.

April 17

Charles Hamilton Houston
September 3, 1895 - April 22, 1950

Charles Hamilton Houston was a prominent African-American lawyer, Dean of Howard University Law School, and National Association for the Advancement of Colored People (NAACP) first special counsel. A graduate of Amherst College and Harvard Law School, Houston played a significant role in dismantling Jim Crow laws, especially attacking segregation in schools and racial housing restrictions. He earned the title "The Man Who Killed Jim Crow".

Houston is well known for having trained and mentored a generation of Black attorneys. He recruited young lawyers to work on the NAACP's litigation campaigns, building connections between Howard's and Harvard's university law schools.

Houston was born in Washington, D.C. His father William Le Pré Houston, the son of a former enslaved African, was an attorney who practiced in the capital for more than forty years. Charles' mother, Mary (née Hamilton) Houston, was as a seamstress.

During World War I, Houston joined the U.S. Army serving as a First Lieutenant in the United States Infantry, with service in France. After being chastised for, during a brief detail as a Judge Advocate, finding a Black sergeant not worthy of prosecution, Houston wrote later:

“The hate and scorn showered on us Negro officers by our fellow Americans convinced me that there was no sense in my dying for a world ruled by them. I made up my mind that if I got through this war I would study law and use my time fighting for men who could not strike back.”

Houston earned a J.D. in 1923 and was admitted to the Washington, DC bar in 1924. He joined his father's practice.

April 18

Marva Collins

August 31, 1936 - June 24, 2015

Marva Delores Collins (née Knight) was an American educator. Collins is best known for creating Westside Preparatory School, a private elementary school in the Garfield Park neighborhood of Chicago, Illinois which opened in 1975.

"All children can learn," says Marva Collins. "For thirty years, we have done what other schools declare impossible," explains Collins, who has trained more than 100,000 teachers, principals, and administrators in the methodology developed and practiced at her Westside Preparatory School in Chicago. "I don't make excuses--I take responsibility. If children fail, it's about me, not them. I tell my students, if you think excellence is difficult, you don't want to try failure."

Collins says the critical element is instilling self-worth and convincing children that they are born to succeed. "Values can be replicated, excellence can be replicated, but it has to begin with the idea that everything is about me, not the other person, and about being proud of my work. Many parents are busy giving their children everything except a sense of self-esteem and self-worth."

Each morning, students begin with a recitation known as the creed--twenty-two verses that stress positive thinking, responsibility, and achievement as individual choices. "We greet two hundred children every day, and each one tells us their plan for the day," says Collins. "They come to lunch and bring a topic they're going to discuss. Man is the only species born to be intellectual, but today's children can't discuss ideas. With my own children, at every dinner they were to bring a topic to the table."

Collins grew up in Atmore, Alabama, where segregation meant limited resources for Black schools and no access to the public library. Her father placed a high value on education, self-reliance and achievement.

April 19

Alvin Ailey, Jr.
January 5, 1931 - December 1, 1989

Alvin Ailey, a.k.a. Alvin Ailey Jr., was an African-American dancer, director, choreographer, and activist who founded the Alvin Ailey American Dance Theater (AAADT). He created AAADT and its affiliated Ailey School as havens for nurturing Black artists and expressing the universality of the African-American experience through dance.

His work fused theatre, modern dance, ballet, and jazz with Black vernacular, creating hope-fueled choreography that continues to spread global awareness of Black life in America. Ailey's choreographic masterpiece *Revelations* is recognized as one of the most popular and most performed ballets in the world

Born in Rogers, Texas, Ailey showed an interest in art at an early age and his experiences growing up in the rural South later inspired some of his best work.

Ailey was first touched by dance on a junior high school field trip to Los Angeles to see the Ballet Russe de Monte Carlo. This led to classes with choreographer Katherine Dunham, widely known for her dance technique that integrated many cultural styles and whose company was the first African-American troupe of dancers, actors and musicians. In 1949, Ailey collaborated with Lester Horton, whose company was racially diverse and included Native American and Japanese influences. Working with Horton significantly influenced Ailey's later dedication to achieving equal rights in the arts.

April 20

Mary Eliza Church Terrell

September 23, 1863 - July 24, 1954

Mary Eliza Church Terrell was one of the first African-American women to earn a college degree and became known as a national activist for civil rights and suffrage. An Oberlin College graduate, Terrell was part of the rising Black middle and upper class who used their position to fight racial discrimination in the late 19th and early 20th centuries.

She taught in the Latin Department at the M Street school (now known as Paul Laurence Dunbar High School)—the first African American public high school in the nation—in Washington, DC. In 1896, she was the first African-American woman in the United States to be appointed to the school board of a major city, serving in the District of Columbia until 1906. Terrell was a charter member of the National Association for the Advancement of Colored People (NAACP) (1909) and the Colored Women's League of Washington (1894). She helped found the National Association of Colored Women (1896) and served as its first national president, and she was a founding member of the National Association of College Women (1910).

The daughter of former enslaved Africans, Terrell was born in Memphis, Tennessee. Her father, Robert Reed Church, was a successful businessman who became one of the South's first African American millionaires. Her mother, Louisa Ayres Church, owned a hair salon.

Her activism was sparked in 1892, when an old friend, Thomas Moss, was lynched in Memphis by whites because his business competed with theirs. Terrell joined Ida B. Wells-Barnett in anti-lynching campaigns, but Terrell's life work focused on the notion of racial uplift, the belief that Blacks would help end racial discrimination by advancing themselves and other members of the race through education, work, and community activism.

April 21

Eunice Kathleen Waymon
February 21, 1933 - April 21, 2003

"I'm a real rebel with a cause." - Nina Simone

Eunice Kathleen Waymon, known professionally as Nina Simone, was an American singer, songwriter, musical arranger, and civil rights activist. Her music spanned a broad range of styles, including classical, jazz, folk, R&B, gospel, and pop. Nina referred to her music as Black Classical Music. She was one of the most extraordinary artists of the twentieth century, an icon of American music.

Simone was the consummate musical storyteller, a griot, who used her remarkable talent to create a legacy of liberation, empowerment, passion, and love through a magnificent body of works. She earned the moniker 'High Priestess of Soul' for she could weave a spell so seductive and hypnotic that the listener lost track of time and space as they became absorbed in the moment. She was who the world would come to know as Nina Simone.

When Nina Simone died she left a timeless treasure trove of musical magic spanning over four decades from *I Loves You Porgy*, to *Young, Gifted and Black*, to *A Single Woman*, with her musical trademark of honest emotion.

Able to play virtually anything by ear, Waymon was soon studying classical European music in her hometown, Tryon, North Carolina. After graduating valedictorian of her high school class, the community raised money for a scholarship for Eunice to study at Julliard in New York City before applying to the prestigious Curtis Institute of Music in Philadelphia. Her hopes for a career as a pioneering African American classical pianist were dashed when the school denied her admission.

She would claim that racism was the reason she was denied admission. While her original dream was unfulfilled, Waymon lived an incredible worldwide career as Nina Simone.

April 22

Sengbe Pieh/ Joseph Cinque

c. 1814 – c. 1879

Joseph Cinqué known as Sengbe Pieh and sometimes referred to as Cinqué, was a West African man of the Mende people who led a revolt of Africans on the Spanish slave ship La Amistad.

After the ship was taken into custody by the United States Revenue Cutter Service, Cinqué and his fellow Africans were eventually tried for mutiny and killing officers on the ship, in a case known as United States v. The Amistad. This reached the U.S. Supreme Court, where Cinqué and his fellow Africans were found to have rightfully defended themselves from being enslaved through the illegal Atlantic slave trade and were released.

Evangelical Christians led by Lewis Tappan, a prominent New York businessman, Joshua Leavitt, a lawyer and journalist who edited the Emancipator in New York, and Simeon Jocelyn, a Congregational minister in New Haven, Connecticut, learned of the Amistad's arrival and decided to publicize the incident to expose the brutalities of slavery and the slave trade. They hoped to launch a massive assault on slavery.

The journey began months earlier, in 1839, when slave trade merchants captured Cinqué, a young man from Mende, Sierra Leone, and about 500 Africans from different West African tribes and took them to the Caribbean.

The journey ended with the clandestine, nighttime entry of the ship into Cuba — in violation of the Anglo-Spanish treaties of 1817 and 1835 that made the African slave trade a capital crime. Slavery itself was legal in Cuba, meaning that once smuggled ashore, the Africans became "slaves" suitable for auction at the Havana barracoons.

In Havana, two Spaniards bought 53 of the Africans — including Cinqué — and chartered the Amistad to transport its human cargo to plantations in another part of Cuba. Cinque said no way.

April 23

Louise Manigault
1947 - 2020

Louise Manigault lived a life of service and sacrifice, a life dedicated to God and the people of God.

She was a licensed realtor, a certified paralegal, a savvy businessperson, a celebrated toastmaster, and the author of eight devotional books filled with daily inspirations and affirmations. And she was a minister of the gospel. Her ministry, Universal Faith Ministry, was international in scope, filled with the Holy Spirit and a treasure to hundreds of thousands who received blessings from her presence on the pages of her work or in person.

Manigault was born in Cleveland, Ohio in November to George McConnell and Maggie Henson. After the passing of her mother at an early age, Manigault's aunt and uncle brought her to live in Brooklyn New York, eventually settling in Queens, New York. She considered herself a native New Yorker.

Her work in the traditional church and in the wider community brought a liberating energy of hope, practical options, and joy to the many people whom she met on her journey.

April 24

Oliver Reginald Kaizana Tambo

October 27, 1917 - April 24, 1993

Oliver Reginald Kaizana Tambo also known as O. R. Tambo, was a South African anti-apartheid politician and revolutionary who served as President of the African National Congress (ANC) from 1967 to 1991.

Oliver Tambo was born on in the village of Nkantolo in Bizana; eastern Pondoland in what is now the Eastern Cape. The village Tambo was born in was made up mostly of farmers.

Tambo was directly responsible for organizing active guerilla units. Along with his comrades Nelson Mandela, Joe Slovo, and Walter Sisulu, Tambo directed and facilitated several attacks against the apartheid state. In a 1985 interview, Tambo was quoted as saying, "In the past, we were saying the ANC will not deliberately take innocent life. But now, looking at what is happening in South Africa, it is difficult to say civilians are not going to die."

The post-apartheid Truth and Reconciliation Commission (TRC) in 1997-1998 identified Tambo as the person who gave final approval for the May 20, 1983 Church Street bombing, which resulted in the death of 19 people and injuries to about 200 people. The attack was orchestrated by a special operations unit of the ANC's Umkhonto we Sizwe (MK), commanded by Aboobaker Ismail. Such units had been authorised by Tambo as President of the ANC in 1979. At the time of the attack, they reported to Joe Slovo as chief of staff.

April 25

Lerone Bennett Jr.
October 17, 1928 - February 14, 2018

Lerone Bennett Jr. was an African-American scholar, author and social historian, known for his analysis of race relations in the United States. His best-known works include *Before the Mayflower: A History of Black America, 1619-1962.* This is a comprehensive examination of the history of African Americans in the United States and it gave Bennett the reputation of a first-class popular historian. In his eight subsequent books, Bennett continued to document the historical forces shaping the Black experience in the United States. His other works included: *What Manner of Man?, Pioneers In Protest, The Shaping of Black America,* and *Forced into Glory* (2000), a book about U.S. President Abraham Lincoln.

Historian Lerone Bennett served as the executive editor of *Ebony* for almost forty years. His written work deftly explored the history of race relations in the United States as well as the current environment in which African Americans strive for equality. Bennett was born in Clarksdale, Mississippi, to Lerone and Alma Reed Bennett. When Bennett was young, his family moved to Jackson, Mississippi, and while attending public schools Bennett's interest in journalism emerged.

Bennett earned a B.A. in 1949 from Morehouse College. He considered Morehouse as the center of his academic development.

After serving in the Korean War, Bennett entered the world of journalism as a reporter for the *Atlanta Daily World.* He became the city editor for the magazine and worked there until 1953, when he began his work as an associate editor at *Jet* magazine in Chicago, Illinois. In 1954, Bennett became an associate editor at *Ebony* and he was promoted to senior editor of the magazine in 1958. His comprehensive articles became one of the magazine's literary hallmarks.

April 26

Mamie Till
November 23, 1921 - January 6, 2003

Mamie Till, born in Mississippi, turned the pain of her son's murder into activism for justice for African Americans.

In 1955, when Emmett was fourteen, his mother Mamie Till put him on a train from Chicago to spend the summer visiting his cousins in Mississippi.

She never saw him alive again.

Her son was abducted and brutally murdered on August 28, 1955, after being accused of interacting inappropriately with a white woman – who years later confessed to lying. The following month, two half-brothers faced trial for Till's kidnapping and murder. They were acquitted by the all-white jury after a five-day trial and a 67-minute deliberation. One juror said, "If we hadn't stopped to drink pop, it wouldn't have taken that long." Only months later, in an interview with *Look* magazine in 1956, protected against double jeopardy, Bryant and Milam admitted to killing Emmett Till.

At her son's funeral, Mamie Till insisted that the **coffin** containing Emmett's body be left open, because, in her words, "I wanted the world to see what they did to my baby." Tens of thousands of people viewed Emmett's body, and photographs were circulated around the country. Through the constant attention it received, the Till case more people became aware of the disparity of justice for Blacks in the South.

The NAACP asked Mamie Till to tour the country relating the events of her son's life, death, and the trial of his murderers.

The National Museum of African American History and Culture in Washington DC carries an exhibit on the Emmett Till story.

April 27
William J. Houston, Department of Justice

Houston served as one of forty five African Americans on the Black Cabinet, or Federal Council of Negro Affairs or Black Brain Trust, the informal term for the group of African Americans who served as public policy advisors to President Franklin D. Roosevelt and his wife Eleanor Roosevelt in his terms in office from 1933 to 1945.

> Mission of the Department of Justice: To enforce the law and defend the interests of the United States according to the law; to ensure public safety against threats foreign and domestic; to provide federal leadership in preventing and controlling crime; to seek just punishment for those guilty of unlawful behavior; and to ensure fair and impartial administration of justice for all Americans.
>
> About the Department of Justice: The Office of the Attorney General was created by the Judiciary Act of 1789 (ch. 20, sec. 35, 1 Stat. 73, 92-93), as a one-person part-time position. The Act specified that the Attorney General was to be "learned in the law," with the duty "to prosecute and conduct all suits in the Supreme Court in which the United States shall be concerned, and to give his advice and opinion upon questions of law when required by the President of the United States, or when requested by the heads of any of the departments, touching any matters that may concern their departments."- https://www.justice.gov/

April 28

Adorah Perrotte
Contributor: Bekeo Adigun, (Grandson)

To my immediate ancestors I give plenty thanks for whom I am. I was born in my mother's mother Adorah Perrotte house in St Andrews, Grenada. From this elder I learned the value of patience, and proper language. I was thirteen years old when I used the (N) word in her presence. She became very upset and said, "Sit down son. This is one of the worst words you should use; it does not put us in a good light. Why should you use words that bring pain sickness? If you must speak, please speak words that are healing and not that which will cause one to be upset or hurt." After that incident I became very careful with the words I use. If words are medicine one must use it with care.

I was fourteen and on my journey to school one morning by bus. At that time I considered myself as part of the revolutionary organization in the country - The New Jewel Movement. On the bus an elder started talking about the government. I did not hesitate to inform him the government will soon be removed and (Maurice) Bishop will be our leader.

After coming from school that afternoon, Grandma called me, "Son please have a seat. Son if you are working to remove the government why should you tell everyone. When you announce your plans on the public bus everyone is listening, and they will come to you when you are not ready. Do not speak your plans to the public. If you feel like talking about your plans get off the bus and walk. Every ear around will not be ready for your words. Be careful with what you speak and where you speak."

April 29

Jo Ann Gibson Robinson
April 17, 1912 - August 29, 1992

Jo Ann Gibson Robinson was an activist during the Civil Rights Movement and an educator in Montgomery, Alabama. Born in Georgia, she excelled in school and earned valedictorian at her high school. She became the first person in her family to become a college graduate at Fort Valley State College with a bachelor's degree in 1934 and a M.A. in English at Atlanta University.

While in Montgomery, Robinson joined the Women's Political Council (WPC), which Mary Fair Burks had founded three years earlier. The WPC was an organization dedicated to inspiring African Americans to rise above the level of mediocrity that they had been conditioned to accept, to fight juvenile delinquency, increase voter registration in the African American community and to improve their status as a group. The WPC was also in the development in women's involvement in civic affairs, worked towards encouraging African Americans to vote, and helping women who were victims of rape.

In 1949, Robinson was verbally attacked by a bus driver for sitting in the front "Whites only" section of the bus. The whites only section was empty. Out of fear that the incident would escalate and that the driver would go from verbal abuse to physical, Robinson left the bus. Her response to the incident was to attempt to start a protest boycott against bus segregation in Alabama. When Robinson approached fellow WPC members with her story and proposal, she was told that it was "a fact of life in Montgomery."

In the late 1950s when City Hall's leaders were of no help, Robinson organized a transportation boycott. She was an outspoken critic of the treatment of African-Americans on public transportation. She was active in the Dexter Avenue Baptist Church.

April 30
Edgar G. Brown, Civilian Conservation Corps

Edgar G. Brown served as one of forty five African Americans on the Black Cabinet, or Federal Council of Negro Affairs or Black Brain Trust, the informal term for the group of African Americans who served as public policy advisors to President Franklin D. Roosevelt and his wife Eleanor Roosevelt in his terms in office from 1933 to 1945.

> The Civilian Conservation Corps (CCC), established by Congress on March 31, 1933, provided jobs for young, unemployed men during the Great Depression. Over its 9-year lifespan, the CCC employed about 3 million men nationwide. The CCC made valuable contributions to forest management, flood control, conservation projects, and the development of state and national parks, forests, and historic sites. In return, the men received the benefits of education and training, a small paycheck, and the dignity of honest work. - https://www.nps.gov/thro/learn/historyculture/civilian-conservation-corps.htm

May 1

Leroy Eldridge Cleaver
August 31, 1935 - May 1, 1998

Leroy Eldridge Cleaver was an American writer, and political activist who became an early leader of the Black Panther Party (1967-1971). He was born in Wabbaseka in Jefferson County, Arkansas.

In 1968, Cleaver wrote *Soul on Ice*, a collection of essays that, at the time of its publication, was praised by *The New York Times Book Review* as "brilliant and revealing". Cleaver stated in *Soul on Ice*: "If a man like Malcolm X could change and repudiate racism, if I myself and other former Muslims can change, if young whites can change, then there is hope for America."

Cleaver went on to become a prominent member of the Black Panthers, having the titles Minister of Information and Head of the International Section of the Panthers, while a fugitive from the United States criminal justice system in Cuba and Algeria. He became a fugitive after leading an ambush on Oakland police officers, during which two officers were wounded. Cleaver was also wounded during the clash and Black Panther member Bobby Hutton was killed. As editor of the official Panthers' newspaper, *The Black Panther*, Cleaver's influence on the direction of the Party was rivaled only by founders Huey P. Newton and Bobby Seale. Cleaver and Newton eventually fell out with each other, resulting in a split that weakened the party.

After spending seven years in exile in Cuba, Algeria, and France, Cleaver returned to the US in 1975, where he became involved in various religious groups before finally joining the Church of Jesus Christ of Latter-day Saints, as well as becoming a conservative Republican, appearing at Republican events.

May 2

Tony Martin

February 21, 1942 - January 17, 2013

Tony Martin was a Trinidad-born scholar of Africana Studies. From 1973 to 2007 he worked at Wellesley College in Wellesley, Massachusetts and over the course of his career published over ten books and a range of scholarly articles.

Born in Port of Spain, Martin moved to the United Kingdom, where he studied law at Gray's Inn, London, and then economics at the University of Hull. Relocating to the U.S., he completed a Ph.D. on the Jamaican political activist Marcus Garvey at Michigan State University in 1973. As an associate professor at Wellesley College, he was a founding member of its Africana Studies Department. During the latter part of the 1970s and 1980s he published several books on Garvey and Garveyism.

Among the subjects that Martin pursued was the place of Jews in the Atlantic slave trade. During the 1990s, he came under public criticism for encouraging his students to read *The Secret Relationship Between Blacks and Jews*, a book compiled by the Nation of Islam that was widely regarded as anti-Semitic. That decade, he also entered into a publicized argument with Classics scholar Mary Lefkowitz, a prominent critic of historical claims made by Afrocentric scholarship. Martin subsequently took Lefkowitz to court for libel, but the case was dismissed. In 1993 he self-published *The Jewish Onslaught*, a book that Wellesley distanced themselves from and which generated further accusations of antisemitism. In 2002 he spoke at a conference organized by a leading Holocaust denial organization, the Institute for Historical Review, alleging that Jewish organizations were trying to stifle free speech. In 2007 he retired from Wellesley.

Martin is the author of *Race First* and editor of Marcus Garvey's *Message to the People: The Course of African Philosophy*.

May 3

Bantu Steve Biko
A Leading Founder of the Black Consciousness Movement in South Africa

December 18, 1946 - September 12, 1977

Steve Biko was born in King William's Town, South Africa. He was thirty-one when he was murdered by South Africa's apartheid government. A leader of the Black Consciousness (BC) movement, Biko helped found the South African Students' Organization (SASO) in 1968 as a breakaway from the multiracial, but white-led, National Union of South African Students.

While the apartheid government initially saw SASO and the BC movement as preaching a racial separatism not detrimental to their own, it soon realized the radical movement was a threat to racial hierarchy in the country. As a series of national strikes broke out among Black workers in the mid-1970s — eventually culminating in the 1976 Soweto uprising — the government cracked down. SASO and BC activist Onkgopotse Tiro was killed in 1974, and three years later Biko died in police custody.

Biko's murder has elevated him to the pantheon of South Africa's great anti-apartheid leaders. Today, many invoke his name to critique the post-apartheid order, which remains brutally unequal.

May 4
Edward H. Lawson, Jr., Works Progress Administration
Alfred Edgar Smith, Works Progress Administration
John W. Whitten, Works Progress Administration

Edward H. Lawson, Alfred Edgar Smith, and John W. Whitten served on the Works Progress Administration team. They were members of the forty five-member African Americans team who served as public policy advisors to President Franklin D. Roosevelt and his wife Eleanor Roosevelt in his terms in office from 1933 to 1945.

> Works Progress Administration: On April 8, 1935, Congress approved the Emergency Relief Appropriation Act of 1935, the work relief bill that funded the Works Progress Administration (WPA). Created by President Franklin Roosevelt to relieve the economic hardship of the **Great Depression**, this national works program (renamed the Work Projects Administration beginning in 1939) employed more than 8.5 million people on 1.4 million public projects before it was disbanded in 1943. The WPA employed skilled and unskilled workers in a great variety of work projects—many of which were public works projects such as creating parks, and building roads, bridges, schools, and other public structures. https://www.loc.gov/item/today-in-history/april-08/

May 5
Arthur Weiseger, Department of Labor

Arthur Weiseger served as a member of the forty five-member team of African Americans who served as public policy advisors to President Franklin D. Roosevelt and his wife Eleanor Roosevelt in his terms in office from 1933 to 1945.

> The bill establishing the Department of Labor was signed on March 4, 1913, by President William Howard Taft, the defeated and departing incumbent just hours before Woodrow Wilson took office. Although Taft had misgivings about creating a new Cabinet-level Department, he realized that the new Congress and new President would surely reenact it if he did apply a veto. A Federal Department was the direct product of a half-century campaign by organized labor for a "Voice in the Cabinet." Also, the Department was an indirect product of the Progressive Movement of the early 1900s which promoted the achievement of better working conditions, conservation of natural resources and a host of other goals through both private and government action.
> https://www.dol.gov/general/aboutdol/history/dolchp01

May 6

Mary Seacole
1805 - 1881

Seacole was a pioneering nurse and heroine of the Crimean War, who as a woman of mixed race overcame a double prejudice.

Mary Seacole was born Mary Joan Grant in Kingston, Jamaica in 1805 to a Creole mother and a Scottish father. It was from her mother that she inherited her interest in nursing. Her mother who was, nicknamed "the Doctress", kept a lodging house at East Street, Kingston where she nursed army officers and their families from Up Park Camp. At age twelve, after much observation, Seacole was allowed to help her mother with the patients.

Although technically free, being of mixed race, Mary and her family had few civil rights - they could not vote, hold public office or enter the professions. In 1836, Mary married Edwin Seacole but the marriage was short-lived as he died in 1844.

Seacole was an inveterate traveller, and before her marriage visited other parts of the Caribbean, including Cuba, Haiti and the Bahamas, as well as Central America and Britain. On these trips she complemented her knowledge of traditional medicine with European medical ideas. In 1854, Seacole travelled to England again, and approached the War Office, asking to be sent as an army nurse to the Crimea where there was known to be poor medical facilities for wounded soldiers. She was refused. Undaunted Seacole funded her own trip to the Crimea where she established the British Hotel near Balaclava to provide 'a mess-table and comfortable quarters for sick and convalescent officers'. She also visited the battlefield, sometimes under fire, to nurse the wounded, and became known as Mother Seacole.

Seacole published her memoirs, *The Wonderful Adventures of Mrs. Seacole in Many Lands* (1857).

May 7

Henry A. Hunt, Farm Credit Administration
October 10, 1866 - October 1, 1938

Henry Alexander Hunt was an American educator who led efforts to reach Blacks in rural areas of Georgia. He was awarded the Spingarn Medal by the National Association for the Advancement of Colored People (NAACP), as well as the Harmon Prize. In addition, he was recruited in the 1930s by President Franklin D. Roosevelt to join the president's Black Cabinet, an informal group of more than 40 prominent African Americans appointed to positions in the executive agencies.

Hunt was born on "Hunt Hill", by the town of Sparta, in Hancock County, Georgia, part of the Black Belt. Hunt was the youngest of eight mixed-race children, four boys and four girls, born to an African-American mother, Mariah Hunt. The Hunts lived in a weather-beaten house on their small farm and the children grew up working on it. Despite his African-American roots, Hunt's appearance led people to assume he was from purely Caucasian descent. After Hunt's death, W. E. B. Du Bois, a personal friend of his, publicly spoke of Henry's Caucasian appearance and reflected on the questions Hunt received about why he did not choose to hide his mixed-race background.

Hunt attended school at Sparta for his early education. At the age of 16, he started at Atlanta University, one of the Historically Black Colleges created after the American Civil War. While attending Atlanta University, Hunt met Florence Johnson, the woman he would eventually marry in 1893. E. A. Johnson, Florence's brother, was the former Assemblyman of New York. Throughout his time as a college student Hunt worked as a carpenter to earn money. Hunt graduated from Atlanta University with a Bachelors of Arts degree and completion of coursework in the Industrial Department in 1890.

May 8

John Oliver Killens

January 14, 1916 - October 27, 1987

John Oliver Killens was an American writer and activist known for his politically charged novels—particularly *Youngblood* (1954)—and his contributions to the Black Arts movement and as a founder of the Harlem Writers Guild.

From an early age Killens was exposed to African American writers and thinkers. His father encouraged him to read Langston Hughes, and his mother introduced him to the work of poet and novelist Paul Laurence Dunbar. Growing up in Georgia under Jim Crow law had a profound impact on Killens's political and social outlook and provided source material for his writings.

While working for the National Labor Relations Board (through 1942), he took night classes and completed a bachelor's degree at Howard University. He then pursued a law degree with evening classes at Terrell Law School but was interrupted by military service during World War II. The racism he experienced while serving in the South Pacific in the highly segregated U.S. Army inspired later writings, especially the novel *And Then We Heard the Thunder* (1963) for which he received Pulitzer Prize nomination.

Killens was active in the civil rights movement, participating in the Montgomery bus boycott and associating with Martin Luther King, Jr. By the early 1960s Killens had become more interested in the philosophy of Malcolm X, and in 1964 he helped cofound the Organization of Afro-American Unity, which encouraged African Americans to look to and embrace their African heritage.

Killens was noted for his teaching, especially for the impact he had on young African American writers such as Ntozake Shange and Nikki Giovanni.

May 9

Joseph Roosevelt Houchins, Department of Commerce

August 9, 1900 - January 5, 1990

Joseph Roosevelt Houchins was an American labor economist, attorney, and academic. He taught at Howard University and was a member of the Black Cabinet who served as public policy advisors to President Franklin D. Roosevelt and his wife Eleanor Roosevelt in his terms in office from 1933 to 1945.

> The Department of Commerce was originally created as the US Department of Commerce and Labor on February 14, 1903. It was subsequently renamed the Department of Commerce on March 4, 1913, as the bureaus and agencies specializing in labor were transferred to the new Department of Labor. As the Federal government grew and evolved, other bureaus were transferred to and from the Commerce Department, giving it a rich history and unique role in the Cabinet.
>
> What do we expect to accomplish by creating a Department of Commerce? The name of the new Department answers the question. We hope to develop new fields of profitable trade and foster old ones. We hope to facilitate industrial development and promote commerce at home and abroad....We will look to this Department to give direction to the energetic campaign that has for its object the conquest of the markets of the world by American merchants and manufacturers."
>
> *-- Congressman Charles F. Cochiran, Congressional Record, January 15, 1903 https://www.commerce.gov/about/history*

May 10
Charles Lionel Franklin, Social Security Board

Charles Lionel Franklin was an economist who served as a member of the Black Cabinet who served as public policy advisors to President Franklin D. Roosevelt and his wife Eleanor Roosevelt in his terms in office from 1933 to 1945.

Franklin, born in New Orleans, earned an undergraduate degree in 1933 from Straight College (established in 1868 as a predominantly African-American school, founded by the American Missionary Association of the Congregational Church) in Louisiana. He earned his masters and doctoral degrees in economics from Columbia University. His doctoral thesis, *The Negro Labor Unionist in New York*, was published in the late 1930s by Columbia University Press.

For about 40 years Franklin was the owner and director of the Economic Statistics Bureau of Washington, a private research organization,. He also edited and published the Bureau's monthly *Handbook of Basic Economic Statistics*.

The Social Security Administration began its life as the Social Security Board: a three-member Board established to administer the Social Security Act. It was responsible for old age insurance, unemployment compensation and public assistance titles of the Social Security Act.

May 11

Frank Smith Horne

1899 - 1974

Frank Smith Horne was an American lyricist, poet, and government official who was an influential figure in the Harlem Renaissance. He was a member of President Franklin Delano Roosevelt's Black Cabinet where he served as Assistant Director of the Division of Negro Affairs, National Youth Administration. Later, Horne worked for the Housing and Home Finance Agency and helped to found the National Committee Against Discrimination in Housing (NCDH).

Horne was born and raised in Brooklyn, New York by Edwin Fletcher Horne and Cora Calhoun Horne. Horne had three brothers, Errol, John Burke, and Edwin Fletcher Junior. Horne's father was a private contractor and builder. His parents were early members of the National Association for the Advancement of Colored People (NAACP) and well-known members of middle class Black New York.

Horne attended the City College of New York, graduating in 1921 with a Bachelor of Science. Horne received an optometry degree from Northern Illinois College of Ophthalmology in 1923. In 1932, he graduated from the University of Southern California with a Master's Degree.

In the 1960s Horne he helped to write the NCDH's Ten Year Plan to end discrimination in housing; helped to set up the Metropolitan Applied Research Center (MARC) training of human relations workers in modern techniques of anti-bias organizations; and was publicly recognized for his dauntless courage… in the battle for open housing.

May 12
William H. Hastie, attorney, Department of the Interior
November 17, 1904 - April 14, 1976

William Henry Hastie Jr. was an American lawyer, judge, educator, public official, and civil rights advocate. He was the first African American to serve as Governor of the United States Virgin Islands, as a federal judge, and as a federal appellate judge. He served as a United States Circuit Judge of the United States Court of Appeals for the Third Circuit and previously served as District Judge of the District Court of the Virgin Islands.

Hastie was born in Knoxville, Tennessee, the son of William Henry Hastie, Sr. and Roberta Childs. His maternal ancestors were African American and Native American, but European American is also a strong possible mix. Family tradition held that one female ancestor was a Malagasy princess. He graduated from Dunbar High School, a top academic school for Black students. Hastie attended Amherst College in Massachusetts, where he graduated first in his class, magna cum laude, and Phi Beta Kappa, receiving an Artium Baccalaureus degree. He received a Bachelor of Laws from Harvard Law School in 1930, followed by a Doctor of Juridical Science from the same institution in 1933.

Hastie entered the private practice of law in Washington, D.C. from 1930 to 1933. From 1933 to 1937 he served as assistant solicitor for the United States Department of the Interior, advising the agency on racial issues. He had worked with Charles Hamilton Houston, former dean of the Howard University Law School, on setting up a joint law practice.

May 13

Esther Rolle
November 8, 1920 - November 17, 1998

Esther Rolle was an American actress. Rolle is best known for her role as Florida Evans, on the CBS television sitcom *Maude*, for two seasons (1972–1974), and its spin-off series *Good Times*, for five seasons (1974–77, 1978–79), for which Rolle was nominated for a Golden Globe Award for Best Actress - Television Series Musical or Comedy in 1976. In 1979, Rolle accepted the Emmy Award for Outstanding Supporting Actress in a Limited Series or Special for the television film Summer of My German Soldier.

Rolle was born in Pompano Beach, Florida. She was the tenth of 18 children. She graduated from Blanche Ely High School in Pompano Beach, Florida and studied at Spelman College in Atlanta, before moving to New York City. While in New York, she attended Hunter College before transferring to The New School and then Yale University in New Haven, Connecticut. For many years, Rolle worked in a traditional day job in New York City's garment district.

Rolle was a member of Asadata Dafora's dance troupe, Shogolo Oloba (later renamed the Federal Theater African Dance Troupe). She became the troupe's director in 1960.

Rolle made her New York stage debut in 1962 in the play *The Blacks*. She was often cast in plays produced by Robert Hooks and the Negro Ensemble Company. She also appeared in productions of *The Crucible and Blues for Mr. Charlie*. Rolle's most prominent early role was as Miss Maybell in the 1973 Melvin Van Peebles play, *Don't Play Us Cheap*. In 1977, Rolle portrayed Lady Macbeth in Orson Welles' Haitian-influenced version of William Shakespeare's *Macbeth* at the Henry Street New Federal Theater in Manhattan.

May 14

Curtis Mayfield
June 3, 1942 - December 26, 1999

Curtis Lee Mayfield was an American singer-songwriter, guitarist, and record producer, and one of the most influential musicians behind soul and politically conscious African-American music. He first achieved success and recognition with The Impressions during the civil rights movement of the late 1950s and 1960s. He later worked as a solo artist.

Mayfield, born in Chicago, Illinois started his musical career in a gospel choir. Moving to the North Side of Chicago, he met Jerry Butler in 1956 at the age of 14, and joined the vocal group The Impressions. As a songwriter, Mayfield became noted as one of the first musicians to bring more prevalent themes of social awareness into soul music.

In 1965, he wrote *People Get Ready* for the Impressions, which displayed his more politically charged songwriting. Ranked at number 24 on *Rolling Stone's* list of the 500 Greatest Songs of All Time, the song received numerous other awards, and was included in the Rock and Roll Hall of Fame 500 Songs that Shaped Rock and Roll, as well as being inducted into the Grammy Hall of Fame in 1998.

May 15

Hubert H. Harrison
April 27, 1883 - December 17, 1927

Born in Concordia, St. Croix, Danish West Indies, Hubert H. Harrison was an influential writer, orator, educator, critic, and political activist in Harlem during the early decades of the 20th century. He played unique, signal roles, in what were the largest class radical movement (socialism) and the largest race radical movement (the New Negro/Garvey movement) of his era.

Labor and civil rights activist A. Philip Randolph described Harrison as "the father of Harlem radicalism" and historian Joel A. Rogers considered him "the foremost Afro-American intellect of his time" and "one of America's greatest minds." Following his death due to complications of an appendectomy, Harrison's important contributions to intellectual and radical thought were much neglected.

In 1900 Harrison moved to New York City where he attended high school, and became interested in freethought and socialism. His first of many published letters to the editor appeared in the *New York Times* in 1903. During his first decade in New York the autodidactic Harrison read and wrote constantly and was active in Black intellectual circles.

In the 1900s Harrison earned a living working as a postal clerk. In 1910 Harrison wrote two letters critical of Booker T. Washington that were published in the *New York Sun*. Subsequent retaliatory efforts it is believed by Washington's "Tuskegee Machine" cost Harrison his postal employment.

For a few years Harrison was the leading Black activist, orator, and theoretician in the Socialist Party of New York and a prominent supporter of the Industrial Workers of the World. Harrison came to the conclusion that Party leaders, like organized labor leaders, put the white "Race first and class after." Harrison pioneered the tradition of Harlem soap-box oratory, which was subsequently carried on by Randolph, Garvey, and Malcolm X.

May 16

Norman Lewis
July 23, 1909 - August 27, 1979

Norman Lewis was an African-American artist known for his incisive depictions of contemporary society and poetic abstractions. "I wanted to be above criticism, so that my work didn't have to be discussed in terms of the fact that I'm Black," he once said.

Born in New York, Lewis began his career as a Social Realist painter, focusing on the inequities caused by poverty and racism, as seen in his work *Girl with Yellow Hat* (1936). In the mid-1940s, his focus shifted towards abstraction and gestural mark-making, drawing inspiration from the work of Wassily Kandinsky and Mark Tobey. He emerged as the sole Black artist in the first generation of Abstract Expressionists alongside Ad Reinhardt, Franz Kline, and Jackson Pollock.

Though his paintings changed Lewis remained committed to social concerns throughout his career, forming the Spiral Group with Romare Bearden, Charles Alston, and Hale Woodruff, the group's primary mission was assisting the Civil Rights Movement during the 1960s. The artist died in New York.

Today, Lewis' works are held in the collections of the Art Institute of Chicago, The Museum of Modern Art in New York, and the National Gallery of Art in Washington, D.C.

May 17

Charles H. Alston
1907 - 1977

Charles Henry Alston was an influential painter during the Harlem Renaissance and the first African American supervisor for the Works Progress Administration (WPA). He supervised the WPA murals created at Harlem Hospital, leading a staff of 35 artists and assistants. Alston was also the first African American to teach at both the Museum of Modern Art and the Art Students League and, in 1969, to have been appointed the painter member of the Art Commission of the City of New York.

Alston, born in Charlotte, North Carolina, was related to renowned artist Romare Bearden through his mother's second marriage. He attended Columbia University as an undergraduate and graduate student, receiving a B.A. from Columbia College in 1929 and an M.F.A. from Columbia University's Teachers College in 1931. After graduating he worked at the Harlem Arts Workshop, and when the program required more space, he secured an additional facility at 306 W. 141st St. The space, known as "306," became a center for the Harlem art community.

The influence of Mexican muralists José Clemente Orozco, Diego Rivera and David Alfaro Siqueiros, who all used murals to inspire people toward social activism, can be seen in Alston's work.

Alston's gift expanded beyond painting. He also worked as a sculptor, and his cartoons and illustrations were published in popular magazines such as *The New Yorker* and *Fortune*. During World War II, he worked at the Office of War Information and Public Information, creating cartoons and posters to mobilize the Black community to join in the American war effort. He also taught at the City University of New York.

Alston's work is in the permanent collections of the Metropolitan Museum of Art, the Whitney Museum of American Art, and the Detroit Institute of Arts.

May 18

Walter Max Ulyate Sisulu
May 18, 1912 - May 5, 2003

Walter Max Ulyate Sisulu was a South African anti-apartheid activist and member of the African National Congress (ANC), serving at times as Secretary-General and Deputy President of the organization. He was incarcerated at Robben Island, where he served more than 25 years of a life imprisonment sentence.

Sisulu was born in Ngcobo in the Union of South Africa and was educated in a local missionary school. He left school to find work and moved to Johannesburg in 1928 where he worked at a wide range of manual jobs.

Sisulu founded Sitha Investments in 1939. It was located in the business district of Johannesburg and its objective was to help Blacks and Indians to buy houses in Apartheid South Africa. During its operations, Sitha was the only Black-owned estate agency in South Africa.

He married Albertina in 1944; the couple had five children, and adopted four more. Sisulu's wife and children were also active in the struggle against apartheid.

Sisulu joined the ANC in 1941. Two years later, Sisulu, Nelson Mandela and Oliver Tambo joined the ANC Youth League, founded by Anton Lembede, and served as the treasurer. He was made secretary general of the ANC in 1949 and served five years in that office.

Sisulu was jailed several times for his anti-apartheid activism. At the Rivonia Trial (1963-1964) for Sisulu and other senior ANC members he was sentenced to life imprisonment. Two years after his release Sisulu was elected ANC deputy president. He functioned in that role until after South Africa's first democratic election in 1994.

In 1992, Walter Sisulu was awarded Isitwalandwe Seaparankoe, the highest honour granted by the ANC, for his contribution to the liberation struggle in South Africa. Several institutions are named after him.

May 19

Alain Leroy Locke
& his Ancestors

September 13, 1885 – June 9, 1954

Alain Leroy Locke was an American writer, philosopher, educator, and patron of the arts. Distinguished in 1907 as the first African-American Rhodes Scholar, Locke became known as the philosophical architect —the acknowledged "Dean"— of the Harlem Renaissance. He is frequently included in listings of influential African Americans. On March 19, 1968, the Rev. Dr. Martin Luther King, Jr. proclaimed: "We're going to let our children know that the only philosophers that lived were not Plato and Aristotle, but W. E. B. Du Bois and Alain Locke came through the universe."

Locke was born Arthur Leroy Locke in Philadelphia, Pennsylvania to parents Pliny Ishmael Locke (1850–1892) and Mary (née Hawkins) Locke (1853–1922), both of whom were descended from prominent families of free Blacks. Called "Roy" as a boy, he was their only child. His father was the first Black employee of the U.S. Postal Service, and his paternal grandfather taught at Philadelphia's Institute for Colored Youth. His mother Mary was a teacher and inspired Locke's passion for education and literature. Mary's grandfather, Charles Shorter, fought as a soldier and was a hero in the War of 1812.

May 20

Ernesto "Che" Guevara

June 14, 1928 - October 9, 1967

Ernesto "Che" Guevara was an Argentine Marxist revolutionary, physician, author, guerrilla leader, diplomat, and military theorist. A major figure of the Cuban Revolution, his stylized visage has become a ubiquitous countercultural symbol of rebellion and global insignia in popular culture.

As a young medical student, Guevara traveled throughout South America and was radicalized by the poverty, hunger, and disease he witnessed. His burgeoning desire to help overturn the capitalist exploitation of Latin America by the United States prompted his involvement in Guatemala's social reforms under President Jacobo Árbenz, whose eventual CIA-assisted overthrow at the behest of the United Fruit Company solidified Guevara's political ideology.

Later in Mexico City, Guevara met Raúl and Fidel Castro, joined their 26th of July Movement, and sailed to Cuba aboard the yacht Granma with the intention of overthrowing U.S.-backed Cuban dictator Fulgencio Batista. Guevara rose to prominence among the insurgents, was promoted to second-in-command, and played a pivotal role in the two-year guerrilla campaign that deposed the Batista regime.

May 21

Norman Washington Manley – One of Jamaica's National Heroes

July 4, 1893 - September 2, 1969

Norman Washington Manley MM, QC, was a Jamaican statesman, a Rhodes Scholar, a veteran of WWI, and was one of Jamaica's leading lawyers in the 1920s. Manley was an advocate of universal suffrage, which was granted by the British to Jamaica in 1944.

Manley helped to launch the People's National Party (PNP) in 1938 which later was tied to the Trade Union Congress and later to the National Workers Union. He led the PNP in every election from 1944 to 1967. Their efforts resulted in the New Constitution of 1944, granting full adult suffrage.

Manley was a strong advocate of the Federation of the West Indies, established in 1958, but when Sir Alexander Bustamante declared that the opposition Jamaica Labour Party (JLP), would take Jamaica out of the Federation, Norman Manley, already renowned for his integrity and commitment to democracy, called a Referendum, unprecedented in Jamaica, to let the people decide. The vote was decisively against Jamaica's continued membership of the Federation. Manley, after arranging Jamaica's orderly withdrawal from the union, set up a committee to decide on a Constitution for the Independence for Jamaica.

In his last public address to an annual conference of the PNP, Manley said: "I say that the mission of my generation was to win self-government for Jamaica, to win political power which is the final power for the black masses of my country from which I spring. I am proud to stand here today and say to you who fought that fight with me, say it with gladness and pride, mission accomplished for my generation. And what is the mission of this generation? … It is… reconstructing the social and economic society and life of Jamaica". https://jis.gov.jm/information/heroes/norman-washington-manley/

May 22

Deolinda Rodrigues
February 10, 1939 - March 2, 1967

Deolinda Rodrigues (also, Deolinda Rodrigues Francisco de Almeida; pseudonym, Langidila; nickname, "Mother of the Revolution") was an Angolan nationalist, militant, writer, and translator, who also taught, wrote poetry, and worked as a radio host. Born into a Methodist family, she received a scholarship to study in Brazil, from where she corresponded with Martin Luther King Jr.

Fearing extradition from Brazil because of the Portuguese Imperial relationship between its colonies and her support of the growing Angolan Independence movement, Rodríguez de Almeida moved to the United States the following year and studied at Drew University before returning to Angola.

Because she wanted to be an active participant in Angola's independence, Rodríguez did not finish school and decided to leave the U.S. in February 1961.

Rodrigues was recruited to participate in the People's Movement for the Liberation of Angola (MPLA) attack on "Fortalesa", gaining the honorary title of "Mother of the Revolution". She co-founded the women's wing of the MPLA, the Organização da Mulher de Angola (Organization of Angolan Women; OMA). She was captured, tortured, and executed by a rival nationalist group in 1967. A documentary of her life was released in 2014.

Rodríguez de Almeida was born in Catete, Angola.

May 23

Marco Mason
1944 - 2011

Marco A. Mason was a medical sociologist, a well-known scholar and activist who achieved a distinguished record of leadership. He is a founding member of the 20 plus year old Caribbean Women's Health Association; where he served as Chief Executive Officer. He was the Chairman/CEO of the Panamanian Council of New York Inc. and President of the Institute for Pan-American Affairs.

Dr. Mason served on the faculty of a number of colleges and universities, including at the State University of New York at Stony Brook; School of Social Work, School of Medicine, and School of Health Management and Technology. He was on the Faculty with the Department of Social and Behavioral Sciences at Medgar Evers College, City University of New York.

Dr. Mason was a technical expert in U.S. Immigration Policy and was duly accredited to practice Immigration Law before the Immigration and Naturalization Court and the Board of Immigration Appeals. He was cited by the US Department of Justice for his "Outstanding services in assisting immigrants with status adjustments. Source: LinkedIn

Dr. Mason wore many hats, but the respected Panamanian-born activist and educator was well-known for his immeasurable support of Caribbean people in New York. A longtime proponent of Caribbean clout, Mason advised politicians, business owners and governmental agencies of the demographics of Caribbean New Yorkers and touted their accomplishments and vast potential. Source: *Daily News*

May 24

Winston Van Horne
1944 - 2013

Winston Van Horne liked to say that Africology was both the newest idea, and the oldest.

Dr. Winston Van Horne, professor of Africolgy, was born in Westmoreland, Jamaica to George and Len. He came to University of Wisconsin Milwaukee (UWM) in 1978, where he served magnanimously until his death. Some of his contributions include navigating the Afro-American Studies Program to the Department of Africology; chairing the Department of Africology three times and being credited with creating the word Africology; serving as principal author of the Ph.D. program in Africology; serving on the faculty senate since 1980 and directing the UWM System Institute on Race and Ethnicity for ten years.

Professor Mensah Aborampah called him "a true brother to me, and a mentor." He said he'd remember two expressions: "He would say that we have to engage in impeccable scholarship, and impregnable social activism. These were the two guiding forces for what we did in the department."

In recognition of his immense contribution and at the request of the Department of Africology, the UWM Faculty Senate unanimously voted in favor of naming a classroom on his behalf in 2012. In 2013, UWM officially re-named Mitchell Hall, Room 206, the Winston Van Horne Seminar Room.

At the time of Van Horne's transition his wife Mary and their son Max were with him listening to Harry Belafonte's song, *Jamaica Farewell.*

Source: http://archive.jsonline.com/news/obituaries/winston-van-horne

May 25

African Liberation Day

African Liberation Day is celebrated by many African communities around the world. It is a permanent mass institution in the worldwide Pan African Movement. The day is observed in countries such as Ghana, Kenya, Spain, Tanzania, the United Kingdom, and the United States.

In the United States the day is commemorated in the form of symposiums, where people are invited to attend and participate in political and social issues relevant to US African communities.

Widely observed on a global scale by various African communities, African Liberation Day is not a federal holiday in many countries. In Ghana May 25 is a public holiday.

African Freedom Day was founded during the first Conference of Independent African States, which attracted African leaders and political activists from various African countries, in Ghana on April 15, 1958. Government representatives from eight independent African states attended the conference, which was the first Pan-African conference in the continent. The purpose of the day was to annually mark the liberation movement's progress and to symbolize the determination of the people of Africa to free themselves from foreign domination and exploitation.

Between 1958 and 1963 the nation/class struggle grew bigger in Africa and around the world. During this period, 17 countries in Africa won their independence and 1960 was proclaimed the Year of Africa. On May 25, 1963, 31 African leaders convened a summit to found the Organization of African Unity (OAU). They renamed Africa Freedom Day as "African Liberation Day" and changed its date from April 15 to May 25. The founding date of the OAU is also referred to as "Africa Day".

African Liberation Day has helped to raise political awareness and the struggles for liberation and development in African communities across the world.

May 26

Tuskegee Airmen

Learn about the determined men and women who either enlisted in the U.S. Army Air Corps or served as civilian support staff in the "Tuskegee Experience."

Three government initiatives occurred between 1938 and 1940 that were instrumental in paving the way for Blacks to participate in the nation's defense and to become military pilots.

1. On December 27, 1938, President Roosevelt announced an experimental civilian pilot training program. That experimental program, which began in early 1939, involved 330 openings at thirteen colleges, none of which were Black. On January 12, 1939, President Roosevelt asked Congress to pass legislation to authorize a permanent Civilian Pilot Training (CPT) Program. The Civilian Pilot Training Act of 1939 was passed on June 27 1939, and funds were appropriated for it in August.

2. In 1940, Congress passed the Selective Service and Training Service Act, which was signed into law by President Franklin Roosevelt on September 16, 1940.

3. That same year, the War Department announced that the Civil Aeronautics Authority, in cooperation with the U.S. Army, would begin development of "colored personnel" for the aviation service. This paved the way for Blacks to train as pilots and vital support personnel.

Individuals came from every part of the country. Each one of them possessed a strong personal desire to serve the United States of America to the best of their ability.

Their legacy continues through the work of:
https://www.tuskegeeairmen.org/legacy/the-people/

May 27

Chinua Achebe
November 16, 1930 - March 21, 2013

Chinua Achebe was a Nigerian novelist and author of *Things Fall Apart* (1958) - a novel that centers on the clash between native African culture and the influence of white Christian missionaries and the colonial government in Nigeria. An unflinching look at the discord, the book was a success and became required reading in many schools and universities across the world. This body of work, in part led to Achebe being called the "patriarch of the African novel."

Things Fall Apart, has sold more than 20 million copies and been translated into more than 50 languages. Achebe followed with novels such as *No Longer at Ease* (1960), for which he was awarded the Nigerian National Trophy for Literature, Arrow *of God* (1964) and *Anthills of the Savannah (*1987), and served as a faculty member at renowned universities in the U.S. and Nigeria.

During the Nigerian Civil War (1967-1970) Achebe became a spokesperson for the Biafran cause in Europe and North America.

Achebe was born Albert Chinualumogu Achebe in the Igbo town of Ogidi in eastern Nigeria. After becoming educated in English at University College (now the University of Ibadan) and a subsequent teaching stint, Achebe joined the Nigerian Broadcasting Corporation in 1961 as director of external broadcasting. He would serve in that role for five years as he continued to write novels.

May 28

Betty Shabazz
May 28, 1934 - June 23, 1997

Betty Shabazz, (born Betty Dean Sanders and also known as Betty X), was an American educator and civil rights advocate. She was the wife of Malcolm X.

Shabazz grew up in Detroit, Michigan, where her foster parents largely sheltered her from racism. She attended the Tuskegee Institute in Alabama, where she had her first encounters with racism. Unhappy with the situation in Alabama, she moved to New York City, where she became a nurse. It was there that she met Malcolm X and, in 1956, joined the Nation of Islam. The couple married in 1958.

Along with her husband, Shabazz left the Nation of Islam in 1964. She witnessed his assassination the following year. Left with the responsibility of raising six daughters as a single mother, Shabazz pursued higher education, earned a Master's degree in health administration and went to work at Medgar Evers College, City University of New York in Brooklyn, New York.

Following the 1995 arrest of her daughter Qubilah for allegedly conspiring to murder Louis Farrakhan, Shabazz took in her ten year old grandson Malcolm. In 1997, he set fire to their apartment. Shabazz suffered severe burns and died three weeks later as a result of her injuries.

May 29

Marielle Franco
July 27, 1979 - March 14, 2018

Sao Paulo, Brazil – "Woman, Black, mother, lesbian, from the favelas, open about sexuality and Rio's problems, and on top of all this, a human rights activist."

That's how Marielle Franco once described herself in an event in Rio de Janeiro, the city where she was elected a councilwoman. And that's also why she was killed.

The Black activist and Rio de Janeiro councilwoman was killed in a drive-by shooting. It took police 363 days to arrest two former policemen allegedly involved in her murder, which authorities say was politically motivated.

A year later, thousands gathered across the country to demand justice and answers for the real question: "Who ordered Marielle's killing?"

"We are all outraged, we are sad," Monica Benicio, Marielle's wife, told Al Jazeera. "But there's also a feeling of courage, of hope. Because Marielle's figure has become a symbol of resistance and the feeling of solidarity is also a big driver for the events today," she said.

Franco was an outspoken defender of women, Black and LGBT rights and often criticized police brutality.

May 30

Muammar Gaddafi

June 7, 1942 - October 20, 2011

Muammar Muhammad Abu Minyar al-Gaddafi, commonly known as Colonel Gaddafi, was a Libyan revolutionary, politician and political theorist.

Gaddafi ruled for 42 years, leading Libya to a significant advance in social, political and economic matters that were recognized and admired by many African and Arab nations at the time. Despite his controversial government, Gaddafi came to represent an important figure for anti-imperialist struggles for his position mainly against the U.S. and the policies carried out from Washington on the Middle East.

May 31

Cyril Lionel Robert James - C.L.R. James

1901-1989

Born in Tunapuna, Trinidad and Tobago to parents one generation removed from emancipation, Cyril Lionel Robert James was a social theorist, historian, writer, and revolutionary whose maturity roughly corresponds to what Eric Hobsbawn called 'the short 20th century.' It was this contextual standpoint of a Caribbean childhood, and later movements to Britain, United States, and West Africa, that shaped his view of the destructive complexity of the modern world and the imperative to break with "old bourgeois civilization" (James cited by Grimshaw, 1991).

In the Global North James is primarily known for two books, *The Black Jacobins* (1938) and *Beyond A Boundary* (1963). Each book is indicative of the various wings of James' wider intellectual project, with the first asking scholars to reconsider the role of racial oppression in capitalism and the second prompting a reconsideration of the role of class formation in popular culture via his treatment of sport, race, and imperialism. These projects combine to provide a Marxist inspired analysis of modernity in which questions of combined and uneven development are foregrounded. The result is to demonstrate the enduring links between advanced capitalist countries and colonized regions along the lines of race, class, and everyday experience.

In the post-independence period James took stock of the various contradictions, competitions, and antagonisms that circulated in the social life in the West Indies and suggested that efforts to induce modernization were shortsighted. This put him in conflict with the post-independence political class, whose budding radicalism was tempered and redirected into cultural nationalism.

James posited that emancipation can best be achieved through a social reconstruction of the way people relate to one another. Much needed, he thought, if one were to escape the "problems of nationality."

June 1

Hope P. White-Davis
June 01, 1952 – April 30, 2009
Contributor: Dr. Gerald White-Davis, (Brother)

Hope White-Davis was a Jamaican born, Columbia University- graduate, and former United Nations intern.

Recognizing that her fellow interns included dynamic and influential people, she co-founded the World Association of Former United Nations Internes and Fellowes (WAFUNIF) in 1978. Its members believe in the mission of "a better – more just, equitable, sustainable, humane, and peaceful world," and are civil servants, industry and world leaders.

Using the WAFUNIF platform, she passionately and selflessly dedicated her life to social justice and development, especially for people of African descent, and introduced many to the international arena through the United Nations programs.

White-Davis earned a doctorate from Columbia University.

June 2

Rayford Whittingham Logan
January 7, 1897 - November 4, 1982

Rayford Whittingham Logan was an African-American historian and Pan-African activist. He was best known for his study of post-Reconstruction America, a period he termed "the nadir of American race relations". In the late 1940s he was the chief advisor to the National Association for the Advancement of Colored People (NAACP) on international affairs. He was professor emeritus of history at Howard University.

Logan served as one of forty five African Americans on the Black Cabinet, or Federal Council of Negro Affairs or Black Brain Trust, the informal term for the group of African Americans who served as public policy advisors to President Franklin D. Roosevelt and his wife Eleanor Roosevelt in his terms in office from 1933 to 1945.

Logan was born and grew up in Washington, DC. He won a scholarship to Williams College, graduating in 1917. During WWI he joined the U.S. Army, and served as a first lieutenant in the all-Black 93rd Infantry Division, which undertook operations with French troops. Once the war ended, Logan remained in France, absorbing both the culture and the language. He helped to co-ordinate the 2nd Pan-African Congress in Paris in 1921. He returned to the US in the early 1920s and began teaching at Virginia Union University, a Historically Black College in Richmond.

During the United States' occupation of Haiti, Logan made a fact finding mission to Haiti to investigate educational efforts and published his findings in *The Journal of Negro History* in October 1930. The main findings indicated there was little improvement in education due to the choice of Southern white Marines as country administrators who had been raised with Jim Crow laws had brought their prejudice with them to Haiti, a majority-Black republic.

June 3

Ambrose Caliver
1894–1962

Ambrose Caliver was an American teacher and Dean who changed the face of Black education on a national scale. Dr. Caliver devoted much of his professional life to adult literacy, although he also took an active role in such matters as displaced persons, human rights, public affairs, aging, and professional development of adult educators.

Born in 1894 in Saltville, Virginia, Caliver graduated from Austin High School and then attended Knoxville College in Tennessee and graduated with a B.A. in 1915. Caliver taught at numerous high schools in Tennessee and also gained experience as a high school principal. By 1917 he was hired to work for the Historically Black College Fisk University in Nashville, Tennessee where he was in charge of their new vocational education program. Caliver earned his M.A. from the University of Wisconsin in 1921 and in 1930 he earned his Ph.D. in Education from Columbia University's Teacher's College. He was the first Black person in the city to earn a Ph. D. and the first to earn such degree in the field of education.

While at Fisk, Caliver was appointed to the new position of Senior Specialist in the Education of Negroes in the U.S. Office of Education by President Herbert Hoover. When Franklin D. Roosevelt was elected President two years later, Caliver kept his post and became a member of F.D.R.'s "Black cabinet". During Caliver's time in the Cabinet, he was highly motivated by the inequity in the education of Blacks and whites and set out to raise national awareness, particularly in the rural South. He traveled and worked fervently to accurately document the lack of funding for public schooling.

June 4

Roscoe Conkling Brown Jr.

March 9, 1922 - July 2, 2016

Roscoe Conkling Brown Jr. was one of the Tuskegee Airmen and a squadron commander of the 100th Fighter Squadron of the 332nd Fighter Group. He was appointed to this position in June 1945, which was after V-E Day (May 8, 1945). During combat, he served as a flight leader and operations officer.

Brown graduated from the Tuskegee Flight School in 1944 as member of class 44-C-SE and served in the U.S. Army Air Forces in Europe during World War II. During this period, Captain Brown shot down an advanced German Me 262 jet fighter and a FW-190 fighter (he is credited as the first pilot to shoot down a jet). He was awarded the Distinguished Flying Cross.

Brown was born in Washington, D.C. His father, Roscoe C. Brown Sr. (1884–1963), was a dentist and an official in the United States Public Health Service who was born as George Brown and changed his name to honor Roscoe Conkling, a strong supporter of the rights of African Americans during Reconstruction. His mother was the former Vivian Berry, a teacher.

After the war, Captain Brown resumed his education. His doctoral dissertation was on exercise physiology and he became a professor at New York University directing their Institute of Afro-American Affairs. He was President of Bronx Community College from 1977 to 1993 and then director for the Center for Education Policy at the City University of New York. In 1992, Brown received an honorary doctor of humanics degree from his alma mater, Springfield College.

Brown served on the Black Cabinet, advising President Franklin D. Roosevelt, and in 2007 Brown and the other Tuskegee Airmen collectively were awarded the Congressional Gold Medal in recognition of their service.

June 5

Robert Clifton Weaver
December 29, 1907 - July 17, 1997

Robert Clifton Weaver was an American economist, academic, and political administrator; he served as the first United States Secretary of Housing and Urban Development (H.U.D.) from 1966 to 1968, when the department was newly established by President Lyndon B. Johnson. Weaver was the first African American to be appointed to a US cabinet-level position.

Prior to his appointment as cabinet officer, Weaver had served in the administration of President John F. Kennedy, in New York State government, and in high-level positions in New York City. During the Franklin D. Roosevelt administration, he was one of 45 prominent African Americans appointed to positions and helped make up the Black Cabinet, an informal group of African-American public policy advisers. Weaver directed federal programs during the administration of the New Deal, at the same time completing his doctorate in economics in 1934 at Harvard University.

Weaver was born into a middle-class family in Washington, D.C. His parents were Mortimer Grover Weaver, a postal worker, and Florence (Freeman) Weaver. His maternal grandfather was Dr. Robert Tanner Freeman, the first African American to graduate from Harvard in dentistry.

The young Weaver attended the M Street High School, now known as the Dunbar High School that was designated for Blacks at a time of racial segregation had a national reputation for academic excellence. Weaver went on to Harvard University, where he earned a Bachelor of Science and Master of Arts degree. He also earned a Doctor of Philosophy degree in Economics, completing his doctorate in 1934.

June 6

Sarah Pringle
December 25, 1921 - December 27, 2011

Contributor: Wesley Pringle Jr. - B.Sc. (Son)

Sarah Pringle was a Black American who was born in South Carolina, United States of America. She was the keeper of the records of children born in Orangeburg, South Carolina.

Pringle lived under the Jim Crow System and attained an elementary education. As a young woman, she married Wesley Pringle Sr. and six children were born from this union.

Pringle stressed getting an education to children and family members because she did not have the opportunity to pursue her education.

She helped families and friends when they were seeking birth information of family members. Having the foresight to take on this responsibility of making note of all children born in the community of Orangeburg – all at-home births at the time - Sara Pringle readily had this information available. She kept this listing in her Bible.

June 7

Mary Jane McLeod Bethune

July 10, 1875 - May 18, 1955

Mary Jane McLeod Bethune was an American educator, stateswoman, philanthropist, humanitarian, womanist, and civil rights activist. Bethune founded the National Council for Negro Women in 1935, established the organization's flagship journal *Aframerican Women's Journal,* and resided as president or leader for myriad African American women's organizations including the National Association for Colored Women and the National Youth Administration's Negro Division. She also was appointed as a national adviser to President Franklin D. Roosevelt, with whom she worked to create the Federal Council on Negro Affairs, also known as the Black Cabinet.

Bethune is well known for starting a private school for African-American students in Daytona Beach, Florida; it grew to become Bethune-Cookman University.

Bethune was the sole African American woman officially a part of the US delegation that created the United Nations charter, and she held a leadership position for the Women's Army Auxiliary Corps. For her lifetime of activism, she was deemed "acknowledged First Lady of Negro America" by *Ebony* magazine in July 1949 and was known by the Black Press as the "Female Booker T. Washington". She was known as "The First Lady of The Struggle" because of her commitment to gain better lives for African Americans.

Born in Mayesville, South Carolina, to parents who were enslaved Africans she started working in fields with her family at age five. She took an early interest in becoming educated and with the help of benefactors Bethune attended college hoping to become a missionary in Africa. She started a school for African-American girls in Daytona Beach, Florida. It later merged with a private institute for African-American boys and was known as the Bethune-Cookman School.

June 8

Lawrence A. Oxley
1887–1973

Lawrence A. Oxley was one among 45 prominent Black community leaders appointed by President Franklin D. Roosevelt to what was called his Black Cabinet, positions in numerous executive agencies and to serve as advisers during his administration. He served with the federal government until 1957. As the Director of the Division of Work among Negroes (1925-1934) in North Carolina, the first state office of its kind, he created programs which other states used as models.

Lawrence A. Oxley was born in 1887 in Massachusetts and attended public schools in Boston and Cambridge, also studying at Harvard. He served with the US Army during World War I, earning the rank of lieutenant.

After working in field community service positions in Ohio, West Virginia and other states, in 1925, Oxley was appointed in North Carolina as Director of the new Division of Work Among Negroes, a branch of the State Board of Charities and Public Welfare. The division was "the first of its kind in the nation" and due to Oxely's success in developing programs, it became a model for other states.

Oxley studied the lives and social conditions of African Americans; and developed self-help initiatives. He promoted social welfare programs that addressed issues of job readiness and social functioning. He emphasized the need to strengthen community efforts with funding and professionally trained social workers, a relatively new profession that developed in the late 19th and early 20th centuries. Oxley was a strong advocate for unemployment assistance, despite North Carolina's reluctance to extend such relief to the Black community. In addition, he improved hospital care and prison reform, as well as encouraged the development of statewide services available to Blacks in Appalachia, such as an orthopedic hospital.

June 9

Dr. William J. Thompkins, Recorder of Deeds for the District of Columbia

July 5, 1884 -August 11, 1944

Born in Jefferson City, Missouri, William J. Thompkins was a physician who was involved in the founding of the General Hospital No. 2 in Kansas City Missouri in 1908. Six years later it became the first hospital in the U.S. to be staffed entirely by African Americans. While he was the hospital's superintendent, its rating improved from class D to class A.

Thompkins was appointed an assistant health commissioner in 1927 and conducted a survey of tuberculosis and housing conditions among Blacks in Kansas City. As a result of this survey, hundreds of houses were condemned, and a new hospital serving African Americans was built. The American Public Health Commission adopted the plan of his survey as a model, and President Hoover presented his housing plan to the National Housing Commission in 1930.

In 1932, Thompkins was named president of the National Colored Democratic Association and helped elect Franklin Roosevelt as president. Roosevelt appointed Thompkins recorder of deeds for the District of Columbia, a position he held from 1934 until his death ten years later.

Recorder of deeds or Deeds registry is a government office responsible for maintaining public records and documents, especially records relating to real estate ownership that provide persons other than the owner of a property with real rights over that property.

June 10

Octavia Estelle Butler
June 22, 1947 - February 24, 2006

Octavia Estelle Butler was an American science fiction author. A multiple recipient of both the Hugo and Nebula awards, she became in 1995 the first science-fiction writer to receive a MacArthur Fellowship.

Born in Pasadena, California, after her father died, Butler was raised by her widowed mother. Extremely shy as a child, Octavia found an outlet at the library reading fantasy, and in writing. She began writing science fiction as a teenager. Butler attended community college during the Black Power movement, and while participating in a local writer's workshop was encouraged to attend the Clarion Workshop, which focused on science fiction.

Butler soon sold her first stories and by the late 1970s became sufficiently successful as an author so she to pursued writing full-time. Butler wrote and published more than 15 books. She wrote in an intriguing and captivating style on the optimism and dangers of the human race revealed through tribalism, race, gender, and sexuality.

Butler's book titles include: *Patternmaster* (1976), *Kindred* (1979), *Wild Seed*: Book 1 in "The Patternist" Series (1980), *Parable of the Sower*: Book #1 in the "Parable" Series (1993), *Bloodchild* (1995), and *Fledgling* (2005). Her papers are held in the research collection of the Huntington Library, Pasadena California.

June 11

Ivan Van Sertima

January 26, 1935 – May 25, 2009

Ivan Van Sertima, probably best known for his work *They Came Before Columbus: The African Presence in Ancient America* (1977) was a linguist, scholar and author whose work transformed the way people viewed and taught African history. Van Sertima was born on January 26, 1935, in Kitty Village, Guyana when it was still a British colony. He returned to Guyana to serve a Press and Broadcasting Officer in the Guyana Information Services in the late 1950s.

As a linguist, he published essays on the dialect of the Sea Islands off the Georgia Coast. He is also the compiler of the Swahili Dictionary of Legal Terms, based on his field work in Tanzania, East Africa, in 1967.

Van Sertima earned degrees at the School of Oriental and African Studies (London University) and the Rutgers Graduate School in African Studies and Anthropology. He served as Professor of African Studies at Rutgers University and as Visiting Professor at Princeton University.

He also authored *Early America Revisited* and appeared before a Congressional Committee in 1987 to challenge the European-presented fabricated and embellished story of Columbus in the Americas.

June 12

Rex Nettleford
February 3, 1933 - February 2, 2010

Ralston Milton Nettleford, better known as Rex Nettleford, was a national patriot, cultural ambassador, international scholar, trade unionist, dancer, choreographer, orator and Vice-Chancellor Emeritus of the University of the West Indies.

Born in Trelawny, Jamaica, Nettleford attended Montego Bay Boys' School, Cornwall College and earned a degree in History from the University College of the West Indies, (now the University of the West Indies) Kingston in 1956. He then joined University College of the West Indies staff as acting Resident Tutor in Trinidad. In that same year, he won the Issa Scholarship but did not take it up. Instead, he accepted the Rhodes Scholarship in 1957 to read for post graduate work in politics at Oxford University. Nettleford was the first West Indian to take this very prestigious degree which was specifically designed to train teachers.

During his stay in Oxford at Oriel College, Nettleford was active in the Oxford University Drama Society, choreographing for the Society's many productions. He was also president of the Ballet Club and encouraged an interest in Afro-Caribbean dance.

As Director of Studies at the Trade Union Education Institute at the University College, he strived to improve the lives of Jamaica's underprivileged, through the Institute's objective, which allowed unionised, factory, and farm workers to unite with scholars to help bridge the education gap between the classes. During his time at the University of the West Indies he was elevated to top position in the University's hierarchy: Deputy Vice Chancellor, 1986-98, then he was made Vice Chancellor, a position he kept until his retirement in 2004. He continued to serve the University as Vice Chancellor Emeritus, Professor of Cultural Studies.

June 13

Pearl Eileen Primus
November 29, 1919 - October 29, 1994

Born in Port of Spain, Trinidad and Tobago, Pearl Eileen Primus was an American dancer, choreographer and anthropologist. Primus played an important role in the presentation of African dance to American audiences. Early in her career she saw the need to promote African dance as an art form worthy of study and performance.

Primus' family emigrated to New York while she was a child. She attended public schools in New York City and earned an undergraduate degree in biology as a pre-med student from Hunter College, CUNY. Her desire to attend medical school was placed on hold as she had to work. Eventually finding steady work in 1941 through the National Youth Administration (part of the Works Progress Administration) in the wardrobe department, working backstage for *America Dances.* A spot opened up for a dancer and Primus stepped into her destiny.

Confronting stereotypes and prejudice through movement, Primus advocated dance as a means of uniting people against discrimination. Her artistry was influenced by her Primus' studies of the Caribbean, Africa and the American South.

Primus made her theatrical debut in 1943 at the 92nd Street Y's concert series to showcase the work of young dancers She performed her own *African Ceremonial, Hard-Time Blues,* and *Rock Daniel* and *Strange Fruit.*

In acknowledgement of her liberating impact on the arts, Primus received many honors, including an honorary doctorate from Spelman College, the Distinguished Service Award from the Association of American Anthropologists and the National Medal of Arts.

June 14

Asadata Dafora
August 4, 1890 - March 4, 1965

Asadata Dafora was born in Freetown, Sierra Leone, the great-grandson of a former enslaved Africans who returned from Nova Scotia to his homeland. His birth name is uncertain but was probably Austin Asadata Dafora Horton. Dafora attended Wesleyan High School in Freetown and moved to Europe in 1910. His life in Europe is not well documented, but he is believed to have studied opera in Germany and Italy from 1910 through 1912. Dafora is also reported to have been a member of the British Army during World War I.

In 1929, Dafora arrived in New York intending to pursue a career in opera. He began working with a group of African men who frequented the National African Union, a social club. From these initial efforts he formed Shogola Oloba, an African troupe of performers. His troupe performed scenes from *Zoonga*, a dance opera of his composition, at the Communist Party Bazaar at Madison Square Garden in New York City in 1933.

The following year Dafora premiered the dance opera *Kykunkor* (*Witch Woman*) at the Little Theater in New York City. A novelty in the United States because of its African theme, *Kykunkor* told the story of a bridegroom who had been cursed by a scorned lover. The performance was a critical success, and by 1935 the group had become the African Dance Troupe of the Federal Theatre Project. It was featured in Orson Welles' production of *Macbeth*.

June 15

Fela Kuti

October 15, 1938 - August 2, 1997

Musician and activist Fela Kuti pioneered Afrobeat music and was repeatedly arrested and beaten for writing lyrics that questioned the Nigerian government.

Beginning in the 1960s, Fela Kuti pioneered his own unique style of music called "Afrobeat." Rebelling against oppressive regimes through his music came at a heavy cost. Kuti was arrested 200 times and endured numerous beatings, but continued to write political lyrics, producing 50 albums before he died on August 2, 1997, in Lagos, Nigeria.

Musician and political activist Fela Kuti was born Olufela Olusegun Oludotun Ransome-Kuti in Abeokuta, Nigeria. Fela was the son of a Protestant minister, Reverend Ransome-Kuti. His mother, Funmilayo, was a political activist.

As a child, Fela learned piano and drums and led his school choir. In the 1950s, Kuti went to England, to study medicine, but enrolled at the Trinity College of Music playing the trumpet. While at Trinity, Kuti studied classical music and developed an awareness of American jazz. He returned to Nigeria and in trying to find an authentic musical voice, he added elements of traditional Yoruba, high life and jazz, and “Afrobeat” was born.

Fela’s Koola Lobitos band traveled to Los Angeles to tour and record in 1969. During his eight months in the US, Fela met Sandra Izsadore, who introduced him to the writings and politics of Malcolm X, Eldridge Cleaver and other proponents of Black nationalism and Afrocentrism.

On his return to Nigeria, Fela’s music served as a rallying cry for the disenfranchised, critiquing the military government, making Fela a pop star and thrust him into political life. People took to the streets singing his songs and the military responded by viciously harassing Fela, jailing him and beating him to near death on several occasions.

June 16

Katherine Mary Dunham
June 22, 1909 - May 21, 2006

Katherine Mary Dunham (also known as Kaye Dunn), born in Glen Ellyn, Illinois, was an African-American dancer, choreographer, author, educator, anthropologist, and social activist. Dunham had one of the most successful dance careers in African-American and European theater of the 20th century, and directed her own dance company - Katherine Dunham School of Arts and Research - for many years. She had schools in New York, Stockholm, Paris, and Rome.

Dunham has been called the "matriarch and queen mother of Black dance." She attended the University of Chicago majoring in anthropology with emphasis on dance and its relation to cultures. She received a fellowship and with that she went to the Caribbean to study dance and ethnography.

Some of Dunham's notable dance/choreography productions include *L'Ag'Ya* (1938), *Tropical Pinafore* (1939), *Carib Song* (1945), *Bal Negre* (1946), *Cakewalk*" (1955), *Aida* (1963), and *Faust* (1965).

June 17

Cheikh Anta Diop
December 29, 1923 - February 7, 1986

Cheikh Anta Diop was a Senegalese scholar historian, anthropologist, physicist, and politician who studied the human race's origins and pre-colonial African culture.

Diop earned his bachelor's degree in Senegal and then he moved to Paris to do graduate work in physics at the Sorbonne. While there, he became involved in the African students' anticolonial movement, where young intellectuals were working for African independence. He helped organize the first Pan-African Student Congress in Paris in 1951 and in 1956 participated in the First World Congress of Black Writers and Artists in Paris. These movements laid the groundwork for a growing African liberation sentiment, supported by the ideological arguments of Negritude, Marxism, and Pan-Africanism.

Diop published three major works that attempt to reconstruct African history and the contributions of Africans to the Foundations of Western civilization: *Precolonial Black Africa*; *African Origin of Civilization*; and *Civilization or Barbarism.*

Cheikh Anta Diop University (French: Université Cheikh Anta Diop or UCAD), also known as the University of Dakar, in Senegal is named for Diop.

June 18

Arthur Schomburg
Jan. 24, 1874 - June 10, 1938

Arthur Schomburg was born in Santurce, Puerto Rico to Mary Josephina, a Black Cruzan mother, and Carlos Federico Schomburg, a Puerto Rican father. He devoted his life to uncovering Africa's glorious heritage after a fifth-grade teacher told him "Black people have no history, no heroes, no great moments."

After studying African literature and commercial printing in the Caribbean, Schomburg emigrated to Harlem in 1891 and seven years later co-founded the Negro Society for Historical Research and served as leader of the American Negro Academy.

Schomburg socialized among African Americans who had moved North in the Great Migration from the South, Pan-African immigrants from the Caribbean, artists of the Harlem Renaissance, exiled Cuban and Puerto Rican nationalists and intellectuals in New York City. He redefined himself as an "Afro Borinqueño," an "African Puerto Rican," He wrote articles for several progressive Black periodicals including *The Crisis* and *Opportunity* magazines, *Negro World*, and the *New York Amsterdam News* newspapers. In 1925 he self-published his inspirational essay, *The Negro Digs Up His Past*, which master teacher Dr. John Henrik Clarke credited as brilliant.

Schomburg, a self-taught bibliophile, amassed a vast collection of rare African artifacts accumulated throughout his global travels, and in 1926 the New York Public Library purchased his collection and displayed them at their 135th St. branch, naming it the Arthur A. Schomburg Collection of Negro Literature and Art. In 1973, the library was renamed the Schomburg Center for Research in Black Culture.

June 19

Juneteenth

Juneteenth is a 155+-year-old holiday celebrating the emancipation of African-Americans from slavery in the U.S.

Juneteenth is the oldest nationally celebrated commemoration of the ending of slavery in the United States.

From its Galveston, Texas origin in 1865, the observance of June 19th as the African American Emancipation Day has spread across the United States and beyond.

Today Juneteenth commemorates African American freedom from chattel slavery and emphasizes education and achievement. It is a day, a week, and in some areas a month marked with celebrations, guest speakers, picnics and family gatherings. It is a time for reflection and rejoicing. It is a time for assessment, self-improvement and for planning the future. Its growing popularity signifies a level of maturity and dignity in America long overdue. In cities across the country, people of all races, nationalities and religions are joining hands to truthfully acknowledge a period in our history that shaped and continues to influence our society today.

Sensitized to the conditions and experiences of others, and with a desire to engage in affecting ideological and systemic change for harmonious living is a way we can make significant and lasting improvements in our society.

June 20

Cheryl Byron
c. 1947 – June 17, 2003

Cheryl Byron was a visual artist, dancer, singer and social and cultural advocate. She started her studies in the land of her birth Trinidad & Tobago. There she also studied dance with Neville Shepard and acted with the Caribbean Theater Guild.

While on tour in New York City, Byron won a scholarship to the New School University, where she studied fine art. Byron earned a Bachelor of Arts and a Master of Arts degrees in English from City College (CUNY) while maintaining her professional life. In 1976 she was the first woman to perform her own original brand of poetry in a calypso tent in Trinidad.

Byron was a pioneering performer of rapso and dub poetry. Considered the Mother of Rapso, she was inspired by the artistry of Lancelot "Kebu" Lane. According to *Rhythms of the Afro-Atlantic World*: *Rituals and Remembrances* by Mamadou Diouf, "Cheryl Byron's poetic performances made visible by the female acts of anticolonial resistance that were carried out in religious and spiritual practice."

She studied dance with Pearl Primus and became a member of the Primus Borde Earth Theater. She became Primus' special assistant, accompanying her on her numerous teaching and choreography assignments, including with the Alvin Ailey American Dance Theater.

Byron founded Something Positive, a New York City-based performing arts and education organization dedicated to preserving the art and culture of the African Diaspora and its cross-cultural influences.

June 21

Tally Beatty
December 22, 1918 - April 29, 1995

Tally Beatty, dancer and choreographer extraordinaire, was born in Shreveport, Louisiana. He left made an indelible impact in dance and choreography as his work artistically spoke to the entrenched racial practices that are a part of the American way of life. He came to be known for his captivating performances and sophisticated choreography with dances that fused lyrical jazz, ballet and modern music. He was a pioneer.

Talley Beatty studied with Martha Graham and Katherine Dunham and became a principal dancer with the Katherine Dunham Company at age sixteen.

After touring with the Dunham Company for five years and appearing in films such as *A Study in Choreography for Camera* and Broadway shows such as *Cabin in the Sky*, *Pins and Needles*, and *Blue Holiday*, Beatty formed his own company and toured throughout Europe, the U.S. and Canada.

For his work on Broadway, Beatty was nominated for a 1977 Tony Award as Best Choreographer for *Your Arm's Too Short to Box with God.* He is considered one of the greatest African American choreographers and his work focuses on the social issues, experiences, and everyday life of *African Americans. Mourner's Bench* is an excerpt from Mr. Beatty's first ballet, *Southern Landscapes*, which takes a dramatic look at the end of the Reconstruction period marked by the end, through destruction, of the thousands of cooperative farms that had been created after the Civil War.

June 22

Sir George Herbert Walter

September 8, 1928 - March 4, 2008

Sir George Herbert Walter, KNH was an Antiguan politician of the Progressive Labour Movement and Premier of Antigua and Barbuda from 1971 to 1976.

Born 1928, Walter was the second premier of Antigua and Barbuda, the founder of the Antigua Workers' Union (AWU) and the Progressive Labour Movement (PLM) and a former general-secretary of the Antigua Trades & Labour Union (AT&LU).

Walter won Premiership in the 1971 elections, defeating Vere Bird four years after the colony became a British dependency with domestic autonomy. He advocated full independence for Antigua and Barbuda and opposed a British proposal to make Antigua and Barbuda an island federation. He was defeated in the 1976 elections by Bird.

The Social Security Act, the Labour Code that was copied in every Caribbean territory, the Representation of the People's Act and the founding of the Antigua & Barbuda Development Bank were all the work of his PLM government.

June 23

Madam C. J. Walker

1867-1919

Madam C. J. Walker is cited as "the first Black woman millionaire in America" and made her fortune thanks to her homemade line of hair care products for Black women.

Born Sarah Breedlove to parents who had been enslaved Africans, she was inspired to create her hair products after an experience with hair loss, which led to the creation of the "Walker system" of hair care.

A talented entrepreneur with a knack for self-promotion, Walker built a business empire, at first selling products directly to Black women, then employing "beauty culturalists" to hand-sell her wares. The self-made millionaire used her fortune to fund scholarships for women at the Tuskegee Institute and donated large parts of her wealth to the National Association for the Advancement of Colored People (NAACP) and the Black Young Men's Christian Association (YMCA) founded in 1853 as a source for building community spirit and a sense of social responsibility among Black Christian men.

June 24

Irene Cohen

Irene Chen was one of five women who died during military combat in the fight for independence in Angola. The martyred group has a certain mythology. They are the only known women to have taken up arms and to have joined an otherwise all-male military detachment tasked with entering Angola crossing both Congos.

Apart from a few articles and Deolinda's diaries, few facts are known about these women's actual lives. What we do know is that Irene and Deolinda's activism began in the church. Both women studied abroad, and both were driven, by the cruel hypocrisy of Portuguese colonialism, to use their relatively privileged positions among Angola's assimilated class to join the anti-colonial movement, the People's Movement for the Liberation of Angola (MPLA).

Annually, they are eulogized on Angolan Women's Day on March 2; their short and tragic lives are made emblematic of African feminism and national pride.

June 25

Participants in Slave Revolts

We remember all the men, women, and children who planned and implemented plans to free themselves, their families and their communities from the oppressors.

June 26

Charles Cogswell Doe
April 11, 1830 - March 9, 1896

Charles Cogswell Doe, born in Derry, New Hampshire, was an Associate Justice of the Supreme Judicial Court of New Hampshire, and after the court was dissolved to be reorganized as the New Hampshire Supreme Court, he served as Chief Justice. Doe has been referred to as one of the ten greatest jurists in American history and the "one judge upon the bench of a state court who stands out as a builder of the law since the Civil War."

In autumn of 1845, Doe entered Harvard College where he stayed for only a year, possibly having been expelled for an incident in which he threw a tree stump through the dormitory window of an upperclassman who had tormented him in a hazing ritual. After leaving Harvard, Doe entered Dartmouth College, from which he graduated in 1849, having been elected to Phi Beta Kappa. Doe was bitter about the education he received at Dartmouth, calling it a "barbaric classical course" of study.

Doe was appointed solicitor of Strafford County, the county's chief prosecuting officer and in 1855 he represented the state in the Hodge Case, a first-degree murder prosecution that marked Doe's first appearance before a jury. The trial ended in a mistrial due to a hung jury. Doe was removed from office as county solicitor on a charge of neglect of his duty, less than two years into his term of six years.

Doe's biographer, John Phillip Reid, suggests that Doe's removal was part of an 1855 "political revolution" in New Hampshire in which hundreds of Democrats were removed from office by the legislature.

Seen as an eccentric, Doe often dressed in the clothes of a farmer and not his judicial attire.

June 27

Emmett Till
July 25, 1941 - August 28, 1955

Emmett Till, a 14-year old African-American boy, was murdered in August 1955 in a racist attack that shocked the nation and provided a catalyst for the emerging civil rights movement.

A Chicago native, Till was visiting relatives in Money, Mississippi, when he was accused of harassing a local white woman. Several days later, relatives of the woman abducted Till, brutally beating and killing him before disposing of his body in a nearby river. Till's devastated mother insisted on a public, open-casket funeral for her son to shed light on the violence inflicted on Blacks in the South. Till's murderers were acquitted, but his death galvanized civil rights activists nationwide.

Emmett Louis Till was born in Chicago, Illinois and he was the only child of Louis and Mamie Till.

June 28

Sojourner Truth

c. 1797 – c. 1883

Sojourner Truth was an African American evangelist, abolitionist, women's rights activist and author who lived a miserable life as an enslaved African, serving several masters throughout New York before escaping to freedom in 1826. After gaining her freedom, Truth became a Christian and, at what she believed was God's urging, preached about abolitionism and equal rights for all, highlighted in her stirring *Ain't I a Woman?* speech, delivered at a women's convention in Ohio in 1851. She continued her crusade for the rest of her life, earning an audience with President Abraham Lincoln and becoming one of the world's best-known human rights crusaders.

Truth was born Isabella Baumfree in 1797 into slavery to James and Elizabeth Baumfree in Ulster County, New York. Around age nine, she was sold at a slave auction to John Neely for $100, along with a flock of sheep.

After the New York Anti-Slavery Law was passed, Dumont illegally sold Isabella's five-year-old son Peter. With the help of the Van Wagenens, she filed a lawsuit to get him back. Months later, Isabella won her case and regained custody of her son. She was the first Black woman to sue a white man in a United States court and prevail.

Engraved on her tombstone are the words, "Is God Dead?," a question she is reported to have once asked a questioning Frederick Douglass to remind him to have faith.

Truth left behind a legacy of courage, faith and fighting for what is right and honorable. She also left a legacy of words and songs including her autobiography, *The Narrative of Sojourner Truth*, which she dictated in 1850 to Olive Gilbert since she never learned to read or write.

June 29

Lucrécia Paím
1939 - 1967

Lucrécia Paím is one of five women who died during military combat in the fight for independence in Angola. The martyred group has a certain mythology. They are the only known women to have taken up arms and to have joined an otherwise all-male military detachment tasked with entering Angola crossing both Congos.

June 30

Charles LeRoy Gittens
August 31, 1928 - July 27, 2011

Charles LeRoy Gittens was an American United States Secret Service agent. Gittens joined the Secret Service in 1956, becoming the agency's first African American agent.

Gittens was born in Cambridge, Massachusetts. His father was a contractor who had immigrated to the United States from Barbados. He left his high school before graduation to enlist in the United States Army. He was promoted to lieutenant in the Army and was stationed in Japan during the Korean War. Gittens earned his GED while serving in the Army. Following the end of the war, Gittens earned a bachelor's degree from present-day North Carolina Central University. He completed the four-year academic program in three years, and graduated magna cum laude with a Bachelor of Arts degree in English and Spanish. As a result, he was bilingual.

Gittens taught at a school in North Carolina and was encouraged to take the civil service exam, which resulted in his recruitment into the United States Secret Service. He began his career at the agency's office in Charlotte, North Carolina. He then became an investigator at the Secret Service's field office in New York City, where he served for ten years. He was assigned to a "special detail" Secret Service unit, which investigated bank fraud and counterfeiting. Gittens was then transferred to the Secret Service's field office in Puerto Rico, where he guarded New York Governor Nelson Rockefeller during his 1969 trip to the Caribbean and Latin America.

Gittens was promoted to the head of the Secret Service's field office in Washington, D.C. After retiring he joined the United States Department of Justice, where he led investigations of Nazi war criminals who were residing in the United States at the Department's Office of Special Investigations.

July 1

Miriam Spied

Contributors: Everett, Lascelles, and Anthony Lewis (Grandnephews)

Born in Portland, Jamaica, Miriam Spied and her father Nathaniel Spied were founders of Merl Grove High School in Kingston, Jamaica in 1920.

The name “MERL” was the initials of Nathaniel’s five children: Miriam, Effey, Reggie & Ruth, and Lucille. The name “GROVE” was derived from the trees on the property.

Merl Grove High School was an all-girls school and the first in Jamaica to have a Parent Teachers Association. The school was initially started to help young ladies living in a disenfranchised community whose parents were unable to send their daughters for a high school education.

Miss Mirrie, as she was affectionately called, also taught boys before they were of high school age. Once in high school Ms. Mirrie would tutor the boys in private lessons after school. Two of those students are Tony Keyes and Hans Barrett.

In addition to the academic studies, Miss Mirrie promoted etiquette and modesty with the girls. She made certain that the hem of the girls’ uniforms had to be two inches below their knees and she held inspections every day to make sure they wore a slip under their uniforms. Miss Mirrie also taught the girls how to sit properly with their legs crossed and to focus on their posture.

Ms. Mirrie retired in 1959 but continued to be active at the school. Her brother Reggie was also a school inspector.

July 2

Adam Clayton Powell, Jr.
November 29, 1908 - April 4, 1972

Adam Clayton Powell Jr. was a Baptist pastor who became politician, who represented the Harlem community of New York City in the United States House of Representatives from 1945 until 1971. He was the first African-American to be elected from New York to Congress.

Re-elected for nearly three decades, Powell became a powerful national politician of the Democratic Party, and served as a national spokesman on civil rights and social issues. He also urged United States presidents to support emerging nations in Africa and Asia as they gained independence after colonialism.

In 1961, after 16 years in the House, Powell became chairman of the Education and Labor Committee, the most powerful position held by an African American in Congress. As chairman, he supported the passage of important social and civil rights legislation under presidents John F. Kennedy and Lyndon B. Johnson.

Following allegations of corruption, in 1967 Powell was excluded from his seat by Democratic Representatives-elect of the 90th United States Congress, but he was re-elected and regained the seat in the 1969 ruling by the Supreme Court of the United States in Powell v. McCormack. He lost his seat in 1970 to Charles Rangel and retired from electoral politics.

July 3

Hulan Jack
December 29, 1906 - December 19, 1986

Hulan Edwin Jack was a prominent Saint Lucian-born New York politician who in 1954 became the highest ranking Caribbean American municipal official up until that time, when he was elected Borough President of Manhattan.

Hulan Edwin Jack was most noted for being the first Black borough president in New York City, representing Manhattan from 1954-1961. He emigrated to the United States at age 16 and later attended New York University.

A Democrat, Jack was elected to the New York State Assembly from 1940-1953 and 1968-1972. As an assemblyman Jack was known as a fighter for civil and human rights, successfully introducing legislation in 1945 to end discrimination in employment as well as discrimination in public and semi-public housing. He also introduced bills for the welfare of laborers, veterans and children.

As borough president Jack helped secure funding for major improvements in highways and public transportation, as well as public works projects.

July 4

Maymie Leona Turpeau DeMena

Maymie Leona Turpeau DeMena, also known as Madame DeMena was a Pan-Africanist, orator, Spanish language interpreter, and international organizer who rose to the top of the Universal Negro Improvement Association and Communities League (UNIA-ACL) like a shooting star. Madame DeMena served the UNIA-ACL as Assistant International Organizer, as Fourth Assistant President General, and Officer in Charge of the American Field.

DeMena's star status was showcased on opening day of the International Convention of the Negro Peoples of the World, August 1, 1929 in Kingston, Jamaica. DeMena sitting astride a white charger, with drawn sword, led a huge, colorful, panoramic procession of African Legions, Black Cross Nurses, African Motor Corps, marching bands, singing choirs, scores of juvenile units, elaborately decorated floats riding high officials and the Honorable Marcus Mosiah Garvey riding in an open car draped in red, black and green, attired in a flowing scarlet robe and cocked hat decorated with white and red plumes bringing up the rear, through the streets of Kingston before an enormous crowd of spectators rivaling the exhibition marking the celebration of Queen Victoria's Diamond Jubilee of 1897.

Madame Maymie Leona Turpeau DeMena was born in Nicaragua, South America of Spanish descent. She married Percival Augusta Aikens who was born in Jamaica and was a master electrician and mechanic. DeMena and Aikens were comrades in their idealism and activism, both fierce freedom fighters in the cause of African redemption who willingly invested their time, effort and money.

Madame DeMena spoke fluent Spanish. She used her literary skills to advocate on behalf of Mr. Garvey and to promote the UNIA among Black people whose primary language was Spanish. Her ability to translate Mr. Garvey's principles and programs from English to Spanish made her an invaluable resource for Garveyism.

July 5

Dr. Karl N. White-Davis
March 16, 1945 - February 4, 2019

Contributor: Dr. Gerald White-Davis, Brother

Working as educators is a White-Davis family tradition. Dr. Karl White-Davis, Jamaican, graduate of the New School of Social Research and Nova Southeastern University, instructed students from middle school to college. His specific area of instruction and expertise was in the field of political and development economics with emphasis on the economics of colonized Africa and the impact of the trans-Atlantic slave trade on western world development.

Two of White-Davis' favored books were: Walter Rodney's *How Europe Underdeveloped Africa* and George Beckford's *Persistent Poverty*. Karl White-Davis sought to impart to his students the important contributions that Africa made to the world.

July 6

Ruby Dee
October 27, 1922 - June 11, 2014

Ruby Dee (born Ruby Ann Wallace) was an American actress, poet, playwright, screenwriter, journalist, and civil rights activist. She originated the role of "Ruth Younger" in the stage and film versions of *A Raisin in the Sun* (1961). Other notable film roles include *The Jackie Robinson Story* (1950) and *Do the Right Thing* (1989).

An acclaimed actor and author, Ruby Dee graced the stage and screen for more than seventy years. Although born in Cleveland, Ohio, Ms. Dee considered herself a product of Harlem, where she grew up and began her career as a member of the American Negro Theatre. She received her B.A. from Hunter College with a degree in Romance languages and she later studied acting with Paul Mann, Lloyd Richards, and Morris Carnovsky.

Dee and Ossie Davis, her husband, wrote an autobiography in which they discussed their political activism and their decision to have an open marriage (later changing their views). Dee was a breast cancer survivor of more than three decades.

Dee and Davis were well-known civil rights activists in the Civil Rights Movement. Dee was a member of the Congress of Racial Equality (CORE), the National Association for the Advancement of Colored People (NAACP), the Student Nonviolent Coordinating Committee (SNCC), Delta Sigma Theta sorority and the Southern Christian Leadership Conference (SCLC). Dee won the Frederick Douglass Award from the New York Urban League.

In 1999, Dee and Davis were arrested at 1 Police Plaza, the headquarters of the New York Police Department, protesting the police shooting of Amadou Diallo.

July 7

Eugene Kinckle Jones
July 30, 1885 - January 11, 1954

Eugene Kinckle Jones was a leader of the National Urban League and one the seven founders (commonly referred to as Seven Jewels) of Alpha Phi Alpha fraternity at Cornell University in 1906. Jones became Alpha chapter's second President.

Jones was born in Richmond, Virginia to Joseph Endom Jones and Rosa Daniel Kinckle. He graduated from Richmond's Virginia Union University in 1905 and Cornell University with a master's degree in 1908. After graduation, he taught high school in Louisville, Kentucky until.

Jones, an organizer for the National Urban League (NUL) founded the Boston Urban League in 1917 and worked for racial equality in employment, housing, and health in Massachusetts. In 1918, Jones became the first Executive Secretary of the NUL. The League, under his direction, significantly expanded its multifaceted campaign to crack the barriers to Black employment, spurred first by the boom years of the 1920s, and then, by the desperate years of the Great Depression. He implemented boycotts against firms that refused to employ Blacks, pressured schools to expand vocational opportunities for young people, constantly prodded Washington officials to include Blacks in New Deal recovery programs, and a drive to get Blacks into previously segregated labor unions.

Together with Charles S. Johnson, Jones helped launch *Opportunity* a journal which addressed problems faced by Blacks. He served first as treasurer and then as Vice President of the National Conference of Social Work as the first African American on its executive board.

In 1933, Jones took a position with the Department of Commerce in Washington, DC as an advisor on Negro Affairs. In this role, Jones was a member of President Franklin D. Roosevelt's Black Cabinet, an informal group of African American public policy advisors to the President.

July 8

Charles Spurgeon Johnson
July 24, 1893 - October 27, 1956

Charles Spurgeon Johnson) was an American sociologist and college administrator, the first Black president of historically Black Fisk University, and a lifelong advocate for racial equality and the advancement of civil rights for African Americans and all ethnic minorities. He preferred to work collaboratively with liberal white groups in the South, quietly as a "sideline activist," to get practical results.

His position is often contrasted with that of W. E. B. Du Bois, who was a powerful and militant advocate for Blacks and described Johnson as "too conservative." During Johnson's academic studies and leadership of Fisk University during the 1930s and 1940s, the South had legal racial segregation and Jim Crow discriminatory laws and practices, including having disfranchised most Black voters in constitutions passed at the turn of the century. Johnson was unwavering in personal terms in his opposition to this oppressive system, yet he worked hard to change race relations in terms of short-term practical gains.

Johnson was born in Bristol, Virginia, to well-educated parents. His father was a respected Baptist minister, and his mother was educated in public schools. He attended a boarding school in Richmond, Virginia, and earned a B.A. in sociology from Virginia Union University. He began graduate study of sociology at the University of Chicago, though his study was interrupted by service in France during World War I as a non-commissioned officer with the US Army. After returning to the US, he resumed graduate work at the University of Chicago, where he earned his Ph.D. in sociology.

In 1920 Johnson married Marie Antoinette Burgette. When he was appointed director of research and investigation of the National Urban League, the couple moved to New York City.

July 9

William Johnson Trent, Jr

1910-1993

William Johnson Trent, Jr. was an African-American economist, non-profit director and civil rights activist from Atlanta, Georgia.

Trent was born in Asheville, North Carolina and moved with his family to Atlanta at an early age. His father, William J. Trent, Sr., was an early organizer of the National Association for the Advancement of Colored People (NAACP). He graduated from a Black private high school in Atlanta and attended Livingstone College, from which he graduated with a bachelor's degree in 1930. His father was president of Livingstone at the time. He then earned a master's degree in economics from the Wharton School of the University of Pennsylvania at the University of Pennsylvania and did graduate work at the University of Chicago. He returned to North Carolina and taught for two years at his alma mater and later Bennett College.

Trent was part of U.S. President Franklin Delano Roosevelt's Black Cabinet, serving as Adviser on Negro Affairs to the Secretary of the Interior Harold L. Ickes and later in the position of race relations officer in the Federal Works Agency. He served as the executive director of the United Negro College Fund (UNCF) from its inception in 1944 until 1964. After leaving UNCF, Trent worked for *Time Inc.* as assistant personnel director where he was concerned with race relations. He served as treasurer and longtime board member of the National Urban League and as board president of St. Luke's Hospital.

During his time at the United Negro College Fund, Trent raised substantial funds for private Historically Black Colleges and Universities (HBCU).

July 10
Founders of Historically Black Colleges and Universities

Historically Black Colleges and Universities (HBCUs) are institutions of higher education in the United States that were established before the Civil Rights Act of 1964 with the intention of primarily serving the African-American community. Most of these institutions were founded in the years after the American Civil War and are concentrated in the Southern United States.

During the period of segregation in the United States prior to the Civil Rights Act, the overwhelming majority of higher education institutions were predominantly white and completely disqualified or limited African-Americans from enrolling; while institutions in other parts of the country regularly employed quotas to limit admissions of African Americans.

HBCUs in the United States, including both public and private institutions, offer doctoral programs, master's degree programs, bachelor's degree programs, and associate degree programs.

July 11

Wilbert Tatum

January 23, 1933 - February 26, 2009

Wilbert Arnold "Bill" Tatum was an American newspaper executive who variously served as the editor, publisher, chairman, and chief executive officer of the *New York Amsterdam News*, a weekly newspaper that still serves the African-American community of New York City. Tatum was part of a group that purchased the paper in the 1970s, the third ownership group in the history of the publication, which included notable investors such as former New York State Comptroller H. Carl McCall and the late Manhattan Borough President Percy E. Sutton.

Tatum was born in Durham, North Carolina and attended Durham's segregated schools, working during the summer in tobacco fields.

He majored in sociology at Lincoln University, the United States' first degree-granting Historically Black University. During the Korean War, he served in the United States Marine Corps as a drill instructor in Japan. . After completing his military service, he attended Yale University as a National Urban Fellow. Tatum was later awarded a master's degree from Occidental College, where he majored in urban studies.

Tatum spent 13 years working as a mayoral appointee in the government of New York City, during the John Lindsay and Abraham Beame administrations. While director of community relations at the New York City Department of Buildings, he spent a cold winter's night in a Queens housing project that lacked heat, to publicize the circumstances of tenants there. He proposed a $6 billion "clothing stamp" program that would provide clothing for the poor nationwide while assisting the City's struggling garment industry.

July 12

Mohamed Mohamed Morsi Issa Al-Ayyat
August 8, 1951 - June 17, 2019

Mohamed Mohamed Morsi Issa Al-Ayyat was an Egyptian politician and engineer who served as the first democratically elected president of Egypt from June 30, 2012 to July 3, 2013. General Abdel Fattah el-Sisi removed him from office in a coup d'état after protests in June.

It was easy to dismiss Morsi then, and it will be easy to dismiss him now, as a footnote in history. Buried without fanfare and under the glare of a near-totalitarian state—the most repressive in Egypt's history—he will be easy to forget. But the brief 12 months in which he found himself in power was an unusual time for Egypt. Morsi was incompetent and polarizing, and managed to alienate nearly everyone outside the Brotherhood.

Ultimately, he and the Muslim Brotherhood failed. But he was not a fascist or a new pharaoh, as his opponents liked to claim. In a previous piece for *The Atlantic*, a colleague and I scored Morsi's one year in power using the Polity IV index, one of the most widely used empirical measures of autocracy and democracy, and then compared it to other cases. We concluded that "decades of transitions show that Morsi, while inept and majoritarian, was no more autocratic than a typical transitional leader and was more democratic than other leaders during societal transitions." Source: https://www.brookings.edu/blog/order-from-chaos/2019/06/19/the-tragedy-of-egypts-mohamed-morsi/

July 13

Wesley Pringle Sr.
October 1921 - October 2005

Contributor: Wesley Pringle Jr. - B.Sc. (Son)

Wesley Pringle Sr. was a Black American who was born in South Carolina, United States of America. He was a Tenant Farmer for many years living under the Jim Crow System which was difficult but he was quite successful working the system. He was responsible for farm crops such as cotton and corn and he trained many young farmers about he process of farming. He helped many youths with opportunities to the science of farming.

As a farmer, there was always an abundance of food in Pringle's environment. He assisted the community by donating food to families in the area. The community adored him and his generosity toward others.

After many years of farming, Pringle left South Carolina and spent time in Washington, D.C. Upon his return to South Carolina, he invested in properties. On these properties he planted and raised various vegetable crops. He continued to share with the community produce from the properties.

July 14

Benjamin "Pap" Singleton
1809-1892

"I started it all; I was the cause of it all," said Benjamin "Pap" Singleton to a Congressional Committee investigating the causes of the great "Exodus of 1879" when tens of thousands of Negroes simply packed up and moved northward from Tennessee, Texas, South Carolina, Mississippi, and Louisiana. In this great movement of Negroes were some sixty to eighty thousand men and women seeking some better place, some more tolerable clime away from the South.

"Pap" Singleton was only partly right in his statement to the Congressmen. Other causes for the migration were economic exploitation, denial of political recognition, and the dreaded activity of the Klu Klux Klan. The Negroes buoyant dreams of early Reconstruction had changed to a nightmare of repression in many parts of the Deep South. "Pap" was the Pied Piper urging them away.

A native of Tennessee, "Pap" Singletary had escaped from slavery. For a time, he lived in Canada. After the Emancipation Proclamation (1863), he returned to the South. In his travels, Singleton discovered thinly populated areas in Kansas. While Negro intellectuals were debating the merits of emigration to Africa and South America, Singleton marched through the South advertising and preaching a haven of ease and dignity over in Kansas.

Singleton had been a carpenter and cabinet-maker during his enslavement and now supported himself through those trades. Source: Great Negroes Past and Present, Russell L. Adams, Afro-Am Publishing Company 1963

July 15

Earl Gilbert Graves Sr.
January 9, 1935 – April 6, 2020

Earl Gilbert Graves Sr. was an American entrepreneur, publisher, businessman, philanthropist, and advocate of African-American businesses. A graduate of Morgan State University, he was the founder of *Black Enterprise* magazine and chairman of the media company Earl G. Graves, Ltd. He was the director for Aetna and Executive Board member of the Boy Scouts of America. He was the father of Earl G. Graves Jr.

Born in Brooklyn, New York, Graves grew up in the Bedford-Stuyvesant section of New York City. A member of Omega Psi Phi fraternity, he received a Bachelor of Arts degree in economics in 1958 from Morgan State University. He was an ROTC graduate and attended Airborne and Ranger Schools.

Having written a letter to the Democratic National Committee, he became a volunteer for the 1964 presidential campaign of Lyndon B. Johnson. His work with the party gave Graves the opportunity to serve as administrative assistant to newly elected Senator Robert F. Kennedy in 1965. Following the assassination of the senator, Graves would land a seat on the advisory board of the Small Business Administration (SBA) in 1968.

Since founding *Black Enterprise Magazine* in 1970, Earl Graves has been named one of the ten most outstanding minority businessmen in the country by the President of the United States, and received the National Award of Excellence in recognition of his achievements in minority business enterprise. Black Enterprise Magazine is recognized as the definitive resource for African American business professionals, entrepreneurs and policy makers in the public and private sectors.

July 16

Ida B. Wells
July 16, 1862 – March 25, 1931

Ida Bell Wells was an American investigative journalist, educator, and an early leader in the civil rights movement. She was one of the founders of the National Association for the Advancement of Colored People (NAACP). Over the course of a lifetime Wells was dedicated to combating prejudice and violence, and the fight for equality for African-American men and women

Born into slavery in Holly Springs, Mississippi, Wells was freed by the Emancipation Proclamation during the American Civil War. At the age of 16, she lost both her parents and her infant brother in the 1878 yellow fever epidemic. She went to work and kept the rest of the family together with the help of her grandmother. Later, moving with some of her siblings to Memphis, Tennessee, she worked as a teacher. She co-owned and wrote for the *Memphis Free Speech and Headlight* newspaper. Her reporting covered incidents of racial segregation and inequality.

In 1884, Wells filed a lawsuit against a train car company in Memphis for unfair treatment. She had been thrown off a first-class train, despite having a ticket. Although she won the case on the local level, the ruling was eventually overturned in federal court.

Wells documented lynching in the United States through her pamphlet called *Southern Horrors: Lynch Law in all its Phases*, investigating frequent claims of whites that lynchings were reserved for Black criminals only. Wells exposed lynching as a barbaric practice of whites in the South used to intimidate and oppress African Americans who created economic and political competition for whites. A white mob destroyed her newspaper office and presses as her investigative reporting was carried nationally in Black-owned newspapers.

In 2020, Wells was posthumously honored with a Pulitzer Prize.

July 17

Eleanora Fagan; professionally known as Billie Holiday
April 7, 1915 - July 17, 1959

Eleanora Fagan was an American jazz and swing music singer with a career spanning 26 years. Nicknamed "Lady Day" by her friend and music partner Lester Young, Holiday had an innovative influence on jazz music and pop singing. Her vocal style, strongly inspired by jazz instrumentalists, pioneered a new way of manipulating phrasing and tempo. She was known for her vocal delivery and improvisational skills.

After a turbulent childhood that included attempted rape by a neighbor, Holiday began singing in nightclubs in Harlem, where she was heard by producer John Hammond, who commended her voice. She signed a recording contract with Brunswick in 1935. Collaborations with Teddy Wilson yielded the hit "What a Little Moonlight Can Do", which became a jazz standard. Throughout the 1930s and 1940s, Holiday had mainstream success on labels such as Columbia and Decca. By the late 1940s, however, she was beset with legal troubles and drug abuse. After a short prison sentence, she performed at a sold-out concert at Carnegie Hall, but her reputation deteriorated because of her drug and alcohol problems.

She was a successful concert performer throughout the 1950s with two further sold-out shows at Carnegie Hall. Because of personal struggles and an altered voice, her final recordings were met with mixed reaction but were mild commercial successes. Her final album, *Lady in Satin*, was released in 1958. Holiday died of cirrhosis in 1959. She won four Grammy Awards, all of them posthumously, for Best Historical Album. She was inducted into the Grammy Hall of Fame in 1973.

"While reading Eleanora Fagan's life story, I am moved by the sorrows she encountered and I am encouraged by her resilience," - Claudette Joy Spence

July 18

Obi Benue Egbuna

July 18, 1938 - January 18, 2014

Obi Benue Egbuna was a Nigerian-born novelist, playwright and political activist, most famous for leading the Universal Coloured People's Association (UCPA) and being a member of the British Black Panther Movement (1968–72) during the years when he lived in England, between 1961 and 1973. Egbuna also published several texts on Marxist–Black Power, including *Destroy This Temple: The Voice of Black Power in Britain* (1971) and *The ABC of Black Power Thought* (1973).

Egbuna was born in Anambra State, Nigeria. He studied at the University of Iowa and Howard University, Washington, DC, moving in 1961 to England, where he lived until 1973.

In London, Egbuna was a member of a group called the Committee of African Organisations that had roots in the West African Students' Union, and which organised Malcolm X's 1965 visit to Britain. Egbuna participated in events organized by the Caribbean Artists Movement, and in 1966 the Negro Theatre Workshop (founded in London by Pearl Connor) took his play *Wind Versus Polygamy* to the World Festival of Negro Arts in Dakar, Senegal.

Egbuna became a pioneer of the Black Power movement in Britain, forming the Universal Coloured People's Association (UCPA) – the first avowed Black Power group in Britain in 1967, following Stokely Carmichael's (Kwame Ture) visit and speaking at a major anti-Vietnam war rally in October that year.

Being heavily influenced by Marxism, Egbuna stressed the importance of an international struggle against capitalism, as a part of the global struggle against racial oppression.

July 19

Hilda Simms
April 15, 1918 - February 6, 1994

Hilda Simms (born Hilda Moses, was an American stage actress, best known for her starring role on Broadway in *Anna Lucasta.*

Hilda Simms was born Hilda Moses in Minneapolis, Minnesota, one of eleven siblings. When Simms starred in the critically acclaimed Broadway hit *Anna Lucasta*, her mother Lydia refused to attend the play on Broadway, stating that she would not watch her daughter play a prostitute as she didn't raise her that way. Simms and her siblings were raised devout Catholics in Minneapolis and walked several miles to school each morning to attend the Basilica of St. Mary on the outskirts of Minneapolis.

Before becoming an actress, Simms planned to enter the teaching profession. She enrolled at the University of Minnesota and engaged in her studies until lack of funds forced her abandon them. Simms relocated to New York, acting in radio dramas and becoming a member of the American Negro Theater, where she gained professional acting experience. As a member of this noted ensemble, she worked on sound effects, props and publicity while learning her new craft.

The United States Department of Justice denied her passport in 1955 and canceled her scheduled 14-week USO tour of the Armed Forces in Europe, even though she had entertained troops and made War Bond tours during World War II. The Defense Department decision was based on speculation about her affiliation with the Communist Party in the late 1930s and early 1940s. That decision caused her dozens of lost opportunities and any chance of a film career evaporated. In 1960, she wrote an article titled I'm *No Benedict Arnold* which told her side of the story.

July 20

Olaudah Equiano
c. 1745 - March 31, 1797

Olaudah Equiano known for most of his life as Gustavus Vassa was a writer and abolitionist from, according to his memoir, the Eboe region of the Kingdom of Benin (today southern Nigeria). Enslaved as a child in Africa, he was taken to the Caribbean and sold as a slave to a Royal Navy officer. He was sold twice more but purchased his freedom in 1766.

As a freedman in London, Equiano supported the British abolitionist movement. He was part of the Sons of Africa, an abolitionist group composed of Africans living in Britain, and he was active among leaders of the anti-slave trade movement in the 1780s.

Equiano published his autobiography, *The Interesting Narrative of the Life of Olaudah Equiano* (1789), which depicted the horrors of slavery. It went through nine editions in his lifetime and helped gain passage of the British Slave Trade Act 1807, which abolished the slave trade. Equiano married an English woman named Susannah Cullen in 1792 and they had two daughters. He died in 1797 in Westminster.

Since the late 20th century, when his autobiography was published in a new edition, he had been increasingly studied by a range of scholars, including from his homeland.

July 21

Ottobah Cugoano
c.1757 - after 1791

Ottobah Cugoano, also known as John Stuart, was an abolitionist, political activist and natural rights philosopher from West Africa who was active in Britain in the latter half of the eighteenth century.

Captured in modern-day Ghana and sold into slavery at the age of 13, Cugoano was shipped to Grenada in the Caribbean, where he worked on a plantation. He was purchased by an English merchant who took him to England, where he was taught to read and write English, and was freed following the ruling in the Somersett Case (1772). Later working for artists Richard and Maria Cosway, he became acquainted with several British political and cultural figures. He joined the Sons of Africa, a group of African abolitionists in Britain.

Ottobah Cugoano was born Quobna Ottobah Cugoano near Ajumako, in modern-day Ghana.

July 22

Josephine St. Pierre Ruffin
August 31, 1842 - March 13, 1924

Josephine St. Pierre Ruffin was an African-American publisher, journalist, civil rights leader, suffragist, and editor of the Woman's Era, the first national newspaper published by and for African-American women.

Ruffin was born in Boston, Massachusetts, to John St. Pierre, of French and African descent from Martinique, and Elizabeth Matilda Menhenick from England. Her father was a successful clothier and founder of a Boston Zion Church. She attended public schools in Charlestown and Salem, and a private school in New York City because of her parents' objections to the segregated schools in Boston. She completed her studies at the Bowdoin School (not to be confused with Bowdoin College), after segregation in Boston schools ended.

Working with her husband, Ruffin became active in the struggle against slavery. During the Civil War, they helped recruit Black soldiers for the Union Army, the 54th and 55th Massachusetts regiments. The couple also worked for the Sanitation Commission, which provided aid for the care of soldiers in the field. After the war ended, Ruffin turned her attention to organizing for the Kansas Freedmen's Relief Association, collecting money and clothes to send to aid southern Blacks resettling in Kansas, known as Exodusters.

Ruffin supported women's suffrage and, in 1869, joined with Julia Ward Howe and Lucy Stone to form the American Woman Suffrage Association (AWSA) in Boston. A group of these women, Howe and Stone also founded the New England Women's Club in 1868. Josephine Ruffin was its first Black member when she joined in the mid-1890s. Ruffin also wrote for the Black weekly paper, The Courant and became a member of the New England Woman's Press Association.

July 23

Pastor Isaac Coachman
1846 - 1934
Contributor: Rev. Phyllis Ida Coachman

It is my pleasure to introduce and pay homage to my Great Grandfather, Isaac Coachman, who was born enslaved in 1846, and later became a Pastor in the African Methodist Episcopal Church, usually called A.M.E Church. The A.M.E church was founded by Richard Allen, Absalom Jones, and others in Philadelphia in 1787. The A.M.E church was founded on racial theological differences because of the discrimination and segregation in the White Methodist Church. The A.M.E Church has always fought for racial, civil, and the human rights of African Americans. The A.M.E Church is an advocate for social improvement, religious autonomy, education, economic and political engagement.

My Great Grand Father, Pastor Isaac Coachman, was mentioned in an article from the Daily Times-Enterprise Newspaper in 1896. There was a 6-day A.M.E. conference in Bainbridge, GA. "The conference made a fine impression on this community". The article states that Isaac Coachman was appointed to Mt. Zion Thomasville District.

As a very soon to be ordained Minister in the United Church of Christ (UCC); it warms my heart to know that I am following in the footsteps of my Great Grandfather, and, his Grandson, (who is my Father): Bishop James Lee Coachman, (transitioned in 1986); and who are now included in "The Great Cloud of Witnesses". (Hebrews 12:1)

With God's help I will declare what is stated in Isaiah 61:1 "The Spirit of the Lord is upon me, because the Lord has anointed me; he has sent me to bring good news to the oppressed, to bind up the brokenhearted, to proclaim liberty to the captives and release the prisoners."

July 24

Bussa

Bussa's rebellion (April 14 – 16, 1816) was the largest slave revolt in Barbadian history. The rebellion takes its name from the enslaved African-born Bussa, who led the rebellion which was defeated by British forces.

Bussa's Rebellion was the first of three large-scale slave rebellions in the British West Indies that shook public faith in slavery in the years leading up to the abolition of slavery in the British Empire and emancipation of former slaves. It was followed by the large-scale rebellion in the Dutch Demerara (present day Guyana) in 1823 and by larger rebellions in Jamaica in 1831–32. Collectively these are often referred to as the "late slave rebellions".

Bussa was born a free man in West Africa of possible Nigerian descent and was captured by African slave merchants, sold to the British, and transported to Barbados (where slavery had been legal since 1661) in the late 18th century as a slave.

Not much is known about Bussa as there are no records of him prior to rebellion date. Since slave owners almost never bothered to keep detailed records about the lives of their slaves (who were considered property), virtually no biographical information about Bussa is available. Records show a slave named "Bussa" worked as a *ranger* (a head officer among the slaves) on "Bayley's Plantation" in the parish of Saint Philip around the time of the rebellion. This position would have given Bussa more freedom of movement than the average slave and would have made it easier for him to plan and coordinate the rebellion.

July 25

Johnny and Sambo
(1725)

Nevis

The Nevis slave conspiracy might initially appear as a minor footnote within the history of the smallest and least politically and economically significant of the Leeward Islands, in the Caribbean. It was a British sugar plantation colony which itself had generally been regarded by historians as a marginal place in comparison with larger Caribbean islands such as Barbados, Jamaica, Haiti, and Cuba. The plans were never put into action and it has been difficult to determine whether or not the plot had actually existed.

Records indicate that the main evidence came from a slave informing his owner of overhearing talk among his fellows of a rising, and of their appointment of leaders'. From this accusation, the tangled trail of hearsay led to a white woman claimed that she had heard a man named Samuel Bayley 'Say that he heard his brother John Bayley say....

None of those enslaved Africans imprisoned or executed confessed to the existence of a plot, let alone their own involvement in it, and it has been impossible to discern whether this conspiracy had actually been organized, and might have succeeded had a single slave not chosen to tell his master about it, or whether it was simply an instance of slaves' wishful thinking, or of planters' deepest anxieties; a question which has been raised in relation to a number of alleged slave conspiracies in the slave societies of the Americas.

It is possible that the Nevis plot of 1725 existed only in the paranoid mind-set of slaveholders, or in the enslaved Africans' expression of their dreams of revenge and freedom, or the best-kept secret among them.

July 26

Cudjoe, Quashie, Cadenda

St. Kitts

One of the many paradoxes upon which Atlantic slavery was based was the idea that a slave was a chattel-living property. Therefore, when a slave ran away from his master, he was not only depriving his owner of labor value, but was also stealing his property.

Runaways were 'slaves who stole themselves'. And because a slave, particularly one young and strong enough to feel confident that he might be able to evade surveillance and survive in the harsh, wild hills of Nevis or Antigua, was a highly valuable piece of property, such 'stealing' was a felony, not an act of petty theft, and had to be punished accordingly.

According to the legislative records of St. Kitts, between February 1740 and June 1746, thirty-eight slaves were executed for felony. They included one woman and a number of men whose African names, such as Cudjoe, Quashie, and Cadenda, may have indicated that they had been born free and had been enslaved and brought to the West Indies as children or young men.

The people who “owned” these executed Africans were compensated in sugar for their loss.

July 27

St. Domingue – 1789

In Saint Domingue, news of the French Revolution of 1789 led the enslaved population to demand the rights proclaimed by the revolutionaries. When it became clear that there were no plans to apply the ideals of liberty, fraternity and equality to Africans, Toussaint L'Ouverture, led almost 400,000 slaves in a successful revolt against the French. Toussaint renamed the independent country Haiti.

July 28

West Indies/Caribbean- 1800s

Enslaved Africans on the plantations retaliated against slavery. Planters used both the law and violence to overpower the rebellious Africans. The King's troops would be called in to force rebels to surrender and receive His Majesty's pardon. Those who failed to obey the King's orders could expect to be tortured, burnt alive or executed if caught. Maroons – runaway Africans- were also transported to the British colony at Sierra Leone.

Emancipation

The struggle for freedom of enslaved Africans began in small resistance movements. After the passing of the Abolition of the Slave Trade Act in 1807, Africans became impatient for their freedom and took part in further revolts. They continued to rebel against their captors on many Caribbean islands until they achieved full emancipation in 1838.

July 29

St. Lucia

Near the end of the century, the French Revolution occurred. A revolutionary tribunal was sent to Saint Lucia, headed by captain La Crosse. Prior to this, the slaves had heard about the revolution and walked off their jobs in 1790-1 to work for themselves. Bringing the ideas of the revolution to Saint Lucia, La Crosse set up a guillotine used to execute Royalists. In 1794,

After the French Revolution, the French governor of the island of St. Lucia declared that all enslaved Africans were free. Shortly thereafter, the British invaded in response to the concerns of the wealthy plantation owners, who wanted to keep sugar production going. In 1795, a group of rebels, led by Victor Hugues, defeated a battalion of British troops and for the next four months, a group of recently freed Africans forced out not only the British army, but every white slave-owner from the island (coloured slave owners were left alone, as in Haiti). In 1796 Castries was burned as part of the conflict.

In 1803, the British finally regained control of the island and restored slavery. Many of the rebels escaped into the thick rain forests, where they evaded capture and established maroon communities.

The British abolished the African slave trade in 1807. They acquired Saint Lucia permanently in 1814 and it was not until 1834 that they abolished the institution of slavery. Even after abolition, all former enslaved Africans had to serve a four-year "apprenticeship," during which they had to work for free for their former masters for at least three-quarters of the work week. They achieved full freedom in 1838. By that time, people of African ethnicity greatly outnumbered those of ethnic European background. Some people of Carib descent also comprised a minority on the island.

July 30

Costa Rica

And I call: Maria and Petrona (Casta Nangu), Juan (caught by slavers Gasper de Acosta Arevalo and Juan Bautista de Retana), Augustina (Yoruba Casta Ana, also captured by Retana), Nicolas, Miguel, Felipe Cubero (from Congo). Antonia Cinitola (from Congo), Micaela (Yoruba Casta Ana), and Miguel Largo (Casta Mina from the upper West African slave coast). They, among others, survived the slave pens of West Africa and the horrific crossing of the Atlantic. They labored, loved, and died in Costa Rica – some gaining freedom, like Augustina, who was the first enslaved woman to appear in the Church register because she married Antonio García in 1733. They were both slaves of Don Juan Francisco de Ibarra.

Enslaved Africans in Costa Rica worked in three areas: on the cattle ranches of Nicoya; on the cacao plantations of Matina; and mostly in domestic servitude in colonial Cartago. Since colonial Costa Rica did not directly import Africans from West Africa, most of the enslaved Africans were brought into the country via Panama – Portobello was a major slave auction site – and along the coasts through smuggling and small purchases.

July 31

King Bayano

Panama is one of the first countries in the Americas to have Africans work as slaves. They were brought in by the Spanish to transport goods at long distances and work in gold mines in Veraguas and Darien. By 1531, the first slave rebellion had occurred in the country. Panama was home to one of the biggest slave markets in 1610 known as the House of Genovese.

In 1552, King Bayano was captured in his village in West Africa. He, along with other people from his village where he ruled, was taken to Panama in the slave trade.

While some sources indicate that Bayano traces to the Mandinka Muslim community of West Africa, another source indicates that he was of Yoruba origin, however, it is more possible that he was indeed a Mandinka king due to the fact that the Spanish and Portuguese first arrived in West Africa around the areas where the Mandinka lived.

The ship that carried King Bayano and 400 captives sank when it was close to Panama. The Africans escaped. They elected Bayano, who was already a royal, as their king and leader. He immediately trained them for war against the Spanish who were plotting to return them into slavery.

In 1552, King Bayano led what is now described as the largest rebellion in Panama now known as the Bayano Wars. He led his army to fight off the Spanish colonists.

August 1

Yaa Asantewaa
October 17, 1840 - October 17, 1921

Yaa Asantewaa was chosen by a number of regional kings to be the war-leader of the Asante fighting force. This is the only example of a woman being given such a role in Asante history.

Queen Mother Nana Yaa Asantewaa led an army of 5,000 warriors in the Ashanti-British "War of the Golden Stool."

Beginning in March 1900 Queen Asantewaa's army sieged the fort at Kumasi where the British had sought refuge. The Gold Coast governor eventually sent in an army of 14,000 to quell the rebellion. Queen Asantewaa and fifteen of her closest advisors were captured and exiled. This rebellion led by the Ashantis represented the final war in the Anglo-Asante series of wars that lasted throughout the 19th century.

On January 1, 1902 the British fully seized the land the Asante army had been defending from the British for almost a century, and the Asante Empire was made a slave state of the British Empire.

Asantewaa is seen by Ghanaians today as a queen mother who exercised her political and social leverage to help defend her kingdom

August 2

Charles A. "Chief" Anderson
February 9, 1907 - April 13, 1996

Charles Alfred Anderson, often called the "Father of Black Aviation," because of his training and mentoring of hundreds of African American pilots, was born in Bryn Mawr, Pennsylvania, a Philadelphia suburb.

Anderson earned the name "Chief" because he was the most ranked and experienced African American pilot before coming to Tuskegee Army Air Field (TAAF) in 1940. By that time he had amassed more than 3,000 hours of flight prompting most of his contemporaries and students to call him by that name as a sign of respect for his accomplishments. Anderson was also the Chief flight instructor for all cadets and flight instructors at Tuskegee, Alabama during World War II.

While growing up in Bryn Mawr, Anderson developed an interest in aviation. At the age of 22, he borrowed money from friends and relatives, bought a used airplane, and taught himself to fly. Anderson received a commercial pilot's license and air-transport pilot license becoming the first African-American to hold both certificates. In the same year he wed his childhood sweetheart, Gertrude Elizabeth Nelson. The couple had two sons.

August 3

Elizabeth Freeman
c.1744 - December 28, 1829

Elizabeth Freeman also known as Bet, Mum Bett, or MumBet, was the first enslaved African American to file and win a freedom suit in Massachusetts. The Massachusetts Supreme Judicial Court ruling, in Freeman's favor, found slavery to be inconsistent with the 1780 Massachusetts State Constitution. Her suit, Brom and Bett v. Ashley (1781), was cited in the Massachusetts Supreme Judicial Court appellate review of Quock Walker's freedom suit. When the court upheld Walker's freedom under the state's constitution, the ruling was considered to have implicitly ended slavery in Massachusetts.

Freeman did not write the language of the dominant group and left no written records of her life. Her early history has been pieced together from the writings of contemporaries to whom she told her story or who heard it indirectly, as well as from historical records: "Any time, any time while I was a slave, if one minute's freedom had been offered to me, and I had been told I must die at the end of that minute, I would have taken it—just to stand one minute on God's airth [sic] a free woman— I would." —
Elizabeth Freeman

August 4

Clement Coxsone Dodd
January 26, 1932 - May 4, 2004

Clement "Sir Coxsone" Dodd is the pioneering producer of Jamaican music associated most readily with roots reggae, although he was active in the development of sound system, as well as in ska and rocksteady. He was an integral part of the careers of nearly every major reggae artist, but is best known for having been the first to record Bob Marley and the Wailers at his Studio One.

Born in Kingston, Jamaica, Dodd got his start in music thanks to his parents. His father was a contractor and mason whose projects included building the Carib Theatre in Jamaica. He also reportedly worked on the docks, which enabled him to obtain recordings from crews on transient ships docked in port. Dodd's mother ran a restaurant in Kingston and his parents also owned a liquor store, where he played American jazz records for customers.

When Dodd finished school he emigrated to the United States, where he worked as a temporary sugar cane cutter in Florida. It was during this time that he was introduced to R&B music and, after a trip to Harlem, New York, amassed more records for his growing collection, just in time for the birth of sound system in Jamaica.

August 5

Constance Baker Motley
September 14, 1921 - September 28, 2005

Constance Baker Motley as a lawyer was a key strategist in the African-American civil rights movement. She was a judge, a New York State Senator representing the 21st District of Brooklyn, and the first African American woman in the Senate, and elected the first woman to serve as Borough President of Manhattan, New York City.

Motley was a member of the team of National Association for the Advancement of Colored People (NAACP) lawyers who brought their training and passion to fight discrimination to work for many African Americans who needed legal representation. She was the first African American woman to argue a case before the U.S. Supreme Court, securing James Meredith's right to attend the University of Mississippi.

Motley served as Chief Judge and a Senior Judge of the United States District Court for the Southern District of New York 1980s to 2005.

Born to Rachel Huggins and McCullough Alva Baker who were immigrants from the Caribbean island Nevis, Motley's interest in becoming a lawyer was sparked when she was a child and had been denied access to a public facility because she was Black.

Motley graduated from Columbia Law School with a Bachelors of Laws and did her undergraduate work at Fisk University a Historically Black College in Tennessee and at New York University.

August 6

Thales Brantley, August 7, 1920 – June 1, 2010
Martha Brantley, January 12, 1928 – April 2, 2009
Contributor: Rev. Reginald Brantley, Esq., M.Div.

My father and mother, Thales and Martha, were patterns which God used, along with other forces, to mold me into the man I am. They descended from giants. I recognize the power of the life-force their ancestors had upon them, their siblings, my siblings, my cousins and me.

Their ancestors were giants because they descended from the noble blood of enslaved Africans who never lost hope that they or their descendants would one day be free. They survived the times of terror of the Ku Klux Klan and lynchings. They preserved their dignity in the emasculating obscenity of Jim Crow society in the South. They answered the call of this country to fight in World War I, World War II, and Korea. Their service and sacrifice were mirrored in that of my brothers and cousins in Vietnam and my nephews in Afghanistan and Iraq.

Thales and Martha were giants because they worked hard to care and provide for their family. My father was a straight A student who dropped out of school to go to work when his father died. He completed an equivalency diploma when I was in high school. Thales was the gift of a *good example* to me and my siblings.

I watched Thales and Martha live in gentleness, an attitude of giving, selflessness, and humility. Their humility was grounded in strength. I came to understand that their strength was grounded in their faith in the Lord Jesus Christ. They were giants in faith and in the love they gave to their children and grandchildren. I am privileged to have lived in their presence and received air from the force of their spirits.

August 7

Walter Francis White
July 1, 1893 - March 21, 1955

Walter Francis White was an African-American civil rights activist who led the National Association for the Advancement of Colored People (NAACP) for almost a quarter of a century, 1929–1955, after joining the organization as an investigator. He directed a broad program of legal challenges to racial segregation and disfranchisement. He was also a journalist, novelist, and essayist. He graduated in 1916 from Atlanta University (now Clark Atlanta University), a Historically Black College.

White oversaw the plans and organizational structure of the fight against public segregation. He worked with President Truman on desegregating the armed forces after the Second World War and gave him a draft for the Executive Order to implement this. Under White's leadership, the NAACP set up its Legal Defense Fund, which conducted numerous legal challenges to segregation and disfranchisement, and achieved many successes. Among these was the Supreme Court ruling in Brown v. Board of Education (1954), which determined that segregated education was inherently unequal.

Born of African and European ancestry, White had physical features that showed the latter. He emphasized in his autobiography, *A Man Called White* (p. 3): "I am a Negro. My skin is white, my eyes are blue, my hair is blond. The traits of my race are nowhere visible upon me."

August 8

Maria L. de Hernández

July 29, 1896 – January 8, 1986

María Rebecca Latigo de Hernández was a Mexican-American rights activist. She was born in San Pedro Garza García, Mexico. During the 1930s, she spoke publicly and demonstrated on behalf of Mexican Americans about their education in the United States. She and her husband, Pedro Hernandez Barrera, founded Orden Caballeros de America on January 10, 1929. She organized the Asociación Protectora de Madres in 1933. In 1970 she was active in the Raza Unida Party.

María Rebecca Latigo de Hernández was born in 1896 in Garza García near Monterrey, Nuevo León, Mexico. Her father was a professor. As a young adult, she taught at an elementary school whilst she lived in Monterrey, Mexico.

The Hernández family owned and ran a grocery store and bakery. She fought and wrote against the segregation, racial oppression, and poor education that the Mexican American children were receiving.

In 1929, the Hernández family helped to organize and found the Order of the Knights of America, or the Orden Caballeros de America. The Order of Knights of America was a committee dedicated to political and civil activists in order to help Mexican Americans as well as Mexican immigrants. They helped with matters including educational and social, but the organization was largely focused on educational matters. The main audience targeted by their organization was Mexican American business owners. However, they also set a goal to help both male and female school aged children.

August 9

Inkosi Albert John Luthuli
c. 1898 – 21 July 1967

Inkosi Albert John Luthuli is also known by his Zulu name Mvumbi and was a South African teacher, activist, Nobel Peace Prize winner, and politician.

Luthuli was elected president of the African National Congress (ANC) in 1952. At this time, it was an umbrella organisation that led opposition to the white minority government in South Africa. Luthuli served then ANC until his death.

Awarded the 1960 Nobel Peace Prize for his role in the non-violent struggle against apartheid, Luthuli was the first person of African heritage to receive this Prize.

Luthuli was a lay preacher of the United Congregational Church of Southern Africa (UCCSA) based at its Groutville Congregational Church in Stanger, KwaZulu-Natal, where Luthuli was laid to rest.

August 10

Edgar Daniel Nixon

July 12, 1899 - February 25, 1987

Edgar Daniel Nixon, known as E. D. Nixon, was an African-American civil rights leader and union organizer in Alabama who played a crucial role in organizing the landmark Montgomery bus boycott there in 1955. The boycott highlighted the issues of segregation in the South, was upheld for more than a year by Black residents, and nearly brought the city-owned bus system to bankruptcy. It ended in December 1956, after the United States Supreme Court ruled in the related case, Browder v. Gayle (1956), that the local and state laws were unconstitutional, and ordered the state to end bus segregation.

After working in a train station baggage room, Nixon rose to become a Pullman car porter, which was a well-respected position with good pay. He traveled around the country and worked steadily. In 1928, he joined the new union, the Brotherhood of Sleeping Car Porters, helping organize its branch in Montgomery. He also served as its president. A

Nixon also served as president of the local chapter of the National Association for the Advancement of Colored People (NAACP), the Montgomery Welfare League, and the Montgomery Voters League.

As a child, Nixon received 16 months of formal education, as Black students were ill-served in the segregated public school system.

August 11

Harriette Vyda Simms Moore
June 19, 1902 – January 3, 1952

Harriette Vyda Simms Moore was an American educator and civil rights worker. She was the wife of Harry T. Moore, who founded the first branch of the National Association for the Advancement of Colored People (NAACP) in Brevard County, Florida. The murder of Harriette and Harry is believed to be first assassination to happen during the civil rights movement, and also to be the only time a husband and wife were both killed for their activism.

Simms attended the segregated Daytona Normal Industrial Institute in Daytona Beach, Florida. She later graduated from Bethune-Cookman College, a Historically Black College in Daytona Beach, with an Associate of Arts degree and a Bachelor of Science degree in 1950.

Simms taught elementary school classes for many years, in Merritt Island and Mims in Brevard County, and in Lake Park, Florida until her death. While teaching in Mims, Simms helped to cook lunch every day for the students.

August 12

Harry Tyson Moore

November 18, 1905 - December 25, 1951

Harry Tyson Moore was an African-American educator, a pioneer leader of the civil rights movement, founder of the first branch of the National Association for the Advancement of Colored People (NAACP) in Brevard County, Florida, and president of the state chapter of the NAACP.

Harry T. Moore and his wife, Harriette Moore, also an educator, were the victims of a bombing of their home in Mims, Florida, on Christmas night 1951. As the local hospital in Titusville would not treat Blacks, he died on the way to the nearest hospital that would treat Blacks. That hospital was in Sanford, Florida, and about 30 miles from where Moore sustained injuries. His wife died from her wounds nine days later at the same hospital. The bombing of their home followed their both having been fired from teaching because of their activism.

Moore also led the Progressive Voters League. Through his leadership there was a significant increase in the registration of Black voters in Florida.

August 13

Marvel Jackson Cooke
April 4, 1903 - November 29, 2000

Marvel Jackson Cooke was a pioneering American journalist, writer, and civil rights activist. She was the first African-American woman to work at a mainstream white-owned newspaper.

Marvel Jackson was the first Black child to be born in Mankato, Minnesota. Her parents were Madison Jackson and Amy Wood Jackson. Her father was an Ohio State University law school graduate who was the first Black member of the South Dakota Bar, but was unable to find employment as a Black lawyer. Her mother once lived on a Native American reservation as a cook and cooking teacher. Amy Wood Jackson left her position on the reservation in South Dakota due to witnessing too much unfair treatment of the Native Americans there. After leaving her cooking job, she became a homemaker and was a mother full-time for Marvel and her three sisters.

Marvel experienced racial discrimination from a young age. When her family moved to upper-class, white neighborhood in Minneapolis, residents demonstrated on the family's lawn.

While enrolled in college, Marvel took a government examination to qualify for a position as a Spanish translator for the War Department. Her score qualified her for hire, but her boss gave her a job as a file clerk telling her the translation department was not yet established. Cooke later found out that the department was established with only white women on staff. With help from her political connections Marvel was reassigned to the translation department.

August 14

James Luther Bevel
October 19, 1936 - December 19, 2008

James Luther Bevel was a minister and a leader of the Civil Rights Movement in the United States. As the Director of Direct Action and of Nonviolent Education of the Southern Christian Leadership Conference (SCLC), he initiated, strategized, directed, and developed SCLC's three major successes of the era: the 1963 Birmingham Children's Crusade, the 1965 Selma voting rights movement, and the 1966 Chicago open housing movement. He suggested that SCLC call for and join a March on Washington in 1963. Bevel strategized the 1965 Selma to Montgomery marches, which contributed to Congressional passage of the 1965 Voting Rights Act.

Bevel's last major action was as co-initiator of the 1995 Day of Atonement/Million Man March in Washington, DC. For his work Bevel has been called a father of voting rights, the strategist and architect of the 1960s Civil Rights Movement, and half of the first-tier team that formulated many of the strategies and actions to gain federal legislation and social changes during the 1960s civil rights era.

Bevel was born in 1936 in Itta Bena, Mississippi, the son of Illie and Dennis Bevel. He was one of seventeen children. He grew up in rural LeFlore County of the Mississippi Delta and in Cleveland. He worked on a cotton plantation for a time as a youth and later in a steel mill. He was educated at segregated local schools in Mississippi and in Cleveland, Ohio. After high school he served in the U.S. Navy.

August 15

James H. Cone
1938 – 2018

James H. Cone is known as the founder of Black Liberation Theology. He served as Bill and Judith Moyers Distinguished Professor of Systematic Theology at Union Theological Seminary.

Cone was an ordained minister in the African Methodist Episcopal Church. It was the northern riots and Stokely Carmichael's (Kwame Ture) call for "Black Power!" during the Meredith March in Mississippi that led him to a crisis in faith. And it was the voice of Malcolm X that first made James Cone question his theology. Malcolm X proclaimed loudly that "Christianity is a white man's religion," and said that Blacks should adopt an understanding of God that grew out of their own history and experience. He railed against a blond-haired, blue-eyed Jesus and a belief in the delayed rewards of heaven.

"For me, the burning theological question was, how can I reconcile Christianity and Black Power, Martin Luther King, Jr.'s idea of nonviolence, and Malcolm X's 'by any means necessary philosophy?'" (Preface to *Black Theology and Black Power*, p. viii.)

Cone received a Master of Divinity degree from Garrett Theological Seminary and an M.A. and Ph.D. (1965) from Northwestern University. His works include: *Black Theology & Black Power* (1969) and *A Black Theology of Liberation* (1970), *God of the Oppressed* (1975), *Martin & Malcolm & America: A Dream or a Nightmare?* (1991), and *The Cross and the Lynching Tree* (2011).

August 16

Gladstone Delroy Rudolph Scarlett

June 26 1924 - October 4, 1995

Contributor: Jasmin Pitter, Natural Therapeutics

My father, Gladstone Scarlett was born in St. James, Jamaica West Indies. After completing his high school education at Cornwall College in Jamaica, he enrolled with the Royal Air Force (RAF), this was during the time of World War II. Jamaica, because it was a British colony and like other British colonies, was immediately involved with the war. Scarlett was the recipient of many medals for his military service.

After returning from the war, Scarlett moved to Kingston, Jamaica and joined the Jamaica Fire Department. Whenever time permitted, he took my siblings and me on Fire Boat to the high seas where he showed us what it was like to be fearless. He was elevated to the rank of officer upon his retirement.

Scarlett married my mother Lucille Mae Marshall and they raised 11 children, nine boys and two girls. His legacy lives on through many grandchildren and great grandchildren with vision, formal education and training, and service to family, community, and country, and good work ethics. We are represented in various facets of life including: decorated military, medical doctor, naturopaths, economist, business owners, accountants, lawyer, engineers, and teachers.

Fond memories on my father include his punctuality wherever he went. Tardiness was not in his DNA. He inspired us to care for ourselves, making sure our appearance was neat and he set the example for that.

His values have left indelible marks on us as we instill them in our children and share them with people who find themselves in our orbit. He was gently in spirit.

August 17

National/International Holiday

Garveyites have long called for August 17 to be a national/international holiday for all Africans. Recognizing all Garveyites who are now among our ancestors.

MAN KNOW THYSELF:" *For man to know himself is for him to feel that for him there is no human master. For him Nature is his servant, and whatsoever he wills in Nature, that shall be his reward. If he wills to be a pigmy, a serf or a slave, that shall he be. If he wills to be a real man in possession of the things common to man, then he shall be his own sovereign.*

"When man fails to grasp his authority he sinks to the level of the lower animals, and whatsoever the real man bids him do, even as if it were of the lower animals, that much shall he do." – *Philosophy and Opinions of Marcus Garvey*

August 18

Frederick Nathaniel "Toots" Hibbert

1950 – 2020

Frederick Nathaniel "Toots" Hibbert was the lead singer and songwriter of Toots and the Maytals and one of reggae's foundational figures.

Hibbert's soulful, electrifying performances thrilled live music lovers for more than 50 years and brought a distinctive Jamaican expression to international audiences. His 1968 song *Do The Reggay* gave a name to Jamaica's signature beat, but his artistry defied boundaries. His vocals are an amalgam of rousing gospel, vintage soul, gritty R&B, and classic country fused with pliant, indigenous Jamaican rhythms. Hibbert brought his guttural voice and that liberating reggae rhythm to Otis Redding's standard (*I've Got*) *Dreams to Remember*, he transformed Ann Peebles' *I Can't Stand The Rain* into a serenade *Love the Rain*, and forever altered John Denver's *Country Roads* into a beloved sing-along reggae anthem *Take Me Home Country Roads*. .

Hibbert's humble demeanor and affable personality belied his towering global stature. Regarded as a national treasure in Jamaica, in 2012 he was conferred the Order of Jamaica, the country's fifth highest honor.

Hibbert was born in Clarendon, Jamaica. His parents were preachers and he was raised singing gospel in what he calls "a salvation church." The hand clapping, foot stomping, and soul-shaking vocals associated with Jamaica's Afro-Christian religious traditions, including Revival Zion and Pocomania, were essential in shaping Hibbert's performances. Hibbert also cites Elvis Presley, gospel icon Mahalia Jackson, and soul superstars James Brown, Wilson Pickett and Otis Redding as influences.

https://www.npr.org/2020/09/12/912245520/toots-hibbert-reggae-ambassador-and-leader-of-toots-and-the-maytals-dies-at-77

August 19

Ellis Louis Marsalis Jr.
November 14, 1934 - April 1, 2020

Ellis Louis Marsalis Jr. was an American jazz pianist and educator. Active since the late 1940s, Marsalis came to greater attention in the 1980s and 1990s as the patriarch of the musical Marsalis family, when sons Branford and Wynton became popular musicians.

Born in New Orleans, Louisiana, Marsalis was the son of Florence Marie (née Robertson) and Ellis Marsalis Sr., a businessman and social activist. Marsalis and his wife Dolores Ferdinand Marsalis had six sons: Branford, Wynton, Ellis III, Delfeayo, Mboya, and Jason. Branford, Wynton, Delfeayo, and Jason also became jazz musicians. Ellis III is a poet and photographer.

Marsalis played saxophone during high school but switched to piano while studying classical music at Dillard University, graduating in 1955. He later attended graduate school at Loyola University New Orleans. In the 1950s and 1960s he worked with Ed Blackwell, Cannonball Adderley, Nat Adderley, and Al Hirt. During the 1970s, he taught at the New Orleans Center for Creative Arts. His students have included Terence Blanchard, Harry Connick Jr., Donald Harrison, Kent Jordan, Marlon Jordan, and Nicholas Payton.

August 20
The Global Struggle for Equality

It is important to understand the Civil Rights movement in the U.S. in the context of worldwide struggles for equality for working Black people, whether from colonial control in the Caribbean and the African continent or racist regimes like the apartheid government in South Africa and other parts of Africa.

August 21

West Indians in the U.S.A.

Among the most prominent non-U.S. "African-Americans" are African peoples who were born in the West Indian and emigrated to the US.

The West Indian, Caribbean, presence in and contributions to American culture and politics began with the start of their (mass) emigration to the US in the early 1900s. For all our pioneering ancestors who contributed in their unique and unheralded ways for creating a better life for all Africans in the US.

African Americans – people of African ancestry who are born in the Americas.

August 22

W.I. Contributions

In 1920, at the start of the era known as the Harlem Renaissance, more than 50% of the Black population of that neighborhood--the center of Black life in the U.S. at the time--was born in the West Indies. Most of these immigrants came from Jamaica, with significant numbers from other Angolophone islands like Trinidad and Tobago and Barbados.

Both of former Attorney General Eric Holder's parents have roots in the West Indies; his father was born in Barbados, and his mother's parents immigrated from there.

Earl G. Graves, Sr., the founder of *Black Enterprise* magazine, was born in 1935 to West Indian parents. He later became an aide to Senator Robert Kennedy and a successful businessman. Graves' philanthropic work involves promoting higher education and entrepreneurship among African-Americans.

August 23

Wenceslaus Hollar July 13, 1607 - March 16th, 1677
7th Great Grandfather Wenceslaus Hollar

Contributor: Leighton Hollar - Author, Poet, Community Activist

The following biography of Hollar was written by one of his contemporaries, John Aubrey (1626–1697). "Hollar was a teacher of drawing to the Prince of Wales in 1640. He fought on the King's side, but was captured by Parliament and escaped to Antwerp. In 1652 he returned to England. He was appointed His Majesty's Designer in 1660.

"Before the introduction of photography, picture painting and engraving were important professions. Hollar's work was exceptional, of which 2733 examples are enumerated. He made copies of famous paintings, illustrating books, executed a fine map of London after the Fire of 1666, illustrated the coronation of Charles II and engraved a series of pictures of women's costumes, which have proved invaluable to historians.

"Hollar's father was a Protestant Knight of The Empire who forfeited his estates, and was ruined by the Roman Catholiques when Prague was captured in the Thirty Years War.

"He told me that when he was a school-boy he took a delight in drawing of maps; but was designed by his father to have been a lawyer, and was put to that profession, when his father's troubles, together with the wars, forced him to leave his country of Bohemia. So that what he did, for his delight and recreation as a boy, proved to be his lively hood when a man."
("Compiled by many biographers, but John Aubrey was his contemporary and I think knew him best,' reports Leighton Hollar on Aubrey.)

August 24

Phyllis Wheatley
May 8, 1753 – December 5, 1784

As a young member of the Old South Congregational Church, Phyllis Wheatley is credited as the first published African American author – in 1773. It would not be far-fetched to say that the white Congregationalists, many of whom were abolitionist, assisted Wheatley in making her *Poems on Various Subjects* possible.

Wheatley gained her freedom from slavery soon after the publication of her work.

Wheatley was kidnapped from West Africa and enslaved in Boston, where she was purchased by John Wheatley as a personal servant to his wife. The Wheatleys educated Wheatley and she mastered Latin and Greek, going on to write highly acclaimed poetry

After Wheatley was freed from slavery, she married and struggled financially and was unable to find a publisher for her second volume of poems.

Wheatley was born in Senegal/Gambia around 1753.

August 25

Alice Moore Dunbar-Nelson
1875 -1935

Alice Moore Dunbar-Nelson was a poet, essayist, diarist, and activist born in New Orleans, Louisiana, to mixed-race parents.

Her African American, Anglo, Native American, and Creole heritage contributed to her complex understandings of gender, race, and ethnicity, subjects she often addressed in her work. She graduated from Straight University (now Dillard University) and taught in the New Orleans public schools.

Dunbar-Nelson's first book, *Violets and Other Tales* (1895), was published when she was 20. Her second collection, *The Goodness of St. Rocque and Other Stories* (1899) explored the lives of creole and anglicized characters. Works exploring racism and racial oppression were largely rejected by publishers during her lifetime.

Dunbar-Nelson organized for the women's suffrage movement in the Mid-Atlantic States and was a field representative for the Woman's Committee of the Council of Defense in 1918. She campaigned for the passage of the Dyer Anti-Lynching Bill of 1924, and in her later years she published poetry in Black newspapers such as the *Crisis, Ebony and Topaz,* and *Opportunity.*

August 26

Richard Claxton Gregory
October 12, 1932 - August 19, 2017

“I've always been insulted when people tell me that my humor has done a lot for race relations. I never thought comedy did anything but make uncomfortable people feel comfortable.” —Dick Gregory

Richard Claxton Gregory, known as Dick Gregory was a pioneering comedian and civil rights activist who took on race with layered, nuanced humor during the turbulent 1960s.

Gregory got a big break performing as a stand-up comedian at the Playboy Club in the early 1960s. Known for his sophisticated, layered humor that took on racial issues of the day, Gregory became a comedy headliner and a trailblazer for other African American comedians including Richard Pryor and Bill Cosby. He also participated as an activist in the Civil Rights Movement and eventually ran for political office. In his later years, he worked as a lecturer and pursued his interests in health and fitness.

August 27

Calypso

Calypsos are musical renditions having their origins in the West African griot tradition. Originally called "Kaiso" in Trinidad and Tobago, these songs, based on West African Yoruba, Ewe-Fon and Akan musical beats, were sung by enslaved Africans and later former enslaved Africans primarily in Trinidad and Tobago during recreation time and about a host of topics – their land of origin, social relationships on the plantations and the lives of community members, including plantation managers, overseers and owners.

Calypso speaks and sings of social commentaries dealing with politics and community issues and the humorous stories of real or imagined experiences created to make the audience laugh.

August 28

Bruce McMarion Wright

December 19, 1917 - March 24, 2005

Bruce McMarion Wright (born Marion Bruce Wright, was an American jurist who served on the New York State Supreme Court. Judge Wright was also the father of Geoffrey D.S. Wright, a New York State Supreme Court Justice, and Keith L.T. Wright, a member of the New York State Assembly.

Born in Baltimore, Maryland, raised in Princeton, New Jersey, Wright spent the majority of his adult life living in Harlem, New York.

Wright was awarded a scholarship to attend Princeton University, but denied admission when he arrived and the Dean of Admissions learned that he was Black. Wright was denied admission to Notre Dame on the same grounds. He studied at Virginia Union University, and graduated from Lincoln University in 1942.

Wright served in a U.S. Army segregated medical unit during World War II and received the Purple Heart with Oak Leaf Cluster. After the war, he travelled to Paris, where he met Senegalese poet Leopold Senghor who later became the president of Senegal.

Wright had ambitions of being a poet (*From the Shaken Tower*, edited by Langston Hughes, 1944) and a doctor. He was unable, however, to make an incision on an anesthetized rabbit during a premedical course and thus decided to study law. He studied at Fordham University Law School, and obtained his law degree from New York Law School.

Wright was a maverick. Called Turn-Em-Loose-Bruce by his detractors, but affectionately so by those who understood the inherent racism in the US justice system, Judge Bruce Wright used his position in New York City's criminal court to right the wrongs of the system against Africans and the poor whose cases came to his courtroom. His book *Black Robes, White Justice* (1987) is a must-read.

August 29

Helen M. Marshall
September 30, 1929 - March 4, 2017

Helen M. Marshall was an American politician from New York City who was the first African American Borough President of Queens from 2002-13. Before being elected to the office of Borough President, Marshall served as a political and community activist in for about 50 years in the Corona-East Elmhurst, Queens community.

Marshall was born in the Bronx to parents who were immigrants of African descent from British Guiana (now Guyana).

She graduated with a B.A. in education from CUNY Queens College. She was a teacher for eight years. In 1969, she left teaching to become the first Director of the Langston Hughes Library in Queens. She was married to Donald Marshall until his death; they had two children, Donald Jr. and Agnes Marie. She entered politics as a Democrat. She was a member of the New York State Assembly for eight years and a member of the New York City Council for ten.

Marshall was elected as Borough President of Queens in November 2001, to succeed the term-limited Claire Shulman.

As Borough President, Marshall made marketing Queens as a tourist destination one of her priorities. She served three terms and influenced health care, education, housing and new park projects in the borough.

August 30

Noel Dexter
1938 - 2019

Reflecting on the life Jamaican musicologist, composer and director Mr. Noel Dexter took us to the following comment made by late United States President Harry Truman: "In reading the lives of great men I found that the first victory they won was over themselves... self-discipline, with all of them, came first."

Mr. Dexter's achievements are no doubt the outcome of enormous self-discipline. It takes a steady focus and dedication to one's craft to produce the type of work he did.

His arrangement of Psalm 150 — O Praise Ye The Lord — as well as his composition of the Jamaican Christmas song, Sing De Chorus, contributed to his status as a legend in local music. It was therefore fitting that he was the recipient of many accolades, among them the Silver Musgrave Medal and the Order of Distinction from the Government of Jamaica.

Dexter was the University Singers' musical director and conductor for near half a century. Throughout that time he shaped the choir into one of the finest in the Caribbean, while nurturing and developing the musical talents of many Jamaicans.

Dexter was born and grew up in Port Antonio, Portland, where his interest in music piqued when he was about ten years old when he returned home to see a piano his father had bought.

Note from Claudette Joy Spence: Noel Dexter taught art and music at Ardenne High School and he was my art teacher when I was in first form at Ardenne.

August 31

Sherona Hall
April 26, 1948 - December 30, 2006

Sherona Hall, along with Dudley Laws, was a co-founder of Toronto's Black Action Defence Committee in response to police shootings of Black people.

Over the years, Hall at various times turned her talent for organizing to protests.

Hall was involved in the freedom struggles in Mozambique, Guinea-Bissau, Zimbabwe; the struggle against apartheid in South Africa, protesting the murders by the racist regime of people in the South African towns of Soweto and Sharpeville.

She also worked against and protested police killings in Toronto.

Les Hart, a Toronto resident and former electoral candidate for the People's National Party in Jamaica, remembers campaigning with Hall in deep rural areas during election campaigns in the 1960s and 1970s.

Sherona Hall was a product of the Democratic Socialist movement led by Michael Manley in Jamaica in the late 1960s.

September 1

Theodore Roosevelt Mason Howard
March 4, 1908 - May 1, 1976

Theodore Roosevelt Mason Howard was an American civil rights leader, fraternal organization leader, entrepreneur and surgeon. He was among the mentors to activists such as Medgar Evers, Charles Evers, Fannie Lou Hamer, Amzie Moore, Aaron Henry, and Jesse Jackson.

Howard founded Mississippi's leading civil rights organization in the 1950s, the Regional Council of Negro Leadership and he played a prominent role in the investigation of the kidnapping and murder of Emmett Till in the late 1950s. He was also president of the National Medical Association, chairman of the board of the National Negro Business League, and a leading national advocate of African-American businesses.

Howard was born in 1908 in Murray, Kentucky to Arthur Howard, a tobacco twister, and Mary Chandler, a cook for Will Mason, a prominent local white doctor and member of the Seventh-day Adventist Church. Mason took note of the boy's work habits, talent, ambition, and charm. He put him to work in his hospital and eventually paid for much of his medical education. Howard later showed his gratitude by adding Mason as one of his middle names.

September 2

Quilombismo

In 1980, Abdias do Nascimento, one of Brazil's greatest Black activists and intellectuals, published an essay titled *Quilombismo: An Afro-Brazilian Political Alternative*. Based on his address to the Second Congress of African Culture in the Americas, the essay was a sweeping declaration of Black rights, asserting "the urgent necessity of Black people to defend their survival and assure their very existence as human beings."

He strategically called this ideology "quilombismo," a derivative of the term "quilombos," which refers to the communities of escaped African who were enslaved in Brazil from the early 16th century to 1888. Similar communities with different names were found throughout the Americas: palenques, cimarrones, and maroons. Quilombismo, then, is an ideology based on an understanding of quilombos as historical beacons of democracy and equality. By offering an alternative to captivity, quilombos allowed Africans to recover their liberty and human dignity by organizing their own viable free societies.

September 3

Amelia Isadora Platts Boynton Robinson

August 18, 1911 - August 26, 2015

Amelia Isadora Platts Boynton Robinson was an African American activist who was a leader of the American Civil Rights Movement in Selma, Alabama, and a key figure in the 1965 Selma to Montgomery marches. In 1984, she became founding vice-president of the Schiller Institute affiliated with Lyndon LaRouche. She was awarded the Martin Luther King Jr. Freedom Medal in 1990.

Amelia Isadora Platts was born in Savannah, Georgia, to George and Anna Eliza (née Hicks) Platts, both of whom were African-American. She also had Cherokee and German ancestry.

Attending church was central to Robinson and her nine siblings. As a young girl, she became involved in campaigning for women's suffrage. Her family encouraged the children to read. Robinson attended Georgia State Industrial College for Colored Youth (now Savannah State University, a Historically Black College)and Tuskegee Institute (now Tuskegee University), earning a degree in home economics in 1927. She also studied at Tennessee State, Virginia State, and Temple University.)

Robinson taught in Georgia before starting with the U.S. Department of Agriculture (USDA) in Selma as the home demonstration agent for Dallas County. She educated the county's largely rural population about food production and processing, nutrition, healthcare, and other subjects related to agriculture and homemaking.

September 4

Victoria and Griffiths Mxenge

Victoria and Griffiths Mxenge, of South Africa, were well-known civil-rights lawyers who took on the cases of political freedom fighters across all political parties, and fought for youths who had been mistreated during imprisonment. As intelligent, well-educated people they were seen as great threats by the apartheid government.

Griffiths was convicted under the Suppression of Communism Act and sent to Robben Island after having been detained by police for 190 days. He survived his incarceration and continued his fight for South Africa's freedom until 1981, when he was abducted, stabbed, and hammered to death. Victoria was murdered four years later in the driveway of her home as her children witnessed the attack.

In 2006, Victoria Mxenge was posthumously awarded the Order of Luthuli in Silver for her excellent contribution to the field of law and sacrifices made in the fight against apartheid and oppression in South Africa.

September 5

Hector Pieterson

The image of a dying 12-year-old Hector Pieterson being carried by a crying youth during the Soweto uprising in 1976 shocked the world, and still stands as a stark reminder of South Africa's apartheid legacy.

Pieterson was a child with no political affiliation, who joined an initially peaceful crowd in protest against the Bantu Education Act. The poignant and deeply telling photograph that captured his last moments has been reproduced thousands of times across the globe in memory of his unjust and untimely death. The young man holding Pieterson, Mbuyisa Makhubo, was so harassed by security police after the photo was published that he fled South Africa.

September 6

Paul Bartholomew

Paul Bartholomew (R), Bekeo Adigun
Contributor: Bekeo Adigun – (Son)

Emerging in my Black consciousness started when I was three years old. One afternoon, in 1965, while coming from town in Grenada with my mom, we saw my father Paul Bartholomew burning his books.

"What are you doing Dad?" I asked.

"I am burning all my Bibles and other religious books. Churches," he said, " was given to us to make us good slaves. Religion will destroy our families and people. That was the best way to keep our people enslaved; imposing on us their religion."

It was on early Sunday mornings that my dad and I had our educational walks. At that time he would explain the suffering and fights our people have been going through with the plantation owners.

I was nine years old in 1971 when Brother Maurice Bishop took up leadership of the New Jewel Movement. My father was with him. It was also around that time that we had a food shortage in the country. Dad said to us if there is a food shortage in the country we will grow our own food. We did.

We needed our road fixed and bridge to be built. Dad organized to get that done. I was involved bringing water to help the men mix the concrete.

When Dad returned to Grenada from the US to bring my three siblings and me to the USA the conversations he had with us was a major learning experience. He told me we are African Americans. We are born on continent of America and we are Africans. It was also at that time he introduced me to the works of Marcus Garvey and building for ourselves. I was 15 years of age. I have been a Garveyite since.

September 7

Myrtle C. Ferguson
1923 - 2015

Myrtle C. Ferguson was born in Brandon Hill, St. Andrew, Jamaica to Elias and Susan Williams. She was an advocate for people who did not know how to access socio-economic opportunities that frequently were not available in their communities.

A strong advocate for education Ma Fergs, as she was affectionately called, guided many children in Kingston and St. Andrew to succeed in the academic arena. This often resulted in their professional success. She helped many too to lay the foundation for financial and economic viability when they purchased their first home in Jamaica with her guidance.

September 8

Don West
June 6, 1906 - September 29, 1992

Don West (born Donald Lee West) was an American writer, poet, educator, trade union organizer, civil-rights activist and a co-founder of the Highlander Folk School.

West was born in Georgia, the child of North Georgia sharecroppers. In high school he led a protest against an on-campus showing of the film *The Birth of a Nation* and was eventually expelled for other conflicts. He was also expelled from Lincoln Memorial University, in Harrogate, Tennessee, for leading another protest against the paternalism of the campus. He returned and graduated in 1929.

West went on to study under Alva Taylor and Willard Uphaus at the Vanderbilt Divinity School in Nashville and was influenced by the Social Gospel movement. He became a Socialist and participated in labor strikes in textile factories and coal mines. Like his eventual collaborator Myles Horton, he travelled to Denmark to tour the Danish folk schools that promoted adult education and community engagement. Upon their return, Horton and West co-founded the Highlander Folk School in Monteagle, Tennessee. West stayed there only a year, before leaving to found his own Southern Folk School and Libraries in Kennesaw, Georgia.

He devoted himself to writing, lectures, and social causes. These included the defense of Angelo Herndon. He was an organizational director of the Kentucky Workers Alliance. He worked in churches in Ohio and Georgia, taught and became a public school superintendent, and joined the faculty of Oglethorpe University in Atlanta. Forced to leave Oglethorpe during the period of Red-baiting, he continued to edit religious publications and teach creative writing.

In the 1940s, his collection of poetry, *Clods of Southern Earth*, became a literary phenomenon.

September 9

Angelo Braxton Herndon
May 6, 1913 - December 9, 1997

Angelo Braxton Herndon, born in Wyoming, Ohio, was an African-American labor organizer arrested and convicted of insurrection after attempting to organize Black and white industrial workers in 1932 in Atlanta, Georgia. The prosecution case rested heavily on Herndon's possession of communist literature which police found in his hotel room.

As a youth, Herndon was introduced to the Communist Manifesto by a white worker in the Unemployed Councils. He was impressed with the Communist Party's campaigning in the South to promote labor reform and interracial cooperation, and its teachings on racial equality and class conflict. He joined the party in 1930.

Herndon was defended by the International Labor Defense, the legal arm of the Communist Party, which hired two young local attorneys, Benjamin J. Davis Jr. and John H. Geer, and provided guidance. Over a five-year period, Herndon's case twice reached the United States Supreme Court, which ruled that Georgia's insurrection law was unconstitutional, as it violated First Amendment rights of free speech and assembly. Herndon became nationally prominent because of his case, and Southern justice was under review. By the end of the 1940s he left the Communist Party, moved to the Midwest and lived a non-public life.

September 10

Nellie Saunders Stone Allen Johnson
December 17, 1905 - April 2, 2002

Nellie Saunders Stone Allen Johnson was an American civil rights activist and union organizer. She was the first Black elected official in Minneapolis and shaped Minnesota politics for 70 years.

Johnson helped form the Minnesota Democratic–Farmer–Labor Party (DFL) and led the effort to create the first Fair Employment Practices department in the nation. She counseled both Hubert Humphrey and Walter Mondale and was on the Democratic National Committee in the 1980s.

Johnson was born, the oldest of eight, in Dakota County, Minnesota, near Lakeville, to William and Gladys (née Foree) Allen, one of the few Black farming families in Minnesota in the early 1900s. Nellie's family owned their first two farms between 1905 and 1918. Her mother was a college-educated schoolteacher from Kentucky and had African American, French, Irish and American Indian ancestry. Their family had a dairy farm and her father was involved with the Nonpartisan League, helping organize farmers and co-founding the Twin Cities Milk Producers Association.

When Johnson was 13, she distributed literature for the Nonpartisan League on her way to school. Allen's family moved to a larger farm east of Hinckley in 1919. She milked cows every morning and earned money by trapping muskrat and mink and she joined the National Association for the Advancement of Colored People (NAACP) as a teenager.

In the 1920s, she worked as an elevator attendant at the all-male Minneapolis Athletic Club, earning $15 per week. When her wages were cut to $12.50, she began quietly organizing workers with the Minneapolis Hotel and Restaurant Workers union. In the 1930s she joined the University of Minnesota's Young Communist League and became a member and then vice president of AFL's Local 665, Hotel and Restaurant Workers union.

September 11

Willa Beatrice Brown

January 22, 1906 – July 18, 1992

Willa Beatrice Brown was an American aviator, lobbyist, teacher, and civil rights activist. She was the first African American woman to earn a pilot's license in the United States, the first African American woman to run for the United States Congress, first African American officer in the Civil Air Patrol, and the first woman in the U.S. to have both a pilot's license and an aircraft mechanic's license.

She was a lifelong advocate for gender and racial equality in the field of aviation as well as in the military. She not only lobbied the U.S. government to integrate the United States Army Air Corps and include African Americans in the Civilian Pilot Training Program (CPTP), she and Cornelius Coffey co-founded the Coffey School of Aeronautics, distinguishing it as the first private flight training academy owned and operated by African Americans in the United States. She trained hundreds of pilots, several of whom went on to become Tuskegee Airmen. The creation of the Tuskegee Airmen has been credited to Brown's training efforts.

Brown remained politically and socially active in Chicago long after the Coffey School closed in 1945. She ran in Congressional primary elections in 1946 and 1950 and taught in the Chicago Public School System until 1971, when she retired at age 65. Following her retirement, she served on the Federal Aviation Administration's Women's Advisory Committee.

September 12
J. Parker Prescott, Housing Authority

The Federal Housing Administration (FHA) is a government agency founded by President Franklin Delano Roosevelt, created in part by the National Housing Act of 1934. The FHA insures mortgages made by private lenders for single family properties, multifamily rental properties, hospitals, and residential care facilities. FHA mortgage insurance protects lenders against losses.

Prescott served as public policy advisors to President Franklin D. Roosevelt and his wife Eleanor Roosevelt in his terms in office from 1933 to 1945.

September 13

Cornelius Robinson Coffey
September 6, 1902 - March 2, 1994

Cornelius Robinson Coffey was the first African American aviator to establish a non-university-affiliated aeronautical school in the United States. His school was also the only aviation program not affiliated with a university or college to become part of the Civilian Pilot Training Program (CPTP).

Coffey was born in Newport (Jackson County), Arkansas to Henry Coffey and Ida Wright Coffey. In 1916, Coffey had his first experience riding in an aircraft and was convinced that aviation was his calling. Coffey and his wife Willa Brown Coffey established their own aeronautics school.

Coffey was a recipient of the Charles Taylor Master Mechanic Award from the Federal Aviation Administration (FAA) and, in 1980, was the first African American to have an aerial navigation intersection named after him by the FAA. The "CO FEY Fix"-only five letters are allowed - is a waypoint located on the VICTOR 7 airway over Lake Calumet that provides electronic course guidance to Chicago Midway Airport Runway 31 Left.

Coffey also designed a carburetor heater that prevented icing and thus allowed airplanes to fly in all kinds of weather. Devices similar to his are still in use on aircrafts today.

Coffey became the first president of the National Airmen's Association of America and flew until he was eighty-nine years old.

September 14

Hubert Alexander Green
Contributor: Ian Edwards

Hubert Alexander Green has always loomed large in family lore and, with every additional bit gleaned about him since my youth, the taller this man has grown in my spirit and esteem: Mom, aunts, uncle, and some contemporaries of Mr. Green's regaled me and others with stories that live on. Quite a gentleman by every account, this Hubert Green, born at Greenfield, Lacovia, (St. Elizabeth, Jamaica, WI.) in 1906 to Edward and Catherine Green.

In adulthood, I began to appreciate the measure of the man most knew as "Dickie" and some as "Prof," for he would write letters or other documents for so many who had lacked the ability to read and write for themselves. Always the dashing, sartorially impeccable presence he cut too (he was a tailor); a respected farmer as well.

He landed in America as a farm worker in the early 1940s, apparently among the earliest enterprising Jamaicans enlisted to fill a labor gap on the nation's farms as legions of American men were shipped out to World War II. This and his subsequent stints in America must have been eye-opening adventures, from what we now know of the role the unheralded Jamaican and other Caribbean farm workers played in tearing down walls of racial strife and segregation in their unique ways. But their determination and resilience spoke for themselves.

Dickie's influence on my life, long after his beautiful soul was snatched from us, was more than met the eye. My mother often said I reminded her of her father in many ways – like he, a left-hander, and a sports reporter with a premium on education as a force for personal and collective liberation.

My grandfather's humility, strength, and exemplary servant of a citizen inspire me.

September 15

John Charles Robinson

November 26, 1905 - March 26, 1954

John Charles Robinson, nicknamed the Brown Condor, was an African American aviator who fought with the Imperial Ethiopian Air Force against Benito Mussolini and Fascist Italy during the Second Italian-Ethiopian War, 1935–1936. He is also known as the Father of the Tuskegee Airmen for his contributions to the aviation programs he began at the Tuskegee Institute in Alabama in the early 1940s.

Born in Carrabelle, Florida, in 1903, Robinson and his family moved to Gulfport, Mississippi, where he spent most of his childhood. With a long-time interest in mechanics and machinery, he traveled to Alabama in 1921 to study mechanical science at the Tuskegee Institute. After graduating, Robinson unofficially attended the Curtiss-Wright School of Aviation in Chicago, Illinois where he worked as a janitor until the faculty assisted him in becoming the school's first Black student.

In early 1935, when much of the world realized Italy was gearing up for war with Ethiopia, Robinson announced that he would help in the war efforts against the Fascist Italian forces. Robinson noted that Ethiopia was the only African nation to have successfully resisted colonial conquest by European imperial forces in the late nineteenth century. Because of this, Robinson argued, the Italian invasion posed a threat to more than just Ethiopia, but the greater idea of independence in Africa.

With the approval of the Ethiopian government, Robinson conducted crucial pilot training near Addis Ababa, the capital of Ethiopia. He was named commander of the Ethiopian Air Force and commanded a fleet of about twenty Potez 25 biplanes which were weaponless and used for reconnaissance and supply. When Ethiopia was defeated by Italy in 1936, Robinson escaped and returned to the United States.

September 16

Adugo Ranglin-Onuora
June 26, 1956 - July 5, 2011

Contributor: Sis. Sophia Lemlem Walsh-Newman

Conscious Queen

I delight in powerful energies of our Ancestral Spirits and share in remembrance of a humble, powerful and dear Sisterfriend. Adugo Ranglin-Onuora lives as a Trelawny Maroon. I no doubt know she continues to lend her Maroon warrior spirit in the fight for the liberation of African peoples, those at home and abroad, especially in Jamaica.

Adugo and I met at a dance class I presented in Jamaica in 2005. Our conversation after class found us reasoning like old girlfriends realizing we knew some of the same people, loved similar things and had lots of ideals in common organically cementing our mutual respect and love for each other.

She was an impassioned dancer and poet, dedicated mother and grandmother, sister and faithful friend. A beloved English teacher at Holy Childhood School, she also taught crafts and empowerment classes to young Maroon women of Jamaica.

She founded Conscious Queens Productions out of her love and promotion of roots, rock, reggae and culture. She loved traveling, traversing France, the Gambia, and Egypt on camelbacks. She visited churches in Ethiopia, purchased goods along her journey, enjoyed sightseeing and attended many events including my 2009 graduation while battling Stage 4 cancer that mistakenly took both of her breasts.

She was a faithful Ethiopian Orthodox observer given the name Wolete Ethiopia and was awarded posthumously with the 1st Conscious Queens Award, created in her honor, at the 1st Jamaica African Dance Arts & Culture Festival in 2016.

September 17

António Agostinho Neto

September 17, 1922 - September 10, 1979

António Agostinho Neto was an Angolan politician and poet. He served as the first President of Angola (1975–1979), and led the Popular Movement for the Liberation of Angola (MPLA) in the war for independence (1961–1974). Also one of Angola's preeminent poets, his birthday is celebrated as National Heroes' Day, a public holiday in Angola.

Neto was born in Bengo Province, Angola and attended high school in the capital city of Luanda. His parents were both school teachers and Methodists, and his father, also called Agostinho Neto, was a pastor. After secondary school he worked in the colonial health services before going on to university. The younger Neto left Angola for Portugal, and studied medicine at the universities of Coimbra and Lisbon.

Neto combined his academic life with covert political activity of a revolutionary sort; and PIDE, the security police force of the Estado Novo regime headed by Portuguese Prime Minister Salazar, arrested him in 1951 for three months for his separatist activism. He was arrested in 1952 for joining the Portuguese Movement for Democratic Youth Unity.

He was arrested again in 1955 and held for two years. He finished his studies, married a 23-year-old Portuguese woman who was born in Trás-os-Montes, Maria Eugénia da Silva, the same day he graduated. He returned to Angola in 1959, was arrested again in 1960. Neto escaped to assume leadership of the armed struggle against colonial rule. When Angola gained independence in 1975 he became President and held the position until his death.

September 18

Romare Bearden
September 2, 1911 - March 12, 1988

Romare Bearden was an American artist, author, and songwriter. He worked with many types of media including cartoons, oils, and collages. Born in Charlotte, North Carolina, Bearden grew up in New York City and Pittsburgh, Pennsylvania, and graduated from New York University in 1935.

He began his artistic career creating scenes of the American South. Later, he worked to express the humanity he felt was lacking in the world after his experience in the US Army during World War II on the European front. He returned to Paris in 1950 and studied art history and philosophy at the Sorbonne.

Bearden's early work focused on unity and cooperation within the African-American community. After a period during the 1950s when he painted more abstractly, this theme reemerged in his collage works of the 1960s. The New York Times described Bearden as "the nation's foremost collagist" in his 1988 obituary. Bearden became a founding member of the Harlem-based art group known as The Spiral, formed to discuss the responsibility of the African-American artist in the civil rights movement.

Bearden was the author and coauthor of several books. He also was a songwriter, known as co-writer of the jazz classic *Sea Breeze*, which was recorded by Billy Eckstine, a former high school classmate at Peabody High School, and Dizzy Gillespie. He supported young, emerging artists, and he and his wife established the Bearden Foundation to continue this work, as well as to support young scholars. In 1987, Bearden was awarded the National Medal of Arts.

September 19

John Birks "Dizzy" Gillespie
October 21, 1917 - January 6, 1993

John Birks "Dizzy" Gillespie was an American jazz trumpeter, bandleader, composer, educator and singer. He was a trumpet virtuoso and improviser, building on the virtuoso style of Roy Eldridge but adding layers of harmonic and rhythmic complexity previously unheard in jazz. His combination of musicianship, showmanship, and wit made him a leading popularizer of the new music called bebop. His beret and horn-rimmed spectacles, his scat singing, his bent horn, pouched cheeks, and his light-hearted personality provided some of bebop's most prominent symbols.

In the 1940s Gillespie, with Charlie Parker, became a major figure in the development of bebop and modern jazz. He taught and influenced many other musicians, including trumpeters Miles Davis, Jon Faddis, Fats Navarro, Clifford Brown, Arturo Sandoval, Lee Morgan, Chuck Mangione, and balladeer Johnny Hartman.

Gillespie's contributions to jazz are legendary and he is considered as one of the greatest jazz trumpeters.

September 20

Hastings Ndlovu

Hastings Ndlovu was another young victim of the Soweto uprising who died a brutal death at the hands of riot police. He was a 15-year-old schoolboy at the time and is believed to have been one of the first youths to have been shot during this bloody freedom battle. He was laid to rest in the same cemetery as Hector Pieterson and is honoured alongside Hector at the Hector Pieterson Memorial Museum.

Nelson Mandela, in his book *Long Walk to Freedom*, said this about that fateful day: “The events of that day reverberated in every town and township of South Africa. The uprising triggered riots and violence across the country. Mass funerals for the victims of state violence became national rallying points. Suddenly the young people of South Africa were fired with the spirit of protest and rebellion. Students boycotted schools all across the country. Bantu education had come back to haunt its creators, for these angry and audacious young people were its progeny.”

September 21

David Webster
December 1, 1944 - May 1, 1989

With a deep interest in anthropology, Rhodesian-born Webster first took a stand against apartheid by joining a peaceful sit-in at Rhodes University in South Africa in protest against Black students' exclusion from the university's rugby team. Later, as a lecturer at Wits University, South Africa, his research led him to the subject of the psychological trauma and torture used on detainees by the South African security forces during interrogation.

In the late sixties and early seventies while doing field work in Mozambique, Webster discovered that 42% of the able-bodied young men were absent for long periods of time working on the South African gold mines. The men had been immigrating from Southern Mozambique to the South African diamond and gold mines since the late nineteenth century. *The Origins of Migrant Labour, Colonialism , and the Under-development of Southern Mozambique* analyzed the problem.

Webster co-authored a report that exposed the intensifying state repression and how liberation movements were finding new and creative methods of resistance. Webster was murdered by apartheid assassin Ferdi Barnard, just nine months before Nelson Mandela was release from prison.

September 22

Neil Aggett
October 6, 1953 - February 5, 1982

At 28 years old, Neil Aggett was the first white South African to die at the hands of South Africa's security police. As a doctor who worked mostly in overcrowded Black appointed hospitals, he was acutely aware of the hardships and poverty-related diseases of workers, and soon became involved in trade unions that were working to champion worker rights. As a result, he became a target of harassment by the Security Branch of the South African Police and was labelled a communist.

His death in 1982 was called suicide, but 16 years later, South Africa's Truth and Reconciliation Commission ruled that being assaulted, blindfolded, and given electric shocks for more than 70 days in detention was directly responsible for Aggett taking his own life.

September 23

Solomon Mahlangu
July 10, 1956 - April 6, 1979

"My blood will nourish the tree that will bear the fruits of freedom. Tell my people that I love them. They must continue the fight." These are the words inscribed on Solomon Mahlangu's tombstone.

He was an Umkhonto we Sizwe soldier who was charged with two counts of murder and several others under South Africa's Terrorism Act. Evidence that emerged during his trial cast doubt over his double murder charge to which Mahlangu pleaded not guilty. However, Mahlangu never did have his fair day in court because he was so brutally beaten while detained that he was deemed unfit to stand trial. Not deterred by this, the apartheid state continued their case against a now-defenceless Mahlangu and found him guilty as charged. He was hanged in 1979.

September 24

Ahmed Timol
November 3, 1941 – October 27, 1971

The life of Ahmed Timol, teacher, freedom fighter, and avid sportsman, was cut short when he reportedly jumped out of a window at the notorious John Vorster Square police station in Johannesburg, South Africa He was arrested after being found in possession of banned African National Congress (ANC) literature. His capture spawned a string of subsequent arrests, with many others being detained, brutally beaten and tortured.

Timol's family were given his body for burial and, after ritual Muslim washing rites, they reported his fingernails to have been removed, his neck broken, and his body covered in bruise and burn marks.

September 25

Willis Boynard Wyatt

October 28, 1882 - August 18, 1945

Contributor: Deirdre FieldsWilson (Grand Daughter of Willis B Wyatt/Mother's Father)

Willis Boynard Wyatt was born in Thunderbolt Georgia. By trade he was a carpenter, farmer, painter, electrician, businessman and plumber. He also learned how to read blueprints, a gift passed down from his father. This gift came in handy when he founded the Mount Sinai Baptist Church, located in the Bedford Stuyvesant section of Brooklyn New York.

Pastor Wyatt used his carpentry skills to physically build several of the church pews where they can be seen today. In 2019 the church celebrated its 100th anniversary. As a businessman he knew the importance of ownership; he bought burial plots for children and grandchildren.

September 26

The Sharpville Victims
South Africa

The Sharpville Massacre (March 21, 1960) brought the inhuman and cruel face of the apartheid regime into the global spotlight, as the freedom fight for South Africa began in earnest. The day began as a peaceful protest march, with a group arriving at a police station in Sharpville to non-violently surrender themselves for refusing to carry pass books (a legal requirement for any non-white during apartheid).

Met by a heavy police contingent, panic soon ensued, shots were fired, stones were thrown, and within two minutes 69 people had died. Many were shot in the back while fleeing. Shortly thereafter, the African National Congress (ANC) and PAC (Pan-African Congress) were banned, eliminating the pathway to peaceful resistance and forcing them to move towards armed resistance.

September 27

Ashley Kriel
October 17, 1966 - July 9, 1987

A cloudy controversy remains over the death of Ashley Kriel, a soft-faced 20-year-old who is still recognized as the quintessential representative of student and youth leadership of the 1980s. He was shot in what was meant to be a safe house in Athlone, Western Cape, South Africa, but it is believed that this was only after beatings with a spade and other forms of torture.

Kriel's funeral was marred by a heavy police presence, with his family never getting the opportunity to say a proper goodbye. His killer, state operative Jeffrey Benzien, testified years later before the Truth and Reconciliation Commission. Questions regarding his torture remained unanswered, with Benzien testifying that he did not recall whom exactly he had tortured.

September 28

Ahmed Kathrada

August 21, 1929 - March 28, 2017

Former South African politician, political prisoner and activist, Ahmed Mohamed Kathrada will be remembered for his involvement in the struggle against Apartheid. He worked alongside Nelson Mandela, Walter Sisulu and other publicly known greats to end racial discrimination in South Africa. In a book, titled *Conversations With a Gentle Soul* (2017), are some highlighted experiences of Ahmed Kathrada's life and work:

He was an anti-war activist by age 12.

Kathrada left school at the age of 17 when he started a full-time position at the offices of the Transvaal Passive Resistance Council. He helped organize the Campaign of Defiance Against Unjust Laws: The 1952 campaign was launched by the African National Congress (ANC) and the SAIC South African Indian Congress (SAIC) and targeted six unjust Apartheid laws.

In December 1962, Kathrada was put under house arrest for 13 hours a day, and over weekends and public holidays. Nonetheless, Kathrada continued to attend secret meetings at the ANC headquarters.

At the age of 34, Kathrada was imprisoned on Robben Island, where he spent 18 years with his comrades of the ANC. Despite being in prison, Kathrada continued his academic studies and obtained four degrees. He was moved to Pollsmoor Maximum Security Prison in Cape Town; there he joined Mandela, Sisulu, Mhlaba, and Mlangeni who had also been moved to Pollsmoor.

Kathrada was 60 when he was released from prison, and was given a hero's welcome in Soweto, where he addressed a crowd of 5000 people.

September 29

Samora Moisés Machel

September 29, 1933 - October 19, 1986

Samora Moisés Machel was a Mozambican military commander, politician and revolutionary who served as the first President of Mozambique from the country's independence in 1975. He was a socialist in the tradition of Marxism–Leninism.

Machel was born in the village of Madragoa (today's Chilembene), to a family of farmers. His grandfather had been an active collaborator of Gungunhana. Under Portuguese rule, his father, like most Black Mozambicans, was classified by the demeaning term "indígena" (native). He was forced to accept lower prices for his crops than White farmers; compelled to grow labour-intensive cotton, which took time away from the food crops needed for his family; and forbidden to brand his mark on his cattle to prevent thievery. Despite that, Machel's father was a successful farmer.

Machel grew up in this farming village and attended mission elementary school. He never completed his secondary education though he had the prerequisite certificate to train as a nurse anywhere in Portugal. However, Machel studied nursing in the capital city of Lourenço Marques (today Maputo - capital and most populous city of Mozambique).

Unable to complete formal training at the Miguel Bombarda Hospital in Lourenço Marques, he got a job working as an aide in the same hospital and earned enough to continue his education at night school. He worked at the hospital until he left the country to join the Mozambican nationalist struggle in neighbouring Tanzania.

Machel was attracted to anti-colonial ideals and began his political activities in the Miguel Bombarda hospital in Lourenço Marques, where he protested against the fact that Black nurses were paid less than whites doing the same job.

Machel died in office in 1986 when his presidential aircraft crashed near the Mozambican-South African border.

September 30

A. Philip Randolph
April 15, 1889 - May 16, 1979

Philip Randolph played a crucial role in gaining recognition of African Americans in labor organizations. A socialist and a pacifist, Randolph founded the Brotherhood of Sleeping Car porters, the first successful Black trade Union and the Negro American Labor Council. The Rev, Dr. Martin Luther King Jr. referred to Randolph as the Dean of Negro leaders.

The youngest son of a preacher deeply committed to racial politics, Randolph was born in Crescent City, Florida. He graduated from Jacksonville's Cookman Institute and relocated to New York City soon afterward. In 1917 Randolph and Chandler Owen founded the *Messenger*, an African American socialist journal critical of American involvement in World War I.

After the 1925 founding of the Brotherhood of Sleeping Car Porters, Randolph succeeded in gaining recognition of the union from the Pullman Palace Car Company. When the union signed its first contract with the company, membership rose to nearly 15,000.

In 1941 Randolph threatened a march on Washington, D.C., if the federal government did not address racial discrimination in the defense industry. In response, President Franklin D. Roosevelt issued Executive Order 8802, which banned discrimination in the defense industry and established the Fair Employment Practices Commission.

Randolph also helped to form the League for Non-Violent Civil Disobedience against Military Segregation, which influenced President Harry S. Truman's decision to desegregate the armed services in 1948.

Randolph devoted his life to the achievement of both racial and economic equality.

October 1

Patrice Émery Lumumba
July 2, 1925 - January 17, 1961

Patrice Émery Lumumba alternatively styled Patrice Hemery Lumumba was a Congolese politician and independence leader who served as the first Prime Minister of the independent Democratic Republic of the Congo (then Republic of the Congo) from June until September 1960.

Lumumba played a significant role in the transformation of the Congo from a colony of Belgium into an independent republic. Ideologically an African nationalist and pan-Africanist, he led the Congolese National Movement (MNC) party from 1958 until his assassination.

Patrice Lumumba, the first legally elected prime minister of the Democratic Republic of the Congo (DRC), was assassinated on 17 January, 1961. This heinous crime was a culmination of two inter-related assassination plots by American and Belgian governments, which used Congolese accomplices and a Belgian execution squad to carry out the deed.

Ludo De Witte, the Belgian author of the best book on this crime, qualifies it as "the most important assassination of the 20th century". *The assassination's historical importance lies in a multitude of factors, the most pertinent being the global context in which it took place, its impact on Congolese politics since then and Lumumba's overall legacy as a nationalist leader.* https://www.theguardian.com/global-development/poverty-matters/2011/jan/17/patrice-lumumba-50th-anniversary-assassination

October 2

James Weldon Johnson
1871-1938

James Weldon Johnson was an influential and notable novelist, poet, songwriter, lawyer, a United States consul to Venezuela and Nicaragua, and served an important role in combating racism through the National Association for the Advancement of Colored People (NAACP).

James Weldon Johnson was born in Jacksonville, Florida. His father was a headwaiter at a hotel and his mother was a teacher at the segregated Stanton School.

He served as a professor at New York University and Fisk University a Historically Black University.

Johnson developed his own philosophy on lessening racism in America. While W.E.B. Du Bois advocated intellectual development and Booker T. Washington advocated industrial training to combat racism, Johnson believed that it was important for Blacks to produce great literature and art. By doing so, Johnson held that Blacks could demonstrate their intellectual equality and advance their placement in America.

Lift Every Voice and Sing, recognized as The Black National Anthem, was written as a poem by Johnson and set to music by his brother John Rosamond Johnson in 1899.

October 3
Sir William Alexander Clarke Bustamante – One of Jamaica's National Heroes
February 24, 1884 - August 6, 1977

Sir William Alexander Clarke Bustamante GBE PC (born William Alexander Clarke) was a Jamaican politician and labour leader, who, in 1962 became the first Prime Minister of Jamaica. He founded the Bustamante Industrial Trade Union following the 1938 labour riots, and the Jamaican Labour Party in 1943. Bustamante is honoured in Jamaica with the title National Hero of Jamaica in recognition of his achievements.

Bustamante travelled the world and worked in many different places. His occupations included working as a policeman in Cuba, as a tramcar conductor in Panama, and as a dietician in a New York City hospital. At the age of 48, he returned to Jamaica in 1932, where he opened offices at 1a Duke Street, as a money lender and a dairy products man. His office was downstairs and living quarters upstairs.

He became a leader in activism against colonial rule and gained recognition by writing frequent letters on the issues to the *Daily Gleaner* newspaper. In 1937 he was elected as treasurer of the Jamaica Workers' Union (JWU), which had been founded by labour activist Allan G.S. Coombs.

During the 1938 labour rebellion, he emerged as the spokesman for striking workers, who were mostly of African and mixed-race descent. After the revolt, JWU became the Bustamante Industrial Trade Union (BITU), and Bustamante became known as "The Chief".

In 1940, he was imprisoned on charges of subversive activities. He was defended by Norman Washington Manley, his cousin, and released from prison in 1943.

The widespread anti-colonial activism resulted in Parliament's granting universal suffrage in 1944 to residents in Jamaica.

October 4

Cordy Tindell Vivian also known as Rev. C. T. Vivian
July 30, 1924 – July 17, 2020

Cordy Tindell Vivian was an American minister, author, organizer, and close friend and lieutenant of Martin Luther King Jr. during the Civil Rights Movement. Vivian resided in Atlanta, Georgia, and founded the C. T. Vivian Leadership Institute, Inc. He was a member of the Alpha Phi Alpha fraternity.

Vivian was born in Boonville, Missouri where the family lost its farm during the Depression and a home to arson.

In 1947, Vivian participated in his first non-violent action to end segregation at lunch counters in Peoria. Because of his strong religious upbringing and beliefs, Vivian said he was called to a life in the ministry. He saw no separation between civil rights, faith and ministry because "racism is a moral issue." With the help of his church, he enrolled in American Baptist Theological Seminary in Nashville in 1955.

Vivian and other ministers founded the Nashville Christian Leadership Conference, an affiliate of the Southern Christian Leadership Conference (SCLC) that organized and trained students to embark on a movement to end segregation in Nashville. He joined Student Nonviolent Coordinating Committee (SNCC) members and other ministers to continue the Freedom Rides into Jackson, Mississippi after a group from the Congress of Racial Equality disbanded. The SNCC group was arrested and Vivian was badly beaten at Parchman Prison.

Vivian worked as a strategist at the SCLC helping to get the Civil Rights Bill and Voting Rights Acts passed. In 1965, he famously confronted Sheriff Jim Clark on the steps of Selma's courthouse while leading Blacks to register to vote.

Vivian was a founder of Capital City Bank, a Black-owned bank in Atlanta and he has provided civil rights counsel to Presidents Johnson, Carter, Reagan and Clinton.

October 5

Derrick Albert Bell Jr.
November 6, 1930 - October 5, 2011

Derrick Bell was an American lawyer, professor, and civil rights activist. In 1971, he became the first tenured African-American professor of law at Harvard Law School, and he is often credited as one of the originators of critical race theory along with Richard Delgado, Charles Lawrence, Mari Matsuda, and Patricia Williams. He was a visiting professor at New York University School of Law from 1991 until his death. He was also a dean of the University of Oregon School of Law.

Derrick Bell was a distinguished legal scholar, prolific writer and tireless champion for equality. He helped to develop critical race theory, a body of legal scholarship that explores how racism is embedded in laws and legal institutions. And more broadly, over the course of his five-decade career, he worked to expose the persistence of racism.

October 6

Dorothy Irene Height
March 24, 1912 - April 20, 2010

Dorothy Irene Height was an American civil rights and women's rights activist. She focused on the issues of African American women, including unemployment, illiteracy, and voter awareness. Height is credited as the first leader in the civil rights movement to recognize inequality for women and African Americans as problems that should be considered as a whole. She was the president of the National Council of Negro Women for forty years.

Dorothy Height was born in Richmond, Virginia. When she was five years old her family moved to Rankin, Pennsylvania, a steel town in the suburbs of Pittsburgh, where she attended racially integrated schools. Height's mother was active in the Pennsylvania Federation of Colored Women's Clubs and regularly took Dorothy along to meetings where she established her "place in the sisterhood." Height's long association with the Young Women's Christian Association (YWCA) began in a Girl Reserve Club in Rankin.

While in high school Height became socially and politically active in anti-lynching campaigns. A talented orator, she won first place and a $1,000 scholarship at a national oratory contest held by the Elks. Height graduated from Rankin High School in 1929.

Height was accepted to Barnard College in 1929, but was denied entrance because the school had an unwritten policy of admitting only two Black students per year. She enrolled at New York University, earned an undergraduate degree in 1932 and a master's degree in educational psychology the following year. She pursued further postgraduate work at Columbia University and the New York School of Social Work (the predecessor of the Columbia University School of Social Work).

October 7
Dr. Wentworth Ofuatey-Kodjoe
Distinguished Political Scientist, Pan-Africanist and Scholar

Wentworth Ofuatey-Kodjoe was emeritus professor of Political Science and African Studies at Queens College City University of New York (CUNY) and at the CUNY Graduate Center. Professor Kodjoe founded the Africana Studies Program at Queens College CUNY, and the graduate programs in African Studies at the Graduate Center of CUNY. In addition he served as a past President of the African Heritage Studies Association and in numerous other organizational and leadership capacities in Africana Studies and in the training of the next generation of Africanists.

As a professor in the political Science department at Queens College he taught and challenged his students' knowledge of the politics and relationships of Africans on the continent and the impact of the European presence.

Note by Claudette Joy Spence: Professor Ofuatey-Kodjoe was one of my professors in Political Science and African Studies. Also, he and Professor Lynn Dozier under the auspices of the African Heritage Studies Association led a group of students, myself included, on our first travel to Ghana - the land of his birth - in the 1970s.

October 8

Rosa Parks
February 4, 1913 - October 24, 2005

She refused to move from her seat on the bus. And while Rosa Parks may not be the first African American to challenge the status quo of segregation laws in the South, her quiet yet courageous act of protest in 1955 earned her the nickname "Mother of the Freedom Movement."

October 9

Omega Smart
Contributor: Bekoe Adigun, (Grandson)

This African-centered-thinking began with my father's mother Omega Smart who was born in Grenada. When I was about five years old, as I was having some oil down (breadfruit) with my grandmother and she started talking about her father.

"He was a real African," she said. "He never gave up our ways. And you too are an African. Don't forget that. We were born in Grenada, but we are not Grenadians. We are Africans that is our home where we were stolen from," she taught me.

In memory of those who took time to nurture my growth, I take a moment to give thanks

October 10

Alex La Guma
February 20, 1924 - October 11, 1985

Alex La Guma was a South African novelist, leader of the South African Coloured People's Organisation (SACPO) and a defendant in the Treason Trial, whose works helped characterise the movement against the apartheid era in South Africa. La Guma's vivid style, distinctive dialogue, and realistic, horrific, sympathetic portrayal of oppressed groups have made him one of the most notable South African writers of the 20th century. La Guma was awarded the 1969 Lotus Prize for Literature.

La Guma was born in Cape Town, South Africa. He was the son of James La Guma, a leading figure in both the Industrial and Commercial Workers' Union and the South African Communist Party.

After graduating from a technical school in 1945, he became an active member of the Plant Workers Union of the Metal Box Company. He was fired after organizing a strike, and he became active in politics, joining the Young Communists League in 1947 and the South African Communist Party in 1948.

In 1956 he helped organize the South Africa representatives who drew up the Freedom Charter, and consequently he was one of the 156 accused at the Treason Trials that same year. He was placed under house arrest, he and his wife Blanche were imprisoned in solitary confinement, and returned to house arrest on their release. With their two children they went into exile to the UK and spent the rest of his life in exile.

He was chief representative of the African National Congress in the Caribbean at the time of his death from a heart attack in Havana, Cuba.

October 11

Babatunde Subair
Contributor: Gbenga Subair

Learning Beyond the Comfort Zone

It has been twenty years since my father Mr. Babatunde Subair left to join the ancestors. Every day, every month and every year goes by that I think about him and wish he was around to see how Africa and the world has changed during these past two decades. I wonder what his views and take would have been on the changes. I know he would have had something to say about it. Whether I agreed with him or not I still would want to hear his fresh perspectives, and in particular how he would have arrived to his conclusions about the many things that have shaped Africa and the world in the last twenty years.

He introduced my older brother and me at a very young age to African issues and world affairs and challenged us to see things beyond our comfort zone. He encouraged us to read, to learn and to understand about people in places far beyond our own home in Nigeria. It was a challenge at an early age I was willing to accept because I was curious and wanted to know what the other countries in the continent and the world was like. We listened to the radio, read books and newspapers, watched the news, documentaries – that is how he empowered my brother and me to learn from any resource available.

Babatunde knew, and taught us that there was a wealth of information available about our African genesis and our contribution to building civilization; he knew the inherent wealth of the people of Africa and the African land because he was a staunch Pan-Africanist and passionate about Africa's issues.

I learned from my father to empower myself and the people around me.

October 12

Daisy Bates
November 11, 1914 - November 4, 1999

Daisy Bates was an American civil rights activist, publisher, journalist, and lecturer who played a leading role in the Little Rock Integration Crisis of 1957.

Bates' mother Hezakiah Gatson was raped and murdered while Daisy was an infant. She was raised by her mother's friends the Smiths. Her adoptive father, Orlee Smith, told her that the killers were never found and that the police showed little interest in the case. Bates wanted justice.

She began to hate white people. Out of concern and hope, her adoptive father gave her some advice from his deathbed:

You're filled with hatred. Hate can destroy you, Daisy. Don't hate white people just because they're white. If you hate, make it count for something. Hate the humiliations we are living under in the South. Hate the discrimination that eats away at the South. Hate the discrimination that eats away at the soul of every Black man and woman. Hate the insults hurled at us by white scum—and then try to do something about it, or your hate won't spell a thing.

Bates said she had never forgotten that. She believed that this memory supported her strength for leadership in the cause of civil rights.

October 13

George T. Raymond

May 10, 1914 - May 9, 1999

George T. Raymond was an African American civil rights leader from Pennsylvania who served as president of the Chester, Pennsylvania branch of the National Association for the Advancement of Colored People (NAACP) from 1942 to 1977. He was integral in the desegregation of businesses, public housing and schools in Chester and co-led the Chester school protests in 1964 which made Chester a key battleground in the civil rights movement.

Raymond was born in Chester, Pennsylvania and graduated from Chester High School in 1933. He studied business administration at Drexel Institute of Technology for one year but economic hardship forced him to leave school and find work. He worked at multiple odd jobs and finally landed at the Chester Boys Club, joined the NAACP and began his career in the civil rights movement.

Raymond became the leader of the Chester branch of the NAACP in 1942 and began to implement programs to end racial discrimination. He partnered with J. Pius Barbour, the pastor of Calvary Baptist Church in Chester and together they adopted a gradualist approach to civil rights.

Raymond was presented the Freedom Award by Supreme Court Justice Thurgood Marshall; in 1991, the George T. Raymond award was established in his honor by the NAACP; and three scrapbooks created by Raymond of newspaper clippings, booklets and photographs chronicling the Chester civil rights movement throughout the 1940s, 1950s and 1960s are available online at the Wolfman Digital Collections at Widener University.

October 14

Julius Kambarage Nyerere
April 13, 1922 - October 14, 1999

Julius Kambarage Nyerere was a Tanzanian anti-colonial activist, politician, and political theorist. He governed Tanganyika as Prime Minister from 1961 to 1962 and then as President from 1963 to 1964, after which he led its successor state, Tanzania, as President from 1964 to 1985. A founding member of the Tanganyika African National Union (TANU) party—which in 1977 became the Chama Cha Mapinduzi party—he chaired it until 1990. Ideologically an African nationalist and African socialist, he promoted a political philosophy known as Ujamaa.

Born in Butiama, then in the British colony of Tanganyika, Nyerere was the son of a Zanaki chief. After completing his schooling, he studied at Makerere College in Uganda and then Edinburgh University in Scotland. In 1952 he returned to Tanganyika, married, and worked as a teacher. In 1954, he helped form TANU, through which he campaigned for Tanganyikan independence from the British Empire. Influenced by the Indian independence leader Mahatma Gandhi, Nyerere preached non-violent protest to achieve this aim.

In 1962, Tanganyika became a republic, with Nyerere elected its first president. His administration pursued decolonisation and the "Africanisation" of the civil service while promoting unity among indigenous Africans and the country's Asian and European minorities. He encouraged the formation of a one-party state and unsuccessfully pursued the Pan-Africanist formation of an East African Federation with Uganda and Kenya.

October 15

Herman Andimba Toivo ya Toivo
August 22, 1924 - June 9, 2017

Herman Andimba Toivo ya Toivo, was a Namibian, a former Robben Island prisoner, a hero and an icon of Namibia's struggle for self-determination.

Ya Toivo was Namibia's longest serving Robben Islander, having served 16 years on the Island with Nelson Mandela and other freedom fighters of the African peoples' struggles following conviction for contravening South Africa's Terrorism Act. His life exemplified solidarity, the quest for self-determination and an unyielding commitment to the liberation of his people.

Ya Toivo was a founding member of the South Western African People's Organization (SWAPO) and its predecessor, the Ovamboland People's Organisation. He advocated for the rights of African and Black mineworkers in South Africa and Namibia and was banished from South Africa for smuggling taped testimonies about the harsh experiences of Black mineworkers to the United Nations.

Speaking at his trial in Pretoria, he denounced South Africa's annexation of Namibia. "We find ourselves here in a foreign country, convicted under laws made by people whom we have always considered as foreigner. We are Namibians, and not South Africans," he said. "We do not now, and will not in the future, recognize your right to govern us, to make laws for us in which we have no say, to treat our country as if it were your property and us as if you were our masters."

October 16

Claude McKay
September 15, 1889 - May 22, 1948

Claude McKay, born Festus Claudius McKay in Sunny Ville, Jamaica in 1889, was a key figure in the Harlem Renaissance, a prominent literary movement of the 1920s. His work ranged from vernacular verse celebrating peasant life in Jamaica to poems that protested racial and economic inequities.

McKay's philosophically ambitious writings, including tales of Black life in both Jamaica and America, addresses instinctual/intellectual duality, which McKay found central to the Black individual's efforts to cope in a racist society. His authorship includes: *The Passion of Claude McKay: Selected Poetry and Prose* (1973), *Harlem Shadows* (1922*), Constab Ballads* (1912), and *Songs of Jamaica* (1912), and *If We Must Die*, written during the Red Summer of 19 , a period of intense racial violence against Black people in .

McKay left Jamaica for the U.S. in 1912 to attend Tuskegee Institute. He was shocked by the intense racism he encountered when he arrived in Charleston, South Carolina, where many public facilities were segregated. This inspired him to write more poetry. At Tuskegee, he disliked the semi-military, machine-like existence there and left to study at Kansas State University. There, he read W. E. B. Du Bois' *Souls of Black Folk*, which had a major impact on him and stirred his political involvement. Despite superior academic performance he decided he did not want to be an agronomist and moved to New York City.

McKay joined the Industrial Workers of the World and was involved with a group of Black people who were unhappy both with Marcus Garvey's nationalism and the middle-class reformist National Association for the Advancement of Colored People. They advocated for Black self-determination within the context of socialist revolution. Together they founded the semi-secret revolutionary organization, the African Blood Brotherhood.

October 17

Edith Mary Rock

April 14, 1924 - April 3, 2019

Edith Mary Rock, a member of faculty at Medgar Evers College, City University of New York had as a mission to preserve the stories of African Americans. Of particular interest to her was to have the stories of the elders written to document their history. In that regard she advocated for a writing workshop to be founded at the College's Center for Black Literature. And so began the Elder Writing Workshop in collaboration with Siloam Presbyterian Church where Rock was a member.

Rock earned a BA, MA and a Ph.D. from New York University. In her honor, after she transitioned, the workshop was named Dr. Edith Rock Elders Writing Workshop.

Here is what the College website says: about the Workshop:

The Dr. Edith Rock Elders Writing Workshop is "intended to preserve the memoirs of elders throughout the African Diaspora whose lives span a major part of the twentieth century and beyond." The writing workshop began as the Writing Project for Older African Americans with the purpose of gathering information from older Black Americans whose history is likely to be distorted or lost for lack of original documentation. The specific purpose of the writing workshop is to encourage elders to recall the past and to help them turn their recollections into inspirational memoirs and stories. Many Blacks from older generations, some descendants of enslaved Africans, made huge sacrifices, such as leaving their families and migrating to various parts of the United States with the hope of a better life; others faced challenges in the forms of discrimination, racism, and segregation during their journey and even after they were settled. Their stories, in turn, have become our history.

October 18

Nickey Iyambo
May 20, 1936 - May 19, 2019

Nickey Iyambo was a Namibian politician and physician who served as the first Vice President of Namibia in 1990.

After Iyambo became a member of the South West Africa People's Organisation (SWAPO) in 1960, he fled into exile with SWAPO in 1964. He travelled on foot to Angola, continuing on to Zambia and Tanzania. He was among the earliest SWAPO members to go into exile and helped establish SWAPO's close relationship with Julius Nyerere's Tanzania.

After Iyambo completed his medical studies in Helsinki, Finland, he moved to Angola and became the head of medical services in the Kwanza Sul refugee camp. Around the time leading up to the independence of Namibia, Iyambo was among the first people in SWAPO leadership to return to Namibia to prepare the country for elections.

October 19

Maurice Rupert Bishop

May 29, 1944 - October 19, 1983

Maurice Rupert Bishop was a Grenadian revolutionary and the leader of New Jewel Movement – a Marxist-Leninist party which sought to prioritise socio-economic development, education, and Black liberation – that came to power during the 13 March 1979 Coup that removed Eric Gairy from office. Bishop headed the People's Revolutionary Government of Grenada from 1979 to 1983, when he was dismissed from his post and shot during a coup by Bernard Coard.

For his secondary education, Bishop received one of the four government scholarships for study at the Roman Catholic Presentation Brothers' College. He was elected president of the Student Council, of the Discussion Club, and of the History Study Group, along with editing the newspaper *Student Voice* and participating in sports. He later recalled: "Here I had much interest in politics, history and sociology." He also established contacts with students from the Anglican Grenada Boys' Secondary School, his own school's competitors.

Bishop was an ardent supporter of the West Indies Federation established in 1958 and the ideas of Caribbean nationalism. He also recalled the great interest the 1959 Cuban Revolution aroused in him. Bishop recalled: "In fact, for us it did not matter what we heard on the radio or read in the colonial press. For us, it comes down to the courage and legendary heroism of Fidel Castro, Che Guevara. ...Nothing could overshadow this aspect of the Cuban Revolution."

Both friends and detractors admired his charisma and good oratory skills, including his skillful use of humor in his speeches.

October 20

Queen Nzinga Mbande
1583-1663

Queen Nzinga Mbande, sometimes referred to as Anna Nzinga, was ruler of the Ndongo and Matamba Kingdoms of the Mbundu people in what is now Angola.

In 1626 Mbande became Queen of the Ndongo following the death of her brother. Her reign began in peril as the Portuguese went back on their deal with her and declared war, as did other neighbouring tribes. Forced into retreat from her own lands, Mbande led her people south to the kingdom of Matamba, which she attacked, capturing Matamba's Queen and routing her army. Mbande then installed herself as the new ruler of Matamba, from where she launched a prolonged campaign of guerrilla warfare against the Portuguese which would last for the next 30 years. Mbande developed a legendary reputation as a warrior,

Mbande continued personally leading her troops into battle until she was in her sixties, but the long war eventually wore both sides down. In 1657 she finally signed a peace treaty with Portugal. She then spent the rest of her life focused on rebuilding a nation which had been devastated by conflict and over-farming. She died of natural causes in 1663, aged 81. Today Nzinga Mbande is a symbol of Angolan independence, memorialized by numerous statues.

October 21

Elombe Brath
Elombe (née Cecil) Brathwaite
1936 – 2014

Elombe was committed to both providing a platform for Africans who were engaging in freedom and anti-imperialist struggles around the world while educating countless others with priceless insight to their struggles.

Through Elombe, as he was called by many, one learned about amazing Freedom Fighters such as Amilcar Cabral and the revolutionary efforts of our people in Guinea-Bissau and the truths behind the rise and fall of one our peoples' greatest heroes - the Pan-African martyr, Patrice Emery Lumumba of the now Democratic Republic of the Congo.

Elombe taught the significance of and connection between our people's current conditions globally and the mis-education we receive of these struggles for freedom whether past or contemporary. With Elombe, one learned in detail how distractions away from understanding the African Independence movements of Osagyefo Kwame Nkrumah's Ghana, Gamal Abdel with Nasser's Egypt, Dedan Kimathi and Jomo Kenyatta's Mau-Mau of Kenya and their Pan-African and African-Internationalist solidarity examples, are calculated attempts by the corrupt super powers to keep our people and global oppressed communities from being inspired and therefore providing the global support they require.

He believed that these forms of struggle are elementary in us realizing our true social, cultural, political and economic potential for true independence and freedom through the continuity of world Afrikan unification.

Elombe Brathwaite was born to Cecil T. Brathwaite and Etelka Margaret Maloney-Brathwaite in Brooklyn, New York who had emigrated from Barbados. He grew up in the Hunt's Point section of the Bronx.

October 22

Cyril Valentine Briggs
May 28, 1888 - October 18, 1966

Cyril Valentine Briggs was an African-Caribbean American writer and communist political activist. He was the founder and editor of *The Crusader*, a New York magazine of the New Negro Movement of the 1920s, and a founder of the African Blood Brotherhood, a small but historically important radical organization dedicated to advancing the cause of Pan-Africanism.

Cyril Valentine Briggs was born on the Caribbean island of Nevis, part of the West Indies. His father, Louis E. Briggs, was a white plantation overseer; his mother, Mary M. Huggins, was of African-Caribbean ancestry. In accord with the racial caste system in colonial Nevis, the biracial Briggs was regarded as "coloured" despite his extremely light complexion. While granted access to a quality colonial education, he was accepted as a potential member of the island's ruling elite because of his ethnically-mixed parentage.

As a youth Briggs worked as an assistant in the library of a local clergyman, where he was first exposed to political works critical of imperialism. He would later move to become a writer, taking jobs with the *St. Kitts Daily Express* and the *St. Christopher Advertiser*.

Recognized for his promise as an aspiring writer, in his later teenaged years Briggs was awarded a scholarship to study journalism at the university level. He ultimately turned down this opportunity, however, emigrating to the United States in 1905 to join his mother, who had already emigrated there. Little is known about Briggs' first seven years in America, as he never wrote of the experience in his extremely short autobiographical notes housed in the Marcus Garvey Papers at UCLA.

Briggs' first American writing job came in 1912 at the *Amsterdam News*.

October 23

Lydia Lili'u Loloku Walania Kamaka'eha

September 2, 1838

The question of whether or not the original natives of Hawaii are truly of African descent has remained one of the biggest puzzles for some. Although their skin, hair and way of life prove that they were of African descent, some scholars with a wide readership have one way or the other refused to dig into their history to provide clear evidence to their story while also sidelining the findings by several historians and anthropology scholars that indicate Africa.

Africans reached Hawaii through their exploratory adventures which took them to lands beyond their continent long before the Europeans came.

The first Hawaiian and their royals were dark skinned with distinctly African features who ruled their people and lived in an African-style community until the forceful invasion of the whites in America and the end of their royal lineage after they destroyed the then Queen Lili'uokalani.

She is known as the last Black royal of Hawaii and was the first and last woman to rule her people between 1891 and 1893.

Lydia Lili'u Loloku Walania Kamaka'eha was born to High Chief Kamanawa II and his wife. Her father was the great-grandson of one of the five Kona chiefs in Hawaii. There is the existence of a Jukun-Kona tribe in Nigeria.

During her short time as queen, she amended laws that did not work in their favor; he founded the Liliuokalani's Savings Bank for women; helped in the establishment of a money-lending group for working women; established orphanages and founded the Lili'uokalani Educational Society to train Black girls from poor homes in various trades. She also created a fund to pay for fees of various intelligent Black women.

October 24

Richard Benjamin Moore
1893 - 1978

Richard Benjamin Moore was a Barbados-born Afro-Caribbean civil rights activist, writer and prominent socialist. He was also one of the earliest advocates of the term African American, as opposed to Negro or "Black".

Richard Benjamin Moore was born in Barbados, West Indies, to Richard Henry Moore and Josephine Thorne Moore. By the age of nine, both of Moore's parents had transitioned and he was raised by his stepmother. Wanting to get the best education and opportunity for Moore, she arranged for him to emigrate to the US.

When Moore arrived in New York City, he was confronted with discrimination based on racism in education and employment. . Although trained in Barbados to do clerical work, he was forced to turn to less-prestigious jobs such as elevator operator and work in a silk manufacturing firm.

The struggles that Moore encountered and observed made him become a strong advocate for the rights of African Americans. In 1919, he joined the African Blood Brotherhood (ABB), which was an organization formed to defend African Americans from race riots and lynching. Moore, along with other African-American advocates, joined the Socialist Party in the early 1920s. Moore joined the Socialist Party, partly because the Socialist Party was then transforming itself into a force to fight against segregation.

Though a frequent political candidate of the Socialist Party, Moore was expelled from it. He was accused of being an African-American nationalist and kept African-American issues on the front burner.

Moore's books include: *The Name Negro, Its Origin and Evil Use* (1960) and *Caribs, Cannibals and Human Relations* (1972). His essays and articles were published in various magazines and journals, including the *Negro Champion*, *Daily Worker*, and *Freedomways.*

October 25

Wilfred Adolphus Domingo

November 26, 1889 - February 14, 1968

Wilfred Adolphus Domingo (W. A. Domingo) was a Jamaican activist and journalist who became the youngest editor of Marcus Garvey's newspaper, the *Negro World.* As an activist and writer, Domingo travelled to the United States advocating for Jamaican sovereignty as a leader of the African Blood Brotherhood and the Harlem branch of the Socialist Party.

Domingo was born in Kingston, Jamaica, the youngest son of a Jamaican mother and a Spanish father. Orphaned early, Domingo was brought up with his siblings by a maternal uncle and was educated at the Kingston Board School, an English-run colonial school specifically for the West Indies. On graduating, he worked as a tailor and began writing newspaper articles.

Domingo left Jamaica for the United States in 1910, settling initially in Boston before moving to New York. Having met Garvey in Jamaica through Jamaica's first nationalist political group, the National Club, Domingo introduced Garvey to people such as Henry Rogowski, who was the printer for *The Call.*

Domingo met Alain Locke and was a contributor to Locke's 1925 anthology *The New Negro: An Interpretation*. Domingo's essay *The Gift of the Black Tropics* gave an account of the sudden immigration of foreign-born Africans of the West Indies to Harlem during the early 1920s.

On an invitation, Domingo returned to Jamaica in after 31 years of living in the United States to help expand the burgeoning People's National Party (PNP), a Jamaican political party with social-democratic views. While in this group, Domingo focused on organizing with others to establish Jamaican self-governance.

Some of Domingo's works include: *What Are We, Negroes or Colored People*? in *Separatism versus Integration*, (1919); *Socialism, The Negroes' Hope* from *Race, Ethnicity, and Gender in Early Twentieth-Century American Socialism*, (1919).

October 26

Margie Hook Mosley
April 19, 1929 - December 15, 2010

Contributor: Rosetta Hook Pringle, M.Sc. (Daughter)

Margie Hook Mosley, Black American was born in South Carolina, United States of America. She was the daughter of sharecropper parents with seven siblings. She grew up during the Jim Crow Era. And she was denied education under this system. She and her family would work from dusk to dawn on the farm. It was a very hard life and they gained very little under the Jim Crow System.

As a young woman in her early twenties she was chosen by an uncle to go live with family members in Washington, DC. This began her migration journey to the northeast in the 1940s.

In the 1950s she moved to New York City where she assisted many family members and friends in the Great Migration. She helped them with finances for traveling and found housing for them in New York. On the arrival of these family and friends Margie helped them with job training and guiding them on travelling around the city.

In New York City, where she finally decided to live she kept the southern tradition of meeting on Sundays with family and friends for meetings, dinners and for supporting each other.

Margie also sponsored the annual family reunion bringing together all who lived in the northeast region.

October 27

To everyone who has transitioned who did not self-identify as African and worked for the liberation of Africans.

October 28

Shero Dovetta Victoria Wilson
Contributor: Rev. Dr. Ruby Wilson (Daughter)

The Enduring Legacy of the African Shero Dovetta Victoria Wilson

In this climate of COVID-Pre 1619, COVID -1619 and COVID-19, I lift up my beloved mother, the late Dovetta Victoria Wilson (nee Crawford, the daughter of a Baptist preacher and Alabaman sharecroppers, Rev. Jeremiah Crawford and Dovetta Crawford (nee Henderson).

She was born amid the 1923 nationwide flu epidemic, in one of the most at-risk rural areas in the country. Her geographical area was hit so hard that she herself, a mere infant, was stricken with the illness. Her parents were told that their baby Dove's body was much too small to fight against this gargantuan virus and she did not stand a chance. She survived and thrived and given a nickname as the only reminder of her harrowing childhood trauma: "Flu."

Oh how she loved learning, though handicapped by the egregious "Jim Crow" segregation educational system whose whole agenda was training her and her 13 siblings for agricultural and domestic work to ensure that the cotton was picked, clothes were washed and whites could live the genteel life to which they felt entitled.

Dovetta, a tiny baby who battled a raging epidemic, beat back the crippling hands of "Jim Crow" and clawed and climbed her way through and up cotton picking and scrubbing floors, reared nine children, along with her husband, David in Harlem's Lincoln Houses. She instilled and infused in her children, the liberating love of God, country, community, and education. And though statistics showed, *It Can't Be Done*, this African Shero whose blood flows back to the Mende tribe of Sierra Leone, produced educators, theologians, business entrepreneurs and a spirit of philanthropy that pours from the heart of her people.

October 29

Wilbert Williamson

Contributor: Errol Williamson (Son)

Wilbert Williamson was born to Clara and Edward Williamson in Golden Grove, St. Ann, Jamaica. He was an ambitious and great man who cared for his family and his community. He often went out to find and purchase land where he would farm planting and harvesting crops such as yam, pumpkin, potatoes, and corn to feed his family.

Wilbert was a hands-on disciplinarian who never spared the rod to spoil the child.

A mason by trade and a jack of all trades, Wilbert and others, during the construction of Bethesda Gospel Chapel church in the early 1930s in Golden Grove, walked two miles carrying stones on their heads that would lay the foundation for community residents to have a church home. Today, in 2020 during the worldwide pandemic of COVID-19 and the social distancing required to help reduce the spread of the virus and with distance teaching and learning, the church that Wilbert helped to build provides WI-FI internet access to students to do their school work.

Light George, as Wilbert was known in the district was a committed Christian who was loyal to the church. At home, he taught his children of seven from the union with Ruth Ann to sing and to study and follow the teachings of the Bible.

Based on my dad's teachings and practice I have learned about commitment to God, family and community and I walk humbly in his footsteps as husband, father and grandfather, and pastor of Bethesda Gospel Chapel.

October 30

Kwaku – Antigua
c. 1694

In 1704, 10-year-old Kwaku was captured form Gold Coast, West Africa which is today Ghana during the massive Eguafo Civil war after the death of King Takyi Kuma, a few years after the end of the Kommenda wars. The several wars that happened in the Gold Coast between the 1680s and 1700s was an advantage to the Danish and British slave traders who captured as many people as possible and sold them off to slavery.

Kwaku was shipped to the Caribbean and was purchased by a rich and prominent sugar planter. At a young age, Kwaku exhibited strength and bravery standing up to white supervisors who harassed him or any of his friends.

Kwaku decided to free himself and all enslaved Africans.

In 1728, Kwaku planned to rid the island of all oppressors, abolish slavery, and make the island of Antigua an African state. After figuring out a great way to execute his plan, he shared details with several like-minded enslaved Africans who helped him develop his plan. The strategy took eight years of planning.

The plan was well-designed and more than ten huge plantations were the target. During an Akan ceremony at one of the planning meetings, Kwaku was initiated as King of the Black community.

The plan was leaked to several slave masters by enslaved African who stayed anonymous. The ball was postponed and Kwaku and several of his allies were captured and executed. Had the plan been successful, the "Antigua's Disputed Slave Conspiracy of 1736", as it is popularly known, would have possibly sparked the beginning of African rule outside of the African continent

Every October 22, the people of Antigua and Barbuda celebrate the execution of Kwaku whose name has been established as Prince Klaas.

☐ October 31

Rice Coast

Bunce Island in Sierra Leone, 20 miles up the Sierra Leone River, and a few miles north of the capital Freetown, was home to one of the most profitable slave trading operations in West Africa. Established in 1670 by English slave traders, it was the largest British slave castle on the Rice Coast where tens of thousands of African were shipped to North America and the West Indies.

The island was part of more than sixty slave-trading forts on the West African coast. It was majorly operated by two companies — the Gambia Adventurers and the Royal African Company of England — from 1670 to 1728. It flourished during private management by a consortium of London firms from 1744 to 1807. Slave trading ceased on the island in 1808 after the slave trade was abolished.

The selection of Africans from the Rice Coast, which stretches from Senegal right to Liberia through Bunce Island, was not random. Africans were particularly targeted on account of Bai Bureh, Sierra Leone's greatest hero who held off British control for months in 1898

South Carolina, which became one of the wealthiest states in North America with an economy based on rice cultivation, benefited the most from these enslaved Africans from the Rice Coast. Nearby Georgia also insisted on using slaves from this region. At the time, during slave auctions in Charlestown (now Charleston), South Carolina, Savana and Georgia, slave selling advertisements specifically mentioned slaves from the Rice Coast or Bunce Island to assure buyers that they would get experienced hands. Buyers would then be willing to pay more for them.

Rice cultivation in America increased as more and more African captives were shipped from Bunce Island to work on rice farms.

November 1

Bai Bureh
February 15, 1840 - August 24, 1908

Bai Bureh, military strategist, Muslim cleric and ruler of Sierra Leone led the foundation to independence as the fight for freedom largely started with his 1898 uprising against British rule. His nickname *Kebalai*, which means "one who never tires of war," is visible in the many months he held off a highly trained, well-equipped British force in 1898 in guerilla warfare.

With only spears, swords, slings and obsolete muskets, Bureh and his men were a thorn in the flesh of the British administration that was then using Sierra Leone's natural harbor Freetown as its capital.

November 2

Audre Lorde

February 18, 1934 - November 17, 1992

Audre Lorde born Audrey Geraldine Lorde was an American writer, feminist, womanist, librarian, and civil rights activist. She was a self-described "Black, lesbian, mother, warrior, poet," who dedicated both her life and her creative talent to confronting and addressing injustices of racism, sexism, classism, heterosexism, and homophobia.

As a poet, she is known for technical mastery and emotional expression, as well as her poems that express anger and outrage at civil and social injustices she observed throughout her life. Her poems and prose largely deal with issues related to civil rights, feminism, lesbianism, illness and disability, and the exploration of Black female identity.

Lorde was born in New York City to Caribbean immigrants, her father from Barbados and her mother Grenadian from the island of Carriacou, Frederick Byron Lorde (known as Byron) and Linda Gertrude Belmar Lorde, who settled in Harlem. Lorde's mother was of mixed ancestry but could "pass" for 'Spanish', which was a source of pride for her family. Lorde's father was darker than the Belmar family liked, and they only allowed the couple to marry because of Byron Lorde's charm, ambition, and persistence.

Nearsighted to the point of being legally blind and the youngest of three daughters, Lorde grew up hearing her mother's stories about the West Indies. At the age of four, she learned to talk while she learned to read, and her mother taught her to write at around the same time. She wrote her first poem when she was in the eighth grade.

Her works include *Sister Outsider* (1984), and *Your Silence Will Not Protect You* (2017).

November 3

David Fagen
c. 1875 - ?

David Fagen was an African-American soldier who defected during the Philippine-American War. He acquired the rank of captain in the Philippine Revolutionary Army.

A native of Tampa, Florida, USA, Fagen served in the 24th Regiment of the U.S. Army, but on November 17, 1899, he defected to the Filipino army. He became a successful guerrilla leader and his capture became an obsession to the U.S. military and American public. His defection was likely the result of differential treatment by white American occupational forces toward African-American soldiers, as well as common white American forces derogatory treatment and views of the Filipino occupational resistance, who were frequently referred to as "niggers" and "gugus".

After two other Black deserters were captured and executed, President Theodore Roosevelt announced he would stop executing captured deserters.

As the war ended, the US gave amnesties to most of their opponents. A substantial reward was offered for Fagen, who was considered a traitor. There are two conflicting versions of his fate: one is that his was the partially decomposed head for which the reward was claimed, the other is that he took a local wife and lived peacefully in the mountains.

November 4

Ralph David Abernathy Sr.
March 11, 1926 - April 17, 1990

Ralph David Abernathy Sr. was an American civil rights activist and Baptist minister ordained in 1948.

As a leader of the civil rights movement, A was a close friend and mentor of Martin Luther King Jr. He collaborated with King to create the Montgomery Improvement Association which led to the Montgomery bus boycott. He also co-founded and was an executive board member of the Southern Christian Leadership Conference (SCLC). He became president of the SCLC following the assassination of King in 1968, where he led the Poor People's Campaign in Washington, D.C. among other marches and demonstrations for disenfranchised Americans. He also served as an advisory committee member of the Congress on Racial Equality (CORE).

In 1971, Abernathy addressed the United Nations about world peace. He also assisted in brokering a deal between the FBI and Indian protestors during the Wounded Knee incident of 1973. He retired from his position as president of the SCLC in 1977 and became president emeritus. Later that year he unsuccessfully ran for the U.S. House of Representatives for the 5th district of Georgia. He later founded the Foundation for Economic Enterprises Development, and he testified before the U.S. Congress in support of extending of the Voting Rights Act in 1982.

In 1989, Abernathy wrote *And the Walls Came Tumbling Down* (1989), a controversial autobiography about his and King's involvement in the Civil Rights Movement.

Abernathy eventually became less active in politics and returned to his work as a minister. His tombstone is engraved with the words "I tried".

November 5
Carlota Lucumí, also known as La Negra Carlota
? – 1844

Carlota Lucumí, also known as La Negra Carlota was an African-born enslaved Cuban woman of Yoruba origin. **Carlota**, alongside enslaved comrade Lucumí Ferminia, was known as one of the leaders of the slave rebellion at the Triunvirato plantation in Matanzas, Cuba during the Year of the Lash in 1843-1844.

Together with Ferminia Lucumí, Carlota led the slave uprising of the sugar mill "Triunvirato" in the province of Matanzas, Cuba in 1843. Her memory has also been utilized throughout history by the Cuban government in connection to 20th century political goals, most notably *Operation Carlota*, or Cuba's intervention in Angola in 1975.

Kidnapped by slavers as child, Carlota was brought from West Africa to the Matanzas province of Cuba.

Known for both her intelligence and musical skill, Carlota sent coded messages using talking drums to coordinate a series of attacks. As the drums were a traditional instrument among the West Africans, the Spanish were unaware that the music was also being used as a form of communication. On November 3rd 1843, Carlota led a raid which freed Fermina and a dozen other slaves from captivity. On November 5th the uprising began at the Triumvirato and Acane sugar plantations, forcibly overthrowing the Spanish owners. These attacks were led personally by Carlota, who went into battle wielding a machete.

The first authorization of the king from Spain to introduce Africans in Cuba, took place in 1512. The fundamental cause to bring them was their strength and performance at work in comparison with the indigenous peoples.

November 6

David Hamilton Jackson
September 28, 1884 - May 30, 1946

David Hamilton Jackson was a labor rights advocate in the Danish West Indies, later the United States Virgin Islands. Jackson was an important figure in the struggle for increased civil rights and workers' rights on the islands. He petitioned for freedom of the press, and organized the islands' first trade union. Following the transfer of the territory to American control in 1917, he lobbied for US citizenship for the islanders.

Jackson worked as an educator, a bookkeeper, and clerk before becoming involved in the politics of the Danish West Indies. He traveled to Denmark and successfully petitioned for the repeal of a 1779 law which prohibited independent newspapers and enforced strict censorship on all publications in the territory. Upon returning home, he established the first free newspaper, *The Herald.* The date of this event, November 1, is celebrated as an annual public holiday known as "Liberty Day", D. Hamilton Jackson Day, or Bull and Bread Day in the U.S. Virgin Islands.

November 7

Barbara Charline Jordan
February 21, 1936 - January 17, 1996

Barbara Charline Jordan was an American lawyer, educator, and politician who was a leader of the Civil Rights Movement. A Democrat, she and Andrew Young (Georgia) were the first African Americans from the South elected to Congress since Reconstruction. They came into office in 1973.

Jordan was the first African American elected to the Texas Senate after Reconstruction and the first Southern African-American woman elected to the United States House of Representatives.

Jordan was well-known for her eloquent opening statement at the House Judiciary Committee hearings during the impeachment process against Richard Nixon, and as the first African-American as well as the first woman to deliver a keynote address at the 1976 Democratic National Convention. She received the Presidential Medal of Freedom, among numerous other honors. She was a member of the Peabody Awards Board of Jurors from 1978 to 1980. She was the first African-American woman to be buried in the Texas State Cemetery.

Jordan's work as chair of the U.S. Commission on Immigration Reform, which recommended reducing legal immigration by about one-third, is frequently cited by American immigration restrictionists.

November 8

The Port Royal Experiment, 1861

The Port Royal Experiment was a program begun during the American Civil War in which former enslaved Africans successfully worked on the land abandoned by planters.

In 1861 the Union captured the Sea Islands off the coast of South Carolina and the main harbor, Port Royal. The white residents fled, leaving behind 10,000 enslaved Africans. Several private Northern charity organizations stepped in to help the former enslaved Africans become self-sufficient. The result was a model of what Reconstruction could have been.

The African Americans demonstrated their ability to work the land efficiently and live independently of white control. They assigned themselves daily tasks for cotton growing and spent their extra time cultivating their own crops, fishing and hunting. By selling their surplus crops, the locals acquired small amounts of property.

November 9

Onkgopotse Tiro

November 9, 1947 - February 1, 1974
A Founding Leader of the Free South Africa Movement

Onkgopotse Tiro was born in Dinokana Village outside the small town of Zeerust, in what is now known as the North West Province, South Africa. These origins automatically define him as son of poor parents.

Like other African young men and women, Tiro managed to make it to university. For him, being of a particular tribal origin, it could only be University of the North, also known as Turfloop, a Blacks-only university for students designated for the Tswana, Sotho, Pedi, Venda and Shangaan tribes, located east of Polokwane. This was the policy of the white apartheid governing state of the time.

The family, social background and experiences that Onkgopotse brought to the university immediately came into conflict with the colonial and racial texture inscribed in every facet of the university life. The critical, questioning mind of the soon to be born philosophy of Black Consciousness soon showed its real character when Tiro and other Black students immersed themselves in debates about how they should organize themselves around their own reality, Black reality.

The anger of the white racist administrators and staff at the university and most likely on behalf of all other white racists was highly provoked when Tiro delivered a graduation speech in 1972, that ignited Black student political uprising throughout the land.

Tiro was a student leader at the University of the North, now University of Limpopo, in the early 1970s and one of the early exponents of the revolutionary Black Consciousness Movement in South Africa. He fled to exile in Botswana, where he was killed by a parcel bomb in 1974. It has always been suspected that it was sent by the apartheid security forces.

November 10

Quilombo of Brazil, 1600's

A Quilombo in Amapá.

A quilombo is a Brazilian hinterland settlement founded by people of African origin. Most of the inhabitants of quilombos, called quilombolas, were maroons, a term used to describe Africans who escaped from slavery.

Documentation about communities of enslaved Africans who ran away from plantations typically uses the term mocambo for settlements, which is an Ambundu word meaning "war camp". A mocambo is typically much smaller than a quilombo. The term quilombo was not used until the 1670s, and then primarily in the more southerly parts of Brazil.

In the Spanish-speaking countries of Latin America, such villages or camps were called a palenque. Its inhabitants are palenqueros. They spoke various Spanish-African-based creole languages such as Palenquero.

A *quilombo* or *mocambo* was a group of Africans who were forcibly brought to Brazil (from present-day Angola, Democratic Republic of Congo, and Congo-Brazzaville) who escaped from slavery and fled into the interior of Brazil to the mountainous region of Pernambuco. As their numbers increased, they formed maroon settlements.

Quilombos are classified as one of the three basic forms of active resistance by enslaved Africans. They also regularly attempted to seize power and conducted armed insurrections at plantations to gain amelioration of conditions. Typically, quilombos were a "pre-19th century phenomenon". In the first half of the 19th-century in Brazil, enslaved Africans typically took armed action as part of their resistance. The colony was undergoing both political transition as it fought for independence from Portugal and new tensions associated with an increased slave trade, which brought in many more native-born Africans.

November 11

Palmares

The most famous quilombo was Palmares, an independent, self-sustaining community near Recife, established in about 1600. Palmares was massive and consisted of several settlements with a combined population of over 30,000 citizens, mostly Blacks. It was the only quilombo to survive almost an entire century, with the second longest-standing quilombo, in Mato Grosso, lasting 25 years.

Part of the reason for the massive size of the quilombo at Palmares was because of its location in Brazil, at the median point between the Atlantic Ocean and Guinea, an important area of the African slave trade. *Quilombo dos Palmares* was a self-sustaining community of escaped Africans who had been enslaved from the Portuguese settlements in Brazil, "a region perhaps the size of Portugal in the hinterland of Bahia".

At its height, Palmares had a population of over 30,000. Forced to defend against repeated attacks by Portuguese colonists, the warriors of Palmares were experts in capoeira, a dance and martial art form.

Ganga Zumba and Zumbi are the two best-known warrior-leaders of Palmares which, after a history of conflict with first Dutch and then Portuguese colonial authorities, finally fell to a Portuguese artillery assault in 1694.

In Brazil, both men are now honored as heroes and symbols of Black pride, freedom, and democracy. As his birthday is unknown, Zumbi's execution date, November 20, is observed as *Dia da Consciência Negra* or "Black Awareness Day" in the states of Rio de Janeiro and São Paulo, and his image has appeared on postage stamps, banknotes, and coins.

November 12

Jerry John Rawlings

June 22, 1947 - November 12, 2020

Jerry Rawlings, the former military leader and then twice-elected president of Ghana, dominated the country's political life for two decades in the 1980s and 90s.

In May 1979, Flt Lt Rawlings of the Ghanaian air force burst on to the country's political scene. With a handful of officers, shortly before a planned election, he launched an unsuccessful coup d'etat against a corrupt and discredited military government headed by Gen Fred Akuffo.

Rawlings was part of a radical underground organisation in the military called the Free Africa Movement. They were mainly young men, and dreamed of a united African continent free of a generation of discredited corrupt leaders close to the European colonial governments and western business interests that dominated so much of the postcolonial landscape.

For the coup attempt, Rawlings was arrested and condemned to death in a military trial. But his blunt statements on the country's urgent need for a new era of social, political and economic justice had fired up his peers, and on 4 June 1979 a group of soldiers forcibly released him from prison before he could be executed.

A second coup led by Rawlings against the Akuffo government succeeded. The scheduled election brought in a civilian government, headed by Hilla Limann, a respected judge, ending the long run of military rule.

With military life behind him, Rawlings had become a charismatic and fearless speaker who was popular among the young soldiers and a militant, impoverished urban working class, and he seized the imagination of many well beyond West Africa. His administration's promises of bold economic and social reform, and of an anti-imperialist foreign policy was reminiscent of that of Ghana's first president after independence, Kwame Nkrumah (1960-64).

November 13

McKinley Morganfield
April 4, 1913 - April 30, 1983

McKinley Morganfield known professionally as Muddy Waters, was an American blues singer-songwriter and musician who was an important figure in the post-war blues scene, and is often cited as the father of modern Chicago blues. His style of playing has been described as raining down Delta beatitude.

Muddy Waters grew up on Stovall Plantation near Clarksdale, Mississippi, and by age 17 was playing the guitar and the harmonica, emulating the local blues artists Son House and Robert Johnson. He was recorded in Mississippi by Alan Lomax for the Library of Congress in 1941. In 1943, he moved to Chicago to become a full-time professional musician. In 1946, he recorded his first records for Columbia Records and then for Aristocrat Records, a newly formed label run by the brothers Leonard and Phil Chess.

In the early 1950s, Muddy Waters and his band—Little Walter Jacobs on harmonica, Jimmy Rogers on guitar, Elga Edmonds (also known as Elgin Evans) on drums and Otis Spann on piano—recorded several blues classics, some with the bassist and songwriter Willie Dixon. These songs included *Hoochie Coochie Man, I Just Want to Make Love to You* and *I'm Ready*.

In 1958, Muddy Waters traveled to England, laying the foundations of the resurgence of interest in the blues there. His performance at the Newport Jazz Festival in 1960 was recorded and released as his first live album, *At Newport 1960.*

Muddy Waters' music has influenced various American music genres, including rock and roll and rock music.

November 14

Vivian Robinson
1926-1996

Vivian Robinson was one who believed if you want something done, don't wait for others to do it, get busy and do it yourself. Ms. Robinson was also an advent lover of the arts, especially the theatrical arts. In 1966 she started working for the *Amsterdam News* as a clerk/typist then became the newspapers theater critic, writing reviews on a regular basis.

Ms. Robinson noticed that many within the Black theatrical community were not receiving their deserved recognition, and awards. In 1973, she and three of her friends started the Audelco Committee Inc. and the Audelco Awards with the idea of showcasing, exposing, and awarding the best in the Black theater including actors, dancers, set designers, costume designers, choreographers and others who many times were over looked.

Ms. Robinson was interested in reshaping the way Blacks were seen and portrayed on stage. She celebrated meaningful portrayals of Blacks in roles that uplifted racial pride and dignity at a time when very few existed.

The AUDELCO (Audience Development Committee, Inc.) is an organization that acknowledges and honors Black Theatre and its artists in New York City. Established and incorporated in 1973 by Vivian Robinson to stimulate interest in and support of performing arts in Black communities.

November 15

Frank Rudolph Crosswaith

1892–1965

Frank Rudolph Crosswaith was a longtime socialist politician and activist and trade union organizer in New York City who founded and chaired the Negro Labor Committee, established in 1935 by the Negro Labor Conference.

Frank R. Crosswaith was born in St. Croix, Danish West Indies (the island was sold to the United States in 1917 and became part of the U.S. Virgin Islands). His parents were William I. Crosswaith and Anne Eliza Crosswaith. He emigrated to the United States in his teens. While finishing high school, he worked as an elevator operator, porter and garment worker. He joined the elevator operators' union and when he finished high school, he won a scholarship from the socialist *The Jewish Daily Forward* to attend the Rand School of Social Science, an educational institute in New York City associated with the Socialist Party of America.

Crosswaith founded an organization called the Trade Union Committee for Organizing Negro Workers in 1925, but this work went by the wayside when Crosswaith accepted a position as an organizer for the at the time fledgling Brotherhood of Sleeping Car Porters. Crosswaith maintained a long association with union head A. Philip Randolph, serving with him as officers of the Negro Labor Committee in the 1930s and 1940s.

Crosswaith was an anti-communist and believed that the best hope for Black workers in the United States was to join bona fide labor unions just as the best hope for the American labor movement was to welcome Black workers into unions in order to promote solidarity and eliminate the use of Black workers as strike breakers.

November 16

Nana Yao Opare Dinizulu
1931 - 1991

Nana Yao Opare Dinizulu founded The Dinizulu Center for African Culture and Research at Aims of Modzawe, Inc. in Jamaica, New York to provide a mechanism for the study and teaching of African Culture. Nana Dinizulu was involved in the study, practice and dissemination of African culture and traditions for over four decades. He was instrumental in introducing hundreds of thousands of people to African culture, through his dance company and other appearances. He was also the founder of the troupe called Dinizulu and His African Dancers, Drummers and Singers.

Nana Dinizulu taught dance at Queens College, City University of New York, through the Africana Studies department where Dr. Wentworth Ofuatey-Kodjoe served as its chairman.

Nana Yao Opare Dinizulu was born in Augusta, Ga., and traced his lineage to Ghana. He traveled to Africa frequently and in Ghana received the titles of Omanhene and Okomfohene, or chief and spiritual leader, of the Akan tribe. Nana is a Ghanaian title of respect. In the United States, he helped promote African customs and traditions with special emphasis on the Akan religion.

November 17

Williana "Liana" Jones Burroughs
January 2, 1882 - December 24, 1945

Williana "Liana" Jones Burroughs was an American teacher, communist political activist, and politician. She is best remembered as one of the first women to run for elective office in New York.

Burroughs was born in Petersburg, Virginia. Her mother had formerly been an enslaved African for 16 years, her father died when Williana was four years old. She was unable to care for her children adequately, and so Williana spent the next seven years in the Colored Orphan Asylum, located at the time on the corner of 143rd Street and Amsterdam Avenue in Harlem. Her mother retrieved her three children from the orphanage when Williana was eleven.

Burroughs attended public school in New York, where she was an excellent student. For college, she attended New York City Normal College, known today as Hunter College, where she achieved credentials to become a teacher. She taught first and second grade children, and was recruited into the New York City Teachers Union and she was active as part of the Communist-led Rank and File caucus.

Burroughs joined the Workers (Communist) Party 1926. She became active in the campaign for defense of the Scottsboro boys and was chairman of the Blumberg Defense Council, an organization formed to defend Isidore Blumberg, a teacher removed from the New York public schools system due to his political views.

After losing of her teaching position, Burroughs became the Communist Party's candidate for New York Comptroller in the fall of 1933 and the candidate for Lieutenant Governor of New York in 1934.

November 18

Chandler Owen

April 5, 1889 - November 2, 1967

Chandler Owen was an African-American writer, editor and early member of the Socialist Party of America. Born in North Carolina, he studied and worked in New York City, then moved to Chicago for much of his career. He established his own public relations company in Chicago and wrote speeches for candidates and presidents including Thomas Dewey, Dwight D. Eisenhower, and Lyndon B. Johnson.

Owen was born in Warrenton, North Carolina, and he graduated from Virginia Union University in 1913. While studying economics at Columbia University in 1916, he joined the Socialist Party of America. He began a lifelong friendship with A. Philip Randolph and together they followed the lead of radical activist Hubert Harrison. They soon became known in Harlem as "Lenin" (Owen) and "Trotsky" (Randolph). The two started a journal in 1917, called *The Messenger*, which published leading literary and political writers. Soon after, while Owen was running for the New York State Assembly, he and Randolph were jailed, where they were mocked and treated cruelly for their Socialist affiliations.

In a 1919 issue of *The Messenger* Owen and Randolph wrote, "We don't thank God for anything...our Deity is the toiling masses of the world and the things for which we thank are their achievement."

In the 1920s, Owen became a Republican. He ran unsuccessfully for a seat in the United States House of Representatives. Following that, he worked in public relations and continued to write speeches.

November 19

The African Blood Brotherhood

The African Blood Brotherhood for African Liberation and Redemption (ABB) was a U.S. Black liberation organization established in 1919 in New York City by journalist Cyril Briggs. The group was established as a propaganda organization built on the model of the secret society. The group's socialist orientation caught the attention of the fledgling American communist movement and the ABB soon evolved into a propaganda arm of the Communist Party of America. The group was terminated in the early 1920s.

November 20

Hamitic League of the World

The Hamitic League of the World was an African American nationalist organization. Its declared aims were:

To inspire the Negro with new hopes; to make him openly proud of his race and of its great contributions to the religious development and civilization of mankind; and to place in the hands of every race man and woman and child the facts which support the League's claim that the Negro Race is the greatest race the world has ever known.

The word Hamitic derives from Ham the son of Noah in the Old Testament. The organisation was founded in 1917 by George Wells Parker. In 1918 it published a pamphlet *Children of the Sun.* At this time Cyril Briggs also became the editor of their journal, *The Crusader* which subsequently became the journal of the African Blood Brotherhood.

November 21
Congress for Racial Equality (CORE)

The Congress of Racial Equality (CORE), founded in 1942, became one of the leading activist organizations in the early years of the American civil rights movement. In the early 1960s, CORE, working with other civil rights groups, launched a series of initiatives: the Freedom Rides, aimed at desegregating public facilities, the Freedom Summer voter registration project and the historic 1963 March on Washington. CORE initially embraced a pacifist, non-violent approach to fighting racial segregation, but by the late 1960s the group's leadership had shifted its focus towards the political ideology of Black nationalism and separatism.

CORE was founded on the University of Chicago campus in 1942 as an outgrowth of the pacifist Fellowship of Reconciliation.

For the next two decades, CORE introduced a small group of civil rights activists to the idea of achieving change through nonviolence, but during these years, its chapters were all in the North and its membership predominantly white and middle class.

In 1955 CORE went into the South and provided nonviolence training to demonstrators during the Montgomery, Alabama, bus boycott. Soon thereafter, CORE hired a small staff to work in the South.

In June 1964, three CORE activists, Andrew Goodman, James Chaney and Michael Schwerner, were murdered by members of the Ku Klux Klan while working as volunteers for CORE's Freedom Summer voter registration project in Mississippi.

November 22

James Farmer

January 12, 1920 - July 9, 1999

James Leonard Farmer, Jr., born in Marshall, Texas, was an American civil rights activist who, as a leader of the Congress of Racial Equality (CORE), helped shape the civil rights movement through his nonviolent activism and organizing of sit-ins and Freedom Rides, which broadened popular support for passage of the Civil Rights and Voting Rights acts in the mid-1960s.

Farmer was educated at Wiley College in Marshall, Texas and at Howard University in Washington, D.C., where his father taught divinity. A conscientious objector on religious grounds, he received a military deferral in World War II, and he joined the pacifist Fellowship of Reconciliation (FOR). In 1942 he cofounded CORE, which originated integrated bus trips through the South, called Freedom Rides, to challenge local efforts to block the desegregation of interstate busing. Farmer, who sought racial justice by means of nonviolence, was often a target of racial violence himself.

He resigned from the leadership of CORE in 1965, and in 1968 he lost a run for a seat in the U.S. House of Representatives to Shirley Chisholm. In 1969–70 he served as assistant secretary of health, education and welfare under President Richard M. Nixon. In 1985 Farmer published his autobiography, *Lay Bare the Heart*, and in 1998 he was awarded the Presidential Medal of Freedom.

November 23

Roy Emile Alfredo Innis
June 6, 1934 - January 8, 2017

Roy Emile Alfredo Innis was an American activist and politician. He was National Chairman of the Congress of Racial Equality (CORE) from 1968 until his death.

Innis was born in Saint Croix, U.S. Virgin Islands in 1934 and moved with his mother from the U.S. Virgin Islands to New York City, where he graduated from Stuyvesant High School in 1952. At age 16, Innis joined the U.S. Army, and after two years of service he received an honorable discharge. He entered a four-year program in chemistry at the City College of New York and worked as a research chemist at Vick Chemical Company and Montefiore Hospital.

CORE is known for its role in organizing acts designed to confront and end apartheid in America, from the Freedom Rides throughout the South to the pivotal March on Washington for Jobs and Freedom in 1963.

Roy Innis, who took control of CORE in 1968, dramatically transformed the group's mission from racial integration to Black separatism.

November 24
POWs - England

During the wars against revolutionary and Napoleonic France of the late 18th and early 19th Centuries, when Britain's Black population numbered no more than 10,000, some 2,000 African-Caribbean people were held as prisoners of war in Portchester Castle in Portsmouth Harbour.

In the intervening 200 years, many POWs' names were forgotten, but now, after years of painstaking research, Abigail Coppins, curator at English Heritage, which manages the castle, has rediscovered their identities.

Ms. Coppins said: "To discover the identities of 2,000 African-Caribbean prisoners of war imprisoned in Portchester Castle was quite astonishing.

"At a time when the entire Black population of Britain was roughly 10 - 15,000, our exhibition completely turns the tables on the views of the period. These names and this exhibition restore a forgotten chapter of Black history to England's story.

"These were not slaves, but free men and women, fighting and in some cases dying for a cause they believed in."

One such name is Delgrès; born free on the Caribbean island of Martinique, Delgrès, of mixed race, was captured on St Vincent in 1796, when the British crushed a force comprised of the island's local population, runaway slaves and French soldiers.

Source: https://www.independent.co.uk/news/uk/home-news/slavery-Black-prisoners-war-race-racism-portchester-castle-english-heritage-exhibition-britain-british-anti-slavery-colonial-history-european-colonialism-imperialism-caribbean-plantations-st-lucia-st-vincent-a7846051.html

November 25

Randolph Samuel Williams
October 26, 1912 - August 11, 1980

Randolph Samuel Williams (Mas Ran) was a dramatist and comedian. He first started his acting career as a child reciting poetry at church, Lodge Hall and schoolrooms in Jamaica.

Born in Colon Panama, Williams came to Jamaica with his family at the age of six.

Williams appeared in pantomimes, films and on television entertaining audiences with his theatrical gifts. . His first pantomime *Bluebeard and Brer Anancy* was in 1942.

Williams was the host of the *Ranny Williams Show* on television and his films include *A High Wind in Jamaica, Oh Dad Poor Dad, White Souls, Jamaica No Problems, Tropical Isles, Zacc Experience,* and *The Marijuana Affair.*

His outstanding achievement in the field of entertainment and drama earned him several awards: The Jamaica Certificate and the Badge of Honour in the Queen's New Year honours list (1968). The Institute of Jamaica Silver Musgrave Medal (1968), Commander of the Order of Distinction (C. D.) for Outstanding Services in the field of Entertainment (1976) and the Centenary Medal (1979). The Ranny Williams Entertainment Centre stands as a monument to his work.

One of Williams' greatest accomplishments is being the recipient of the love of the people of Jamaica .This love comes from the fact that he also gave service outside of entertainment. He was a social worker, worked with Jamaica Movement for the Advancement of Literacy (JAMAL), founder of the Ranny Williams Youth Club, and a participant on The Nugget for the Needy show.

Source: https://jis.gov.jm/information/famous-jamaicans/randolph-samuel-williams/

November 26

Panama Black Movement

In the years following the 1989 U.S. invasion of Panama, there was an observable increase in racial discrimination, overt racist practices, and social disparity there that was the consequence of the defeat of the popular forces, the embrace of neoliberalism by wide sectors of the political and economic class, and the disarray of the Black movement.

During the 90s, Afro-Panamanian groups and popular organizations had to adjust to the post-invasion political and economic environment dominated by the so-called transition to democracy, which was accompanied by the implementation of neoliberal policies by the white political elite in the governmental and opposition parties. This chapter seeks to address the challenges and opportunities for mobilization faced by the Panamanian Black movement since the 1989 invasion, and particularly in the decade between 1994 and 2004.

Source: https://link.springer.com/chapter/10.1057/9780230104570_4

November 27

John Elroy Sanford aka Redd Foxx
December 9, 1922 - October 11, 1991

Notorious for his frank, tell-it-like-it-is style, Redd Foxx (his stage name) broke new ground for Blacks and comedians alike. By joking about everything from sex to color barriers, he brought simmering and taboo issues into the open. His candor onstage not only jump-started what is now considered a war with censors, but also inspired and enabled other comedians to achieve more than had ever been possible. Foxx was not only "The King of Comedy," but also a talented artist. He took a sketchbook with him whenever possible, and enjoyed creating his own fantastic images or capturing the essence of those whom he loved or admired.

John Elroy Sanford was born in St. Louis, Missouri. With a ruddy complexion, Redd fast became a nickname. He derived Foxx from admirable Major League Baseball player, Jimmie Foxx. He left St. Louis for Chicago when he was 13, and supported himself by playing the washboard in a band. When the band broke up three years later, he hopped a train to New York City. It was there that he met Malcolm Little, a man who would later be known as Malcolm X. In *The Autobiography of Malcolm X*, he is referred to as "Chicago Red, the funniest dishwasher on this earth."

Foxx began performing as a comedian/actor in Black theaters and nightclubs, often referred to as the "Chitlin Circuit." From 1951-1955 he teamed with comic Slappy White, a lifelong friend who would also act alongside him on *Sanford and Son* and *The Redd Foxx Comedy Hour*. He produced more than 50 comedic albums, made his film debut in Ossie Davis' *Cotton Comes to Harlem*, and was signed by NBC for the *Sanford and Son* television sitcom.

November 28

Loretta Mary Aiken
c. 1894 - May 23, 1975

Moms Mabley was a trailblazing African American 20th century comedian known for warm yet raunchy stand-up routines and hit albums.

Moms Mabley was born in Brevard, North Carolina in the 1890s, and went on to establish a career as the top standup comedienne of her time. She starred in several films, became a headliner at the Apollo Theater and in the 1960s had hit comedy albums. She was also a top draw for a number of TV variety shows. She died in New York on May 23, 1975. Comedian Whoopi Goldberg directed a documentary on Mabley's life.

The woman who would become known as famed comedian Moms Mabley was born Loretta Mary Aiken in Brevard, North Carolina to a large family. She experienced a horrifying, traumatic childhood. Her firefighter father was killed in an explosion when she was 11 and her mother was later hit and killed by a truck on Christmas Day. And by the beginning of her teens, Aiken had been raped twice and become pregnant from both encounters, with both children being given away.

Aiken left home at the age of 14 and pursued a show business career, joining the African American vaudeville circuit as a comedian under the Theatre Owners Booking Association. Fellow performer Jack Mabley became her close friend for a short time, and she took on his name, becoming Jackie Mabley, with "Moms" coming from her eventual reputation as a mentoring, mothering spirit.

November 29

Henrietta Vinton-Davis
1860 – 1941

Henrietta Vinton Davis was born in Baltimore, Maryland to Mansfield Vinton and Mary Ann (Johnson) Davis. Her father, a pianist, died when she was very young. Her mother remarried George Alexander Hackett who was one of the founders of the Chesapeake Marine Railway Dry-dock Company, an African American owned ship-building company that operated from 1855 to 1873.

On April 25, 1883, Frederick Douglas introduced Davis in her debut at Marini's Hall, and for nearly 40 years she performed professionally as an elocutionist, Shakespearian actor, and dramatic reader.

As a member of the Universal Negro Improvement Association (UNIA), Davis was one of signatories to The Declaration of the Rights of the Negro Peoples of the World. She was a stellar organizer, establishing UNIA Divisions in Cuba, Guadeloupe, St, Thomas (Virgin Islands), Port-au-Prince (Haiti), Trinidad and Tobago, and Jamaica.

Vinton was the founder of the Black Cross Nurses – an auxiliary of the UNIA that was formed to provide care to the Africans returning to the US after serving in WWII who were denied medical care in US hospitals.

November 30

Gordon Roger Alexander Buchanan Parks

November 30, 1912 – March 7, 2006

Gordon Roger Alexander Buchanan Parks was an American photographer, musician, writer and film director, who became prominent in U.S. documentary photojournalism in the 1940s through 1970s—particularly in issues of civil rights, poverty and African-Americans, and in glamour photography.

Gordon Parks was one of the most groundbreaking figures in 20th century photography. His photojournalism during the 1940s to the 1970s reveals important aspects of American culture, and he became known for focusing on issues of civil rights, poverty, race relations and urban life.

Parks wrote, directed, and scored the first major Hollywood film to be directed by a Black American, *The Learning Tree* (1969) based on his semi-autobiographical novel of the same name. He created short documentaries and direct the iconic film *Shaft*.

December 1

Horace Edward Steve Carter
November 7, 1929 - September 15, 2020

Horace Edward "Steve" Carter Jr. was an American playwright, best known for his plays involving Caribbean immigrants living in the United States.

Born Horace Edward Carter Jr. in New York City to Horace Sr., an African-American longshoreman from Richmond, Virginia, and Carmen, who was from Trinidad and Tobago, he is professionally known as steve carter (spelled in all lowercase letters).

Carter's first interest in the theatre was to be a set designer. As a youngster, he made models of sets inspired by motion pictures and the occasional play he would see with his mother. Soon he would populate these models with cutout figures. This led to him creating dialog for the figures as he moved them around the set.

In 1948, he graduated from the High School of Music and Art in New York City. His professional career as a playwright began in 1965 at the American Community Theater with the production of the short play *Terraced Apartment*. This work would evolve years later into an expanded version titled *Terraces*.

In 1967, *One Last Look* premiered off-off-Broadway at the Old Reliable Theatre Tavern under the direction of Arthur French. It is a dark comedy set during the funeral of a family patriarch. It features the character of Eustace Baylor that would later be found in *Eden*, the first of Carter's trilogy of plays featuring Caribbean families in New York City.

In 1968, Carter joined the staff of the Negro Ensemble Company (NEC), where he would become director of the NEC Playwrights Workshop. While Carter was at NEC, several of his plays were produced, including the first two of his Caribbean trilogy.

December 2

Andrew Cooper

August 21, 1927 - January 28, 2002

Andrew W. Cooper was an African-American activist during the Civil Rights Movement, businessman, and journalist. He was the founder, along with Utrice C. Leid, the publisher and editor-in-chief of *The City Sun.*

Cooper was born in Brooklyn, New York where he attended Boys High School and Adelphi University. From 1951 through 1971, he was an executive of the F. & M. Schaefer Brewing Company.

In 1966, a year after the Voting Rights Act began opening the polls to millions of southern Blacks, Black New Yorkers challenged a political system that weakened their voting power. Cooper, while employed at the brewing company, sued state officials in a case called Cooper vs. Power. In 1968, the courts agreed that Black citizens were denied the right to elect authentic representatives of their community. The 12th Congressional District in Brooklyn was redrawn. Shirley Chisholm ran for the new seat and made history as the first Black woman elected to Congress.

Cooper became a journalist, a political columnist, and then founder of Trans Urban News Service and the City Sun, a fiesty Brooklyn-based weekly that published from 1984 to 1996. Whether the stories were about Mayor Koch or Rev. Al Sharpton, Howard Beach or Crown Heights, Tawana Brawley's rape allegations, the Daily News Four trial, or Spike Lee's filmmaking career, Cooper's City Sun commanded attention and moved officials and readers to action.

Cooper's leadership also gave Brooklyn -- particularly predominantly Black central Brooklyn -- an identity. It was no accident that in the twenty-first century the borough crackles with energy. Cooper fought tirelessly for the community's vitality when it was virtually abandoned by the civic and business establishments in the mid-to-late twentieth century.

Additionally, scores of journalists trained by Cooper are keeping his spirit alive.

December 3

Patricia E. Boothe

I regret to announce the passing of Patricia Boothe, *EVERYBODY'S* Magazine editor. Pat was very dedicated to me and primarily responsible for the editorial growth of the magazine especially during the decades of the 1980s and 1990s. She preferred to be a behind-the-scene person and shunned the limelight. She declined to do interviews with personalities. She took delight in arranging for me and others to do them.

She could have easily interviewed Bob Marley, members of Third World, Steele Pulse, Michael Manley, Maurice Bishop and other groups and personalities. Instead she took delight in transcribing the interviews and editing them for publication.

In 1987, the 10th anniversary of EVERYBODY'S, Pat made a massive montage of almost every photograph that appeared in the magazine. Today most visitors to the magazine are attracted by it. You can say the history of the Caribbean between1977-1987 is in the montage from Janelle Penny Commissiong of Trinidad & Tobago becoming Miss Universe, Mary Eugenia Charles of Dominica becoming the first female prime minister in the region to Eric Gairy at his hotel suite in New York City upon learning his Grenada Government was overthrown, to President Ronald Reagan visit to Jamaica and Barbados.

Although she was not involved in the planning and implementing the magazine's cultural events including plays and concerts, Pat attended almost each program and encouraged friends to purchase tickets.

I am shattered over Pat's passing. She inspired me and without her *EVERYBODY'S* would have folded years ago. - Herman Hall, Publisher, *EVERYBODY'S*, the Caribbean-American magazine.

(Claudette Joy's note: Pat was born in Jamaica, W.I. and she also was the editor of my first book *Nurturing The Garden of Joy: Provocative Essays on Relationships.*)

December 4

James H. Anderson

The *New York Amsterdam News* was started more than a century ago, with a $10 investment. It has gone on to become one of the most important Black newspapers in the country and today remains one of the most influential Black-owned and -operated media businesses in the nation.

On Dec. 4, 1909, James H. Anderson put out the first edition of the *Amsterdam News* with six sheets of paper, a lead pencil, a dressmaker's table and that $10 investment. The *Amsterdam News* was one of only 50 Black newspapers in the country at that time. Copies were sold for two-cents apiece from his home at 132 W. 65th St. in Manhattan. The paper was named after the avenue where Anderson lived in New York's San Juan Hill section of Manhattan.

The *Amsterdam News* (also known as *New York Amsterdam News*) was and is a weekly African American newspaper speaking of the life and concerns of African Americans. It is one of the oldest in the United States and has published columns by notable people including W. E. B. Du Bois, Roy Wilkins, and Adam Clayton Powell, Jr., and was the first to recognize and publish Malcolm X.

By the mid-1940s the *New York Amsterdam News* was one of the four leading Black newspapers in the country, along with *The Pittsburgh Courier*, *The Afro-American (*Baltimore), and *The Chicago Defender*.

December 5

Shirley Chisolm
November 30, 1924 - January 1, 2005

The struggle to increase participation by groups historically excluded from politics such as African Americans, women, and immigrants, is one of the continuing stories in the, A Changing America: 1968 and Beyond exhibition. Shirley Chisholm personifies this story. Chisholm was the first African American woman elected to Congress, representing residents of the 12th Congressional District, Brooklyn, New York where she served for seven terms beginning in 1969.

The daughter of immigrants from Barbados and Guyana, Chisolm had a significant impact on anti-poverty policy and educational reform. In 1971, she was a founding member of both the Congressional Black Caucus and the National Women's Political Caucus.

Chisholm was also the first African American woman to campaign for the Democratic Party presidential nomination in 1972 with the slogan "Unbought and Unbossed." Beset by both racist and sexist opposition, she failed to win her party's nomination, losing to anti-Vietnam War candidate Senator George McGovern. Always an advocate for poor, inner-city residents, Chisolm said, "I am and always will be a catalyst for change." She served another eleven years in Congress.

December 6

Frantz Omar Fanon

July 20, 1925 - December 6, 1961

Frantz Omar Fanon, also known as Ibrahim Frantz Fanon, was a French West Indian psychiatrist and political philosopher from the French colony of Martinique (today a French department). His works have become influential in the fields of post-colonial studies, critical theory and Marxism. As well as being an intellectual, Fanon was a political radical, Pan-Africanist, and Marxist humanist concerned with the psychopathology of colonization and the human, social, and cultural consequences of decolonization.

In the course of his work as a physician and psychiatrist, Fanon supported Algeria's War of independence from France and was a member of the Algerian National Liberation Front.

For more than five decades, the life and works of Frantz Fanon have inspired national-liberation movements and other radical political organizations in Palestine, Sri Lanka, South Africa, and the United States. He formulated a model for community psychology, believing that many mental-health patients would do better if they were integrated into their family and community instead of being treated with institutionalized care. He also helped found the field of institutional psychotherapy.

In *What Fanon Said: A Philosophical Introduction To His Life And Thought*, Lewis R. Gordon an American philosopher remarked that:

Fanon's contributions to the history of ideas are manifold. He is influential not only because of the originality of his thought but also because of the astuteness of his criticisms. He developed a profound social existential analysis of anti-Black racism, which led him to identify conditions of skewed rationality and reason in contemporary discourses on the human being.

Fanon published numerous books, including *The Wretched of the Earth* (1961). This influential work focuses on what he believed is the necessary role of violence by activists in conducting decolonization struggles.

December 7

Nannie Helen Burroughs
May 2, 1879 - May 20, 1961

Nannie Helen Burroughs was an African-American educator, orator, religious leader, civil rights activist, feminist, and businesswoman in the United States. Her speech *How the Sisters Are Hindered from Helping*, at the 1900 National Baptist Convention in Virginia, brought her fame and recognition. In 1908-1909, she founded the National Training School for Women and Girls in Washington, DC. Burroughs worked for equal rights in races as well as furthered opportunities for women beyond the duties of domestic housework. She continued to work for those rights until her death.

In 1964, the school Burroughs founded was renamed the Nannie Helen Burroughs School in her honor and began operating as a co-ed elementary school.

In its early years, the school, founded in a small farmhouse attracted women from around the country and provided evening classes for women who had no other means for education. Burroughs created history courses and she taught the classes which were designed to uplift the race and obtain a livelihood.

Nannie H. Burroughs was born in Orange, Virginia. She is thought to be the eldest of the daughters of John and Jennie Burroughs who were former enslaved Africans who purchased their freedom and so did one of her grandfathers.

December 8

Felipe Pazos Roque

September 27, 1912 - February 26, 2001

Felipe Pazos Roque was a Cuban economist who initially supported the Cuban Revolution of Fidel Castro, but became disillusioned with the increasingly radical nature of the revolutionary government. Born in Havana, Pazos earned a doctorate from the University of Havana in 1938. He was a member of the Cuban delegation to the 1944 Bretton Woods Conference. In 1946, he joined the staff of the fledgling International Monetary Fund that had been established at the Bretton Woods Conference. He worked there for three years before returning to Cuba in 1950 to be the president of the newly established National Bank of Cuba for two years at the behest of Cuban President Carlos Prío Socarrás.

After Fulgencio Batista took power in Cuba through a military coup d'état in 1952, Pazos became active in supporting the resistance against Batista. Batista's rule came under increasing assault during the 1950s, and he and the Cuban military soon found themselves fighting against a young Castro and the forces of his 26th of July Movement. At the time, Castro was waging a guerrilla campaign in the mountainous Sierra Maestra region of Cuba. Batista had declared that Castro had been killed. Pazos arranged for *The New York Times* reporter Herbert Matthews to come and meet Castro in February 1957. The resulting interview refuted Batista's claims and gave Castro and his revolutionaries international attention.

After Castro's victory in 1959, Pazos returned to Cuba and again served as the president of the National Bank of Cuba. Later that year he tendered his resignation. The presidency of the National Bank of Cuba was given to Che Guevara in November, 1959. Pazos was allowed to leave Cuba shortly thereafter.

December 9

Anna Julia Haywood Cooper
August 10, 1858 - February 27, 1964

Anna Julia Haywood Cooper was an American author, educator, sociologist, speaker, Black liberation activist, and one of the most prominent African-American scholars in United States history.

Born into slavery in 1858 in Raleigh, North Carolina, Cooper received a world-class education and claimed power and prestige in academic and social circles. Upon receiving her Ph.D. in history from the Sorbonne in 1924, Cooper became the fourth African-American woman to earn a doctoral degree. She was also a prominent member of Washington, D.C.'s African-American community and a member of Alpha Kappa Alpha sorority.

Cooper made contributions to social science fields, particularly in sociology. Her first book, *A Voice from the South: By a Black Woman of the South*, is widely acknowledged as one of the first articulations of Black feminism, giving Cooper the often-used title of "the Mother of Black Feminism."

Cooper, who worked as a domestic worker, teacher, and principal, articulated a vision of self-determination through education and social uplift for African-American women. She posited that the educational, moral, and spiritual progress of Black women would improve the general standing of the entire African-American community. She thought the violent natures of men often run counter to the goals of higher education, so it was important to foster more female intellectuals because they would bring more elegance to education; and that it was the duty of educated and successful Black women to support their underprivileged peers in achieving their goals.

December 10

Erica Garner-Snipes

May 29, 1990 - December 30, 2017

Erica Garner-Snipes was an American activist who advocated for police reform, particularly in the use of force during arrests. Garner became involved in activism following the 2014 death of her father, Eric Garner, after a New York City police officer placed him in a lethal chokehold during an arrest.

December 11

Alberta Odell Jones
November 12, 1930 - August 5, 1965

Alberta Odell Jones was an African-American attorney and civil rights icon. She was one of the first African-American women to pass the Kentucky bar and the first woman appointed city attorney in Jefferson County. She was murdered by an unknown person.

Jones graduated from Louisville Central High School and went to the Louisville Municipal College (LMC) for Black people. LMC later merged with the University of Louisville during desegregation and Jones graduated third in her class. She attended the University of Louisville Law School for one year, transferring to Howard University School of Law for her degree, graduating fourth in her class.

After graduating Jones began practicing law and took on a prominent client early in her career, a young boxer who later changed his name from Cassius Clay to Muhammed Ali, introducing him to trainer Archie Moore of California. She was appointed in 1965 to the Louisville Domestic Relations Court, where she was a prosecutor.

Jones rented voting machines and taught African Americans how to use the machines to vote; engineered a fundraising effort to pay the medical bills of a young man, James "Bulky" Welch, who lost his arms saving his dog trapped under a train, purchasing him prosthetic arms by auctioning a car.

December 12

Dovey Johnson Roundtree

April 17, 1914 - May 21, 2018

Dovey Johnson Roundtree was an African-American civil rights activist, ordained minister, and attorney. Her 1955 victory before the Interstate Commerce Commission (ICC) was the first bus desegregation case to be brought before the ICC which resulted in the only explicit repudiation of the "separate but equal" doctrine in the field of interstate bus transportation by a court or federal administrative body. That case, Sarah Keys v. Carolina Coach Company (64 MCC 769 (1955)), which Dovey Roundtree brought before the ICC with her law partner and mentor Julius Winfield Robertson, was invoked by Attorney General Robert F. Kennedy during the 1961 Freedom Riders' campaign in his successful battle to compel the Interstate Commerce Commission to enforce its rulings and end Jim Crow laws in public transportation.

A protégé of Black activist and educator Mary McLeod Bethune, Roundtree was selected by Bethune for the first class of African-American women to be trained as officers in the newly created Women's Army Auxiliary Corps (later the Women's Army Corps) during World War II.

Roundtree, in 1961, became one of the first women to receive full ministerial status in the African Methodist Episcopal Church. With her controversial admission to the all-white Women's Bar of the District of Columbia in 1962, she broke the color bar for Black women in the Washington legal community. In one of Washington's most sensational and widely covered murder cases, United States v. Ray Crump, tried in the summer of 1965 on the eve of the Watts riots, Roundtree won acquittal for the Black laborer accused of the murder of Georgetown socialite (and former wife of a CIA officer).

December 13

Ella Jo Baker
December 13, 1903 - December 13, 1986

"The major job was getting people to understand that they had something within their power that they could use, and it could only be used if they understood what was happening and how group action could counter violence..." – Ella Jo Baker

Her work sparked change by unlocking the power of every person to strengthen their communities and shape their future.

Ella Jo Baker was born in Norfolk, Virginia. While growing up in North Carolina, she developed a sense for social justice early on, due in part to her grandmother's stories about life under slavery.

As an enslaved African, her grandmother had been whipped for refusing to marry a man chosen for her by the slave owner. Her grandmother's pride and resilience in the face of racism and injustice inspired Baker throughout her life.

Baker studied at Shaw University in Raleigh, North Carolina. As a student she challenged school policies that she thought were unfair. After graduating in 1927 as class valedictorian, she moved to New York City and joined social activist organizations.

In 1930, she joined the Young Negroes Cooperative League, whose purpose was to develop Black economic power through collective planning. She also involved herself with several women's organizations. She was committed to economic justice for all people and once said, "People cannot be free until there is enough work in this land to give everybody a job."

Baker played key roles in some of the most influential organizations of the time, including the National Association for the Advancement for Colored People (NAACP), the Southern Christian Leadership Conference (SCLC), and the Student Nonviolent Coordinating Committee (SNCC).

December 14

Rev. Dr. Neville Carlyle Brathwaite
May 15, 1935 – May 16, 2000

Neville Carlyle Brathwaite was an ordained minister in the American Baptist Church and he served as the first African American chaplain in New York State Corrections. Born in Barbados, Brathwaite immigrated to New York where he worked for the New York City Transit System and he also served in the U.S. Army in the Vietnam War.

Brathwaite counselled many and brought hope and practical optimism to those who sought his wisdom.

December 15

St. Clair C. Bourne

February 16, 1943 - December 15, 2007

St. Clair C. Bourne was an American documentary filmmaker, who focused on African-American social issues and themes. He also developed projects that explored African-American cultural figures, such as Langston Hughes and Paul Robeson. Not only was Bourne a towering figure in the documentary film world but also an activist, teacher, and organizer.

Born in Harlem, New York, his family moved to Brooklyn when he was two years old. He completed two years at the Georgetown School of Foreign Service before joining the Peace Corps. In 1965, the Peace Corps sent Bourne to Peru where he helped publish a Spanish newspaper, *El Comeno,* in Comas, a settlement adjacent to Lima. The November 1965 issue of *Ebony* magazine featured an article about Bourne's efforts in Comas.

Bourne graduated from Syracuse University in 1967 with a dual degree in Journalism and Political Science.

In 1988, a retrospective of his films was shown at the Whitney Museum of American Art. In a 36-year career in which he made more than 40 films, either producing or directing or doing both, Bourne's works were seen on public television, commercial networks and at film festivals around the country.

The St. Clair Bourne Collection can be found at the Black Film Center/Archive at Indiana University, Bloomington, Indiana.

December 16

Venture Smith
c. 1729

Venture Smith was born in Guinea, West Africa. He was enslaved as a child and brought to Barbados in the Caribbean and later to Rhode Island and Connecticut in New England. Determined to become free, he purchased his own freedom by 1765, and, by 1775, he earned and saved enough money to purchase freedom for his entire family—his wife, son, and two daughters. - http://historymatters.gmu.edu/d/6536

December 17

Whitney Moore Young Jr.

July 31, 1921 - March 11, 1971

Whitney Moore Young Jr. was an American civil rights leader. He spent most of his career working to end employment discrimination in the United States and turning the National Urban League from a relatively passive civil rights organization into one that aggressively worked for equitable access to socioeconomic opportunity for the historically disenfranchised.

During World War II, Young was trained in electrical engineering at the Massachusetts Institute of Technology. He was then assigned to a road construction crew of Black soldiers supervised by Southern white officers. After just three weeks, he was promoted from private to first sergeant, creating hostility on both sides. Despite the tension, Young effectively mediated between his white officers and Black soldiers angry at their poor treatment. This situation propelled Young into a career in race relations.

In 1968, Young was invited to address the American Institute of Architects (AIA) National Convention in Portland, Oregon through the keynote speech. At the time, he was the executive director of the National Urban League and had spoken before on the concerns of the AIA regarding social and racial inequality in housing and cities. In his speech, he addressed the Institute's silent stance on the turmoil in the country and urged them to stand up and endorse the efforts of John F. Kennedy and Martin Luther King Jr.

In response to Young's message, the Institute created two separate resolutions to advance the organizations initiative for diversity and social equality: one created a scholarship program, the AIA/Architects Foundation Diversity Advancement Scholarship, specifically for Blacks who wanted to study architecture and another for architects to be actively engaged in the current social issues.

Source: https://www.nyul.org/whitney-young-scholarship-1

December 18

Marian Anderson
February 27, 1897 - April 8, 1993

On April 9, 1939, contralto Marian Anderson sang before an estimated 75,000 people gathered at the Lincoln Memorial in Washington. The outdoor location was chosen because Constitution Hall, which was owned by the Daughters of the American Revolution, refused to host Anderson because she was Black. A center of political storm emerged from the refusal, even as it was reported that Anderson insisted that she had no interest in being a social campaigner.

She would grace the estimated 250,000 people gathered at the 1963 March on Washington for Jobs and Freedom (a show of determination to work for the African American community's full social, political, and economic rights) in song with her gifted contralto voice. She sang one of her beloved spirituals.

Anderson was born in Philadelphia, Pennsylvania and her home there where she lived for most of her life has been restored as a museum of her life and career.

December 19

Jack Roosevelt Robinson
January 31, 1919 - October 24, 1972

Jack Roosevelt Robinson was an American professional baseball player who became the first African American to play in Major League Baseball (MLB) in the modern era. Robinson broke the baseball color line when he started at first base for the Brooklyn Dodgers in 1947. When the Dodgers signed Robinson, they heralded the end of racial segregation in professional baseball that had relegated Black players to the Negro leagues since the 1880s. Robinson was inducted into the Baseball Hall of Fame in 1962.

In 1942, Robinson was drafted and assigned to a segregated Army cavalry unit in Fort Riley, Kansas. Having the requisite qualifications, Robinson and several other Black soldiers applied for admission to an Officer Candidate School (OCS). Although the Army's initial July 1941 guidelines for OCS had been drafted as race neutral, few Black applicants were admitted into OCS until after subsequent directives by Army leadership. As a result, the applications of Robinson and his colleagues were delayed for several months. After protests by heavyweight boxing champion Joe Louis (then stationed at Fort Riley) and the help of Truman Gibson (then an assistant civilian aide to the Secretary of War), the men were accepted into OCS. The experience led to a personal friendship between Robinson and Louis. Upon finishing OCS, Robinson was commissioned as a second lieutenant in January 1943.

Robinson's character, his use of nonviolence, and his talent challenged the traditional basis of segregation that had then marked many other aspects of American life. In the 1960s, he helped establish the Freedom National Bank, an African-American-owned financial institution based in Harlem, New York.

Robinson was posthumously awarded the Congressional Gold Medal and Presidential Medal of Freedom in recognition of his achievements on and off the field.

December 20

Elsie Ofuatey-Kodjoe

"And as I was surrounded by my family I noticed some very old pictures of my grandmother hanging on the wall. She passed 25 years ago but I remember her vividly sitting in her room commenting on my outfits when I was 10, or telling me to make funny faces and then laughing at them, which left me amazed because she was blind."

"Mrs. Elsie Ofuatey-Kodjoe was born in 1901. She was very active in government and even started the Girl Guides in Ghana to help girls and young women develop their potential and become outspoken citizens of society who fight for equality, inclusion, and parity across gender lines.

"She was a beautiful, strong, proactive trailblazer, who was one of my grandfather's three wives, a friend of the honorable Kwame Nkrumah, who has her own stamp, and who takes portraits with a sheep.

"We honored her today by being together and remembering those family members who had passed."

https://www.ghanaweb.com/GhanaHomePage/entertainment/My-last-day-in-Accra-was-great-Boris-Kodjoe-615450

December 21

Elizabeth Keckley
c. 1818

Elizabeth Keckley, enslaved in Virginia, North Carolina, and St. Louis, Missouri, tried to purchase freedom for herself and her son. Her slaveholder finally agreed to a sum of $1200, but her plans to go to New York and raise money as a seamstress were thwarted when she was unable to acquire enough signed guarantees that she would return.

Help arrived from her clients among the wealthy women of St. Louis, as Keckley relates in her autobiography. Later in Washington, DC, she became a valued dressmaker and seamstress to Mary Lincoln and other women of the governing elite.

December 22

Gil Noble
February 22, 1932 - April 5, 2012

Gilbert Edward Noble was a pianist, producer, professor, news anchor, television host, and documentarian. His entry into media was largely due to the Civil Rights and Black Power Movements. Born in Harlem, New York to Jamaican parents Iris Villiers Noble, a teacher, and Gilbert Robert Noble, an auto-mechanic shop owner, he grew up in a middle-class household in Harlem's famed Sugar Hill.

A 1949 graduate of DeWitt Clinton High, which also graduated Countee Cullen and James Baldwin, Noble served as a medic in the US Army during the Korean War and worked at a New York City public library while attending City College of New York. He also occasionally modeled while employed at Union Carbide.

Noble became a WABC-TV correspondent which at the time was one of the three major T.V. stations in New York City in 1967. He was promoted to weekend co-anchor in February and he initially co-hosted *Like It Is* with actor Robert Hooks. When Hooks left the show to star in *N.Y.P.D.*, Noble hosted *Like It Is* alone for 43 years as it became the second longest-running US Black public affairs program after *American Black Journal*.

In 1984, Noble established the National Black Archives of Film and Broadcasting in New York City to preserve and distribute materials on the Black experience. After his death his children moved the collection to Montclair, New Jersey where the New Jersey City University's Hagan Africana Studies Center holds about 850 *Like It Is* interviews.

December 23

David Norman Dinkins
July 10, 1927 - November 23, 2020

David Norman Dinkins was an American politician, lawyer, and author who served as the 106th Mayor of New York City from 1990 to 1993. He was the first African American to hold that office. Dinkins was widely regarded as a calm, deliberate leader.

Dinkins had also served in the New York State Assembly and as the Borough President of Manhattan.

Dinkins also teamed with other entrepreneurial African Americans to form partnerships and corporations to benefit African American people, their culture and their economics.

Dinkins was born in 1927 in Trenton, New Jersey and he was a graduate of Howard University and Brooklyn Law School.

As mayor, Dinkins can be credited for promoting policies that helped the poor, aggrandizing the National Tennis Center, laying the groundwork for a record drop in crime, and he was a racial reconciliatory, and a mentor to others to serve in public office.

December 24

Charles Conliff Mende Roach
September 1933 - October 2012

Charles Conliff Mende Roach was a Canadian civil rights lawyer and an activist in the Black community in Toronto. Born in Belmont, Trinidad and Tobago, the son of a trade union organizer, Roach arrived in Canada in 1955 as an aspiring priest to study at the University of Saskatchewan. Roach was politicized by the civil rights movement, stating: "after the '50s, I started being more political... This was the spirit of the times. I'm really from the civil-rights era." He then studied law at the University of Toronto and was called to the bar in 1963.

Roach opened his own law practice in 1968. It grew to be the firm of Roach and Schwartz Associates. Among his clients were Black Panthers attempting to seek refuge in Canada from prosecution in the United States and other asylum seekers. He also represented domestic workers being deported in the 1970s. He further became a vocal critic of the police, accusing them of racism. In 1999, Roach went to Rwanda to represent Hutu journalist Mathieu Ngirumpatse against human rights abuse charges before the International Criminal Tribunal for Rwanda.

Through his work, Roach became a leading figure in Toronto's Black community. He was a founder of the Caribana festival. He established the Movement of Minority Electors in 1978 to encourage non-Caucasians to enter electoral politics and was a founding member of the Black Action Defence Committee.

December 25

Loretta Robinson
Contributor: Devon Harris, Olympian, Motivational Speaker

I Called her Mama

My paternal grandmother was Loretta Robinson. Everyone called her Miss Carmen. I called her "mama". She was born in Greenfield - a small rural district in the parish of St Elizabeth, Jamaica but lived in the adjoining district of Haughton. She transitioned in 1975. Haughton was a community of mainly subsistence farmers with men finding employment on the sugar plantation in nearby Holland.

I don't remember much about my grandmother's physical appearance except that she was of a lighter complexion, had soft brown eyes and false teeth which she left in a glass of water on the table overnight. What I remember though is that she loved me like no one else has since.

Mama was an amazing storyteller. The stories that had the greatest impact on me were the ones she told me about soldiers and the amazing feats they could perform without getting hurt. I remember her saying that *"they could jump in a gully and don't bruk dem foot!"* She made them sound almost superhuman and although I had no idea how I would fare on any of those incredible adventures on which soldiers embark, I knew I wanted to be one.

Mama's stories lit up my five year-old imagination and made me want to pursue dreams that everyone else thought was impossible or at least too difficult. They installed in me the kind of thinking that allowed me to rise from the violent impoverished enclave of Waterhouse in Kingston to become a graduate of the prestigious Royal Military Academy Sandhurst, to serving in the officer corps of the Jamaica Defence Force, to become a three-time Olympian and founding member of the original Jamaica Bobsled team.

Thank you Mama. I love you.

December 26

Unity (Umoja)

Kwanzaa is a seven day festival that celebrates African and African American culture and history from 26th December to 1st January. It is founded on traditional African principles and brought forward into the 20th century in 1966 by Dr. Maulana Karenga, professor and chairman of Black Studies at California State University, Long Beach, created Kwanzaa in 1966.

African theologists and philosophers say Ma'at is an ancient Kemetic concept. The Nguzo Saba is a term popularized by Dr. Maulana Karenga. As used by the Ancient Africans, Ma'at was a concept that stood for "universal order." Ma'at represents realty in all its manifestations both spiritual and material. It is the divine force that encompasses and embraces everything that is alive and exists. As an ethical system, Ma'at is often discussed as seven cardinal virtues (truth, justice, righteousness, harmony, balance, reciprocity, and order). As part of Karenga's Kawaida philosophy, the Nguzo Saba are seven principles (Umoja, Unity; Kujichagulia, Self-determination; Ujima, Cooperative Work and Responsibility; Ujamaa, Collective Economics; Nia, Purpose; Kuumba, Creativity; and Imani, Faith). The Nguzo Saba is most widely recognized in relation to the seven days of Kwanzaa.

Unity in family and unity in community is an ideal worth pursuing. Where are you on the unity spectrum as we seek to celebrate Umoja?

Live and Celebrate Umoja

December 27

Self-determination (Kujichagulia)

How does one prepare for self-determination as an individual and as a community of Africans? A foundational step in that direction is the study and understanding of the history of African peoples taught in our all institutions that influence our minds from an early age: family, school, religious institutions, community and civic organizations.

Live and Celebrate Getting to Kujichagulia

December 28
Collective work and responsibility (Ujima)

Making and keeping commitments to work together for the common good of Africans as agreed-on by all involved. Each of us brings self-interest to the table which must be articulated in the group so that together we can "make it work." Hidden agendas are major barriers to collective work and living into our responsibility with self-respect.

Live and Celebrate Ujima

December 29

Cooperative economics (Ujamaa)

Discovering ways to pool our resources to strengthen individual and community in the financial realm is a pathway to Ujamaa. Step with transparency and mutual accountability. Support Black-owned businesses that support community. This is a tenet of Race First. Get knowledge about credit, financing, and tax laws. Build and maintain trust. Build financial wealth.

Live and Celebrate Ujima

December 30

Purpose (Nia)

The purpose for which I was placed on this earth at this time…. Explore, discover and live it, helping to peace, harmony, and satisfaction to my life. Could my purpose be to "serve our Creator, our universe, and our community while maintaining our innate joy, peace, and harmony?"

Live and Celebrate Nia

December 31

Creativity (Kuumba)

Call on the creativity that is within you. Let it spark the purpose for which you live. Unleash and be thankful.

Live and Celebrate Kuumba

Sources

James Weldon Johnson, *The Autobiography of an Ex-Colored Man* (Sherman, French, & Co, 1912)
C. L. R. James, The Black Jacobins (Secker & Warburg Ltd 1938)
15/marielle-lives-brazil-remembers-slain-activist
Alex Haley and Malcolm X, *Autobiography of Malcolm X* (Grove Press 1965)
Atlanta Black Star – Black News, Culture and Information
atlantablackstar.com
Booker T. Washington, *Up From Slavery* (1901)
Cheikh Anta Diop, *Precolonial Black Africa* (Lawrence Hill & Company, 1987)
Chinua Achebe, *Things Fall Apart* (Heinemann 1958)
Cornell West, *Race Matters* (First Vintage Books Edition, 1994)
Derrick Bell, *Faces at the Bottom of the Well* (1992)
Eric Williams, *Capitalism and Slavery* (1944)
Garvey's Voice, November-December 2019, Official Publication of the Universal Negro Improvement Association and African Communities League
Global Social Theory:
Gordon K. Lewis, *The Growth of the Modern West Indies* (Ian Randle Publishers, 2004)
Russell L. Adams, *Great Negroes Past and Present* (Afro-Am Publishing Company 1963)
Henry Louis Gates, Jr. and Cornell West, *The Future of the Race* (Alfred A. Knopf, New York, NY 1996)
How the last and only black queen of Hawaii was overthrown by the U.S. in the 1800s
http://amistadresearchcenter.tulane.edu/archon/?p=creators/creator&id=70
http://amsterdamnews.com/about/
http://amsterdamnews.com/news/2015/may/14/dr-yosef-ben-jochannan-transitioning-immortality/
http://amsterdamnews.com/news/2020/jan/23/arthur-schomburg-and-harlem-renaissance/
http://aponte.hosting.nyu.edu/
http://archive.jsonline.com/news/obituaries/winston-van-horne-started-department-of-africology-at-uwm-b9936439z1-212027301.html/
http://archives.nypl.org/scm/21049
http://findingfela.com/about-fela/
http://maatlaws.blogspot.com/2010/06/42-laws-of-maat.html
http://nationalhumanitiescenter.org/pds/maai/emancipation/text1/text1read.htm
http://saintluciamissionun.org/about-saint-lucia/#:~:text=In%201794%2C%20the%20French%20governor,also%20happened%20on%20Saint%2DDomingue.&text=The%20British%20abolished%20the%20African,abolished%20the%20institution%20of%20slavery.
http://unaclarkeassociates.com/drmarcomason.html
http://www.artnet.com/artists/elizabeth-catlett/
http://www.artnet.com/artists/grant-wood/
http://www.artnet.com/artists/norman-lewis/
http://www.bbc.co.uk/history/historic_figures/seacole_mary.shtml
http://www.blackhistoryheroes.com/2020/02/carlos-alexander-cook-and-black.html
http://www.columbia.edu/cu/lweb/archival/collections/ldpd_6134799/
http://www.hunter.cuny.edu/afprl/dr.-john-henrik-clarke
http://www.jamaicaobserver.com/editorial/mr-noel-dexter-a-great-but-humble-man_172875
http://www.jamesbrown.com/
http://www.jpanafrican.org/docs/vol11no8/11.8-16-WHorne.pdf
http://www.myblackhistory.net/Percy_Sutton.htm
http://www.pbs.org/black-culture/explore/rosa-parks/
http://www.raceandhistory.com/Historians/eric_williams.htm

http://www.samsharpeproject.org/sam-sharpe
http://www.visionaryproject.org/dinkinsdavid/
http://www.visionaryproject.org/vivianct/
http://www.youthforhumanrights.org/news/2014-alvin-ailey.html
https://aaprp-intl.org/african-liberation-day/
https://aaregistry.org/story/the-black-ymca-a-community-and-a-home/
https://aaregistry.org/story/the-new-york-amsterdam-news-founded/
https://achievement.org/achiever/congressman-john-r-lewis/
https://aflcio.org/about/history/labor-history-people/asa-philip-randolph
https://alicenter.org/about-us/muhammad-ali/
https://alumni.columbia.edu/content/city-son-andrew-w-coopers-impact-modern-day-brooklyn
https://archives.history.ac.uk/history-in-focus/Slavery/articles/zacek.html
https://biography.jrank.org/pages/2781/Wright-Bruce-McMarion.html
https://blackbooksmatter.com/black-history-makers-dr-frances-cress-welsing/
https://blackhistory.news.columbia.edu/people/charles-h-alston
https://blackthen.com/empress-menen-asfaw-ethiopia/
https://centerforblackliterature.com/dr-edith-rock-elders-writing-workshop/
https://docsouth.unc.edu/fpn/washington/bio.html
https://ellabakercenter.org/who-was-ella-baker/
https://en.unesco.org/womeninafrica/miriam-makeba/biography
https://en.wikipedia.org/wiki/Albert_Luthuli
https://en.wikipedia.org/wiki/Am%C3%ADlcar_Cabral
https://en.wikipedia.org/wiki/Andrew_W._Cooper
https://en.wikipedia.org/wiki/Aretha_Franklin
https://en.wikipedia.org/wiki/Barbara_Jordan
https://en.wikipedia.org/wiki/Bayard_Rustin
https://en.wikipedia.org/wiki/Black_Cabinet
https://en.wikipedia.org/wiki/Booker_T._Washington
https://en.wikipedia.org/wiki/Bruce_M._Wright
https://en.wikipedia.org/wiki/Bussa%27s_rebellion#:~:text=Bussa's%20rebellion%20(14%E2%80%9316%20April,was%20defeated%20by%20British%20forces.&text=Collectively%20these%20are%20often%20referred,the%20%22late%20slave%20rebellions%22.
https://en.wikipedia.org/wiki/Calypsonian
https://en.wikipedia.org/wiki/Carlota_(rebel_leader)
https://en.wikipedia.org/wiki/Charles_Cogswell_Doe
https://en.wikipedia.org/wiki/Charles_Roach
https://en.wikipedia.org/wiki/Che_Guevara
https://en.wikipedia.org/wiki/Daisy_Bates_(activist)
https://en.wikipedia.org/wiki/Deolinda_Rodrigues_Francisco_de_Almeida
https://en.wikipedia.org/wiki/Derrick_Bell
https://en.wikipedia.org/wiki/Dudley_Laws#:~:text=Dudley%20Laws%20(May%207%2C%201934,the%20Black%20Action%20Defence%20Committee.&text=In%201965%2C%20he%20relocated%20to,Improvement%20Association%2C%20a%20Garveyite%20organization.
https://en.wikipedia.org/wiki/E._D._Nixon
https://en.wikipedia.org/wiki/Earl_G._Graves_Sr.
https://en.wikipedia.org/wiki/Eduardo_Mondlane
https://en.wikipedia.org/wiki/Eldridge_Cleaver
https://en.wikipedia.org/wiki/Elizabeth_Freeman
https://en.wikipedia.org/wiki/Ellis_Marsalis_Jr.
https://en.wikipedia.org/wiki/Felipe_Pazos
https://en.wikipedia.org/wiki/Fidel_Castro
https://en.wikipedia.org/wiki/Ganga_Zumba

https://en.wikipedia.org/wiki/George_W._Lee
https://en.wikipedia.org/wiki/George_Walter
https://en.wikipedia.org/wiki/Haile_Selassie
https://en.wikipedia.org/wiki/Harry_T._Moore
https://en.wikipedia.org/wiki/Helen_M._Marshall
https://en.wikipedia.org/wiki/Historically_black_colleges_and_universities
https://en.wikipedia.org/wiki/Ida_B._Wells
https://en.wikipedia.org/wiki/James_Baldwin
https://en.wikipedia.org/wiki/James_Bevel
https://en.wikipedia.org/wiki/John_Henrik_Clarke
https://en.wikipedia.org/wiki/Josephine_St._Pierre_Ruffin
https://en.wikipedia.org/wiki/Lamar_Smith_(activist)
https://en.wikipedia.org/wiki/Lerone_Bennett_Jr.
https://en.wikipedia.org/wiki/List_of_civil_rights_leaders
https://en.wikipedia.org/wiki/Little_Richard
https://en.wikipedia.org/wiki/Lorraine_Hansberry
https://en.wikipedia.org/wiki/Marvel_Cooke
https://en.wikipedia.org/wiki/Mohamed_Morsi
https://en.wikipedia.org/wiki/Murder_of_Jimmie_Lee_Jackson
https://en.wikipedia.org/wiki/Murders_of_Chaney,_Goodman,_and_Schwerner
https://en.wikipedia.org/wiki/Nannie_Helen_Burroughs
https://en.wikipedia.org/wiki/National_Union_of_Freedom_Fighters
https://en.wikipedia.org/wiki/Nellie_Stone_Johnson
https://en.wikipedia.org/wiki/Nnamdi_Azikiwe
https://en.wikipedia.org/wiki/Olaudah_Equiano
https://en.wikipedia.org/wiki/Oliver_Tambo
https://en.wikipedia.org/wiki/Ottobah_Cugoano
https://en.wikipedia.org/wiki/Port_Royal_Experiment
https://en.wikipedia.org/wiki/Quilombo#Palmares
https://en.wikipedia.org/wiki/Ralph_Abernathy
https://en.wikipedia.org/wiki/Rayford_Logan
https://en.wikipedia.org/wiki/Roscoe_Brown
https://en.wikipedia.org/wiki/Ruby_Dee
https://en.wikipedia.org/wiki/St._Clair_Bourne
https://en.wikipedia.org/wiki/Steve_Carter_(playwright)
https://en.wikipedia.org/wiki/Thomas_Sankara
https://en.wikipedia.org/wiki/Thurgood_Marshall
https://en.wikipedia.org/wiki/Tony_Martin_(professor)
https://en.wikipedia.org/wiki/Walter_Francis_White
https://en.wikipedia.org/wiki/Walter_Sisulu
https://en.wikipedia.org/wiki/Wilfred_Adolphus_Domingo
https://everybodysmag.com/pat-boothe/
https://face2faceafrica.com/article/bai-bureh-sierra-leones-greatest-hero-who-held-off-british-control-for-months-in-1898
https://face2faceafrica.com/article/how-the-last-and-only-black-queen-of-hawaii-was-overthrown-by-the-u-s-in-the-1800s
https://face2faceafrica.com/article/king-bayano-the-mandinka-king-who-escaped-slavery-in-the-1600s-and-fought-off-the-spanish-for-several-years#:~:text=By%201531%2C%20the%20first%20slave%20rebellion%20had%20occurred%20in%20the%20country.&text=Later%20in%201552%2C%20King%20Bayano,fight%20off%20the%20Spanish%20colonists.
https://face2faceafrica.com/article/the-horrifying-execution-of-prince-klaas-the-slave-from-ghana-who-planned-to-make-antigua-an-african-state
https://felakuti.com/story/1976

https://globalsocialtheory.org/thinkers/cabral-amilcar/
https://jis.gov.jm/information/famous-jamaicans/louise-bennett-coverley/
https://jis.gov.jm/information/heroes/norman-washington-manley/
https://jis.gov.jm/information/heroes/samuel-sharpe/
https://kinginstitute.stanford.edu/encyclopedia/jackson-jimmie-lee
https://kinginstitute.stanford.edu/encyclopedia/nkrumah-kwame
https://kinginstitute.stanford.edu/encyclopedia/randolph-philip
https://library.richmond.edu/collections/rare/walker.html
https://lists.h-net.org/cgi-bin/logbrowse.pl?trx=vx&list=h-afro-am&month=0903&week=c&msg=QOXpvg5kW7ix265C9a%2B6RA&user=&pw=
https://livinginmontserrat.wordpress.com/2019/01/08/the-cudjoe-montserrat-slave-rebellion-march-17-1768-africans-attack-irish-planters/
https://livingnewdeal.org/tag/black-cabinet/
https://mg.mail.yahoo.com/neo/launch?.rand=494rngagtr3gb#5372516104
https://nlj.gov.jm/project/nettleford-rex-choreography-education-1933-2010/
https://nlj.gov.jm/project/rt-hon-norman-washington-manley-1893-1969/
https://nmaahc.si.edu/shirley-chisholm-president
https://nymag.com/intelligencer/2020/11/new-york-city-mayor-david-dinkins-deserved-better.html
https://ossieandruby.com/
https://ossieandruby.com/ruby-dee-biography/
https://pendergastkc.org/article/biography/dr-william-j-thompkins
https://republic.com.ng/june-july-2020/feminist-freedom-modern-angola/
https://search.proquest.com/openview/76f749e84743bbabc5116f590eead561/1?pq-origsite=gscholar&cbl=44042
https://theconversation.com/onkgopotse-tiro-revolutionary-who-paid-a-heavy-price-for-shaking-apartheid-to-its-core-124813
https://theculturetrip.com/africa/south-africa/articles/10-freedom-fighters-who-completely-altered-south-africas-fate/
https://theculturetrip.com/africa/south-africa/articles/10-things-to-know-about-ahmed-kathrada-south-africas-eminent-freedom-fighter/
https://the-female-soldier.tumblr.com/post/128481094040/carlota-was-a-lucum%C3%AD-yoruba-resistance-fighter-who
https://the-female-soldier.tumblr.com/post/140560698072/queen-nzinga-mbande-1583-1663-sometimes?is_highlighted_post=1
https://theintercept.com/2015/08/17/core-went-leading-civil-rights-movement-protesting-support-police-exxonmobil/
https://thekingcenter.org/about-dr-king/
https://ticotimes.net/2016/07/11/rare-find-african-voices-costa-rican-national-archives
https://today.law.harvard.edu/derrick-bell-1930-2011/
https://utsnyc.edu/faculty/james-h-cone/
https://uwm.edu/african-diaspora-studies/our-people/about-winston-van-horne/
https://wbssmedia.com/artists/detail/2375
https://www.anb.org/view/10.1093/anb/9780198606697.001.0001/anb-9780198606697-e-1501356;jsessionid=BC4B00E3C15B57F58294D3E26871 1DD7
https://www.arkavhs.com/cornelius-robinson-coffey
https://www.audelco.org/about/
https://www.bbc.com/news/entertainment-arts-26936950
https://www.biography.com/activist/coretta-scott-king
https://www.biography.com/activist/frederick-douglass
https://www.biography.com/musician/marvin-gaye
https://www.biography.com/performer/dick-gregory
https://www.biography.com/performer/moms-mabley
https://www.biography.com/scholar/carter-g-woodson

https://www.biography.com/writer/chinua-achebe
https://www.biography.com/writer/james-baldwin
https://www.biography.com/writer/toni-morrison
https://www.blackenterprise.com/percy-e-sutton-a-titan-worthy-of-emulation/
https://www.blackhistorybuff.com/blogs/the-black-history-buff-blog/zumbi-dos-palmares-hero-of-brazil
https://www.blackhistorymonth.org.uk/article/section/bhm-heroes/haile-selassie-king-god-or-redeemer/
https://www.blackpast.org/african-american-history/anderson-charles-chief-1907-1996/
https://www.blackpast.org/african-american-history/carmichael-stokely-kwame-ture-1941-1998/
https://www.blackpast.org/african-american-history/people-african-american-history/gil-noble-1932-2012/
https://www.blackpast.org/african-american-history/robinson-john-charles-1903-1954/
https://www.blackpast.org/global-african-history/diop-cheikh-anta-1923-1986/
https://www.blackpast.org/global-african-history/kenyatta-jomo-c-1894-1978/
https://www.britannica.com/biography/Hattie-McDaniel
https://www.britannica.com/biography/James-Farmer
https://www.britannica.com/biography/John-Oliver-Killens
https://www.britannica.com/biography/Richard-Allen
https://www.brookings.edu/blog/order-from-chaos/2019/06/19/the-tragedy-of-egypts-mohamed-morsi/
https://www.caribbeanlifenews.com/marco-mason-prominent-immigrant-advocate-and-scholar-passes/
https://www.chipublib.org/lorraine-hansberry-biography/
https://www.christianitytoday.com/history/people/denominationalfounders/richard-allen.html
https://www.cookman.edu/about_BCU/history/our_founder.html
https://www.cubahistory.org/en/spanish-settlement/slavery-and-rebellion-in-cuba.html
https://www.dinizuluarts.org/nanayao
https://www.dol.gov/general/aboutdol/history/dolchp01
https://www.dw.com/en/eduardo-mondlane-the-architect-of-mozambiques-national-unity/a-52448404
https://www.dw.com/en/l%C3%A9opold-s%C3%A9dar-senghor-from-prisoner-to-president/a-52448430
https://www.elombebrathfoundation.org/legacy
https://www.encyclopedia.com/education/news-wires-white-papers-and-books/dodd-clement-coxsone
https://www.google.com/search
https://www.google.com/search?q=slave+revolts+in+cuba&rlz=1C1VASU_enUS553US555&oq=slave+revolts+in+cuba&aqs=chrome..69i57.5911j0j7&sourceid=chrome&ie=UTF-8
https://www.govtrack.us/congress/members/john_lewis/400240
https://www.harlemheritage.com/cultural-harlem-blog/harlem-heritage-tours-loves-the-legacy-of-ms-vivian-robinson/
https://www.historians.org/teaching-and-learning/teaching-resources-for-historians/teaching-and-learning-in-the-digital-age/through-the-lens-of-history-biafra-nigeria-the-west-and-the-world/the-first-nigerian-republic-formation-and-operation/nnamdi-azikiwe
https://www.history.com/news/the-man-behind-black-history-month
https://www.history.com/topics/black-history/alex-haley
https://www.history.com/topics/black-history/congress-of-racial-equality
https://www.history.com/topics/black-history/emmett-till-1
https://www.history.com/topics/black-history/madame-c-j-walker
https://www.history.com/topics/black-history/sojourner-truth

https://www.independent.co.uk/travel/news-and-advice/traveller-s-guide-saint-lucia-8344633.html
https://www.jacobinmag.com/2020/09/steve-biko-south-africa-black-consciousness-movement
https://www.loc.gov/item/today-in-history/april-08/
https://www.localprayers.com/US/Jamaica/406539879383263/The-Dinizulu-Center-for-African-Culture-and-Research?__cf_chl_jschl_tk__=b3e1ea0bbe4341c816adb1a57690f8925fb2694e-1604499487-0-AW17NGIINObzmUEqe1B1xz9rTZymUJidQtVvBqLYTExGehGCxzkcz4LAug95xp4qFP4SKQDN2PIMZqBjj9sge6xSAjCCLxAlWnVd2T-RjvP0RnzPDXOswnJ_pljEnoQOvrU0yFfwQGHatsAAUPQpyw5VJ3b_DCSewHtAsLpCRxTOYsa2HqsfJuTsyhdmqsDnbSKIF-EuyLiuWZbbTpj6MoXT8CazGOYIT5J_2-3G0hAVJTIQGj2NaGfE0zUakwKPwPK113LLTv1GvxdPkliX_a6hhau6IJh2chhNQSOFyvG-Cja9g_J-hjUSakLYXywPJiAG5vChJtNak4i0VomZfO1yT82aFfZWYk3AdKolu2j14sseESH-iMmw4LJ_WvYLognH_VFGPVtnuHl_DY8P888uCdqgbBuxWatHIiat-Dpmv9JNwOJiUtz3Pkf7C6TSgg
https://www.naacp.org/julian-bond/
https://www.naacp.org/naacp-history-medgar-evers/
https://www.naacp.org/naacp-history-roy-wilkins/
https://www.nationalarchives.gov.uk/pathways/blackhistory/africa_caribbean/caribbean_resistance.htm
https://www.neh.gov/about/awards/national-humanities-medals/marva-collins
https://www.ninasimone.com/biography/
https://www.noi.org/honorable-elijah-muhammad/
https://www.npr.org/2020/07/19/890796423/civil-rights-leader-john-lewis-never-gave-up-or-gave-in
https://www.npr.org/2020/09/12/912245520/toots-hibbert-reggae-ambassador-and-leader-of-toots-and-the-maytals-dies-at-77
https://www.nps.gov/features/malu/feat0002/wof/Michael_Manley.htm
https://www.nps.gov/thro/learn/historyculture/civilian-conservation-corps.htm
https://www.nycaribnews.com/articles/jamaican-noel-dexter-dies-at-80/
https://www.nypl.org/blog/2020/10/05/arturo-schomburg-his-life-and-legacy
https://www.nytimes.com/1991/02/16/obituaries/yao-opare-dinizulu-troupe-founder-60.html
https://www.nyul.org/whitney-young-scholarship-1
https://www.pbs.org/thisfarbyfaith/people/james_cone.html
https://www.pbs.org/wgbh/aia/part4/4p1535.html
https://www.pbs.org/wgbh/americanexperience/features/freedomsummer-hamer/
https://www.pbs.org/wgbh/americanexperience/features/garvey-unia/
https://www.pdcnet.org/clrjames/content/clrjames_2017_0023_43102_0267_0305?file_type=pdf
https://www.peacewomen.org/content/angola-womens-contribution-liberation-struggle-highlighted
https://www.poetryfoundation.org/poets/agostinho-neto
https://www.poetryfoundation.org/poets/claude-mckay
https://www.poetryfoundation.org/poets/langston-hughes
https://www.qgazette.com/articles/former-borough-president-helen-marshall/
https://www.reddfoxx.com/
https://www.reuters.com/article/us-people-david-dinkins/former-new-york-city-mayor-david-dinkins-dies-at-93-police-idUSKBN2840DZ
https://www.rockhall.com/sister-rosetta-tharpe
https://www.sahistory.org.za/people/miriam-makeba

https://www.siksewomen.com/content/the-story-of-beverly-jones-the-woman-who-engaged-in-guerrilla-warfare-during-the-black-power-movement
https://www.splcenter.org/rev-george-lee
https://www.sunypress.edu/p-2257-clr-james.aspx
https://www.telesurenglish.net/analysis/Libya-Before-and-After-Muammar-Gaddafi-20200115-0011.html
https://www.theglobeandmail.com/opinion/article-to-shape-the-future-look-to-past-black-canadian-activism/
https://www.theguardian.com/global-development/poverty-matters/2011/jan/17/patrice-lumumba-50th-anniversary-assassination
https://www.theguardian.com/global-development/poverty-matters/2011/jan/17/patrice-lumumba-50th-anniversary-assassination
https://www.theguardian.com/music/2020/mar/27/jamaican-reggae-vocalist-bob-andy-dies-aged-75-young-gifted-black
https://www.theguardian.com/music/2020/may/06/millie-small-obituary
https://www.theguardian.com/world/2020/nov/13/jerry-rawlings-obituary
https://www.thehistorymakers.org/biography/earl-g-graves-sr-40
https://www.thehistorymakers.org/biography/lerone-bennett-39
https://www.themilitant.com/1989/5313/MIL5313.pdf
https://www.thestar.com/news/2007/01/09/sherona_hall_59_fighter_for_justice.html
https://www.thestar.com/news/gta/2011/03/24/fearless_black_activist_dudley_laws_dies_at_age_76.html
https://www.thirteen.org/freetodance/biographies/dafora.html
https://www.thirteen.org/wnet/supremecourt/rights/robes_marshall.html
https://www.timeanddate.com/holidays/world/african-liberation-day
https://www.timeanddate.com/holidays/world/african-liberation-day
https://www.trtworld.com/africa/ahmed-sekou-toure-an-indispensable-yet-forgotten-african-leader-31967
https://www.tuskegee.edu/discover-tu/tu-presidents/booker-t-washington
https://www.tuskegeeairmen.org/legacy/the-people/
https://www.un.org/en/sections/nobel-peace-prize/ralph-bunche-united-nations-mediator-palestine-during-1948-conflict/index.html
https://www.walterrodneyfoundation.org/biography/
https://www.wesleyan.edu/mlk/posters/malcolmx.html
https://www.womenshistory.org/education-resources/biographies/coretta-scott-king
https://www.womenshistory.org/education-resources/biographies/ida-b-wells-barnett
https://www.womenshistory.org/education-resources/biographies/mary-church-terrell
https://www.womenshistory.org/education-resources/biographies/mary-mcleod-bethune
https://www.youtube.com/watch?v=JNUHavCZl0c; James Early and Devyn Springer on Cuba, Socialism and Race
https://www.zoranealehurston.com/about/
Ivan Van Sertima, *They Came Before Columbus* (Random House Trade Paperbacks 1976)
Martin Luther King, Jr. *Strength to Love* (Harper & Row 1963)
Edited by Tony Martin, *Message to the People: The Course of African Philosophies* (The Majority Press, MA 1986)
Oliver Tambo - Have You Heard From Johannesburg
Philosophy and Opinions of Marcus Garvey
Sister Rosetta Tharpe | Rock & Roll Hall of Fame
The Universal Negro Improvement Association and African Communities League Women of the UNIA (Our Ancestors) by Gwendolyn Martin, Brenda Amoakon, T.M. Myers; published by Sir Isaiah Morter Division 401 Chicago, Second Edition 2018"
Tony Martin, *Race First* (The Majority Press, Inc., 1976)
W. E. B. Du Bois, *The Soul of Black Folk* (A. C. McClurg & Co., Chicago 1903)
Winnie Mandela, *Part of My Soul Went with Him* (Penguin Books Canada Ltd. 1985)

www.clarityfilms.org › biographies
www.facebook.com › posts › mrs-elsie-ofuatey-kodjoe-.
www.juneteenth.com
www.rockhall.com › inductees › sister-rosetta-tharpe

About the Author

Claudette Joy Spence, M.Sc.

Claudette Joy Spence describes herself, culturally, as an African American. This allows her to claim her African ancestry while telling us she was born in the Americas - Jamaica, to be exact. She spent her years through high school (Ardenne) in the land of her birth and grew into adulthood in the USA. Her self-identification allows her to connect her love and service to Africans at home and abroad.

A Pan-Africanist for most of her adult life, Claudette Joy serves in the roles of educator, interpersonal, social, and economic justice advocate, journalist, author, friend, and a people empowerment facilitator - with a special interest in influencing harmonious and victorious relationships between and among men, women and families. Her living is influenced by the teachings and practices of Jesus, the Brahma Kumaris World Spiritual Organization, and her paternal grandmother Lilleth Spence. She likes to believe that she, more often than not, has grown to show up with and sharing love, compassion and peace.

Claudette Joy's service has, in collaboration with community, leveraged access to capital and credit for communities marginalized by the banking industry in New York; significantly increased lending to modest-income homeowners to complete needed repairs to their major financial asset in East Flatbush, Brooklyn; and she has developed and implements curriculum for a women's empowerment program that can be appreciated by men, women, and children.

Claudette Joy earned a BA degree in Political Science and Communications from Queens College (CUNY) and a M.Sc. degree in Mass Communications from Brooklyn College (CUNY). She served as an adjunct assistant professor at St. John's University, NY teaching in the School of Professional Studies and the School of Liberal Arts.

Published since 2005, Claudette Joy is the author of *Not My Mother's Daughter*; *Sunday Afternoon Energy*; *Garden of Wisdom & Faith*; and the most popular is *Nurturing The Garden of Joy: Provocative Essays on Relationships*.

She enjoys the sounds of laughter, water lapping on the beach ... and sheer silence. She also enjoys experimenting in the kitchen with vegetable dishes.

Made in the USA
Middletown, DE
26 August 2021

46924694R00214